In My Wake

IN MY WAKE

A Commercial Fisherman's Story
1953 - 2016

JAMES A. MCCAULEY

Printed in the United States of America

First Printing: 2016

ISBN 978-1-365-55124-6

Published by:

James A. McCauley
Wakefield, RI 02879

For more information or contact: Jim McCauley, 34 Blossom Court,
Wakefield, RI 02879

Dedication

"In My Wake" is dedicated to my wife Joan and three daughters, Lynn Sabina, Pamela Scott, and Wendy Rifkin for their love and patience.

Also, in memory of the many people named in this narrative who have passed.

Contents

Acknowledgements

I have been fortunate to have been able to acquire photographs from a number of sources that have contributed to the understanding of commercial fishing.

The photographs of the University of Rhode Island, School of Fisheries were the property of Professor Richard A. "Dick" Wing who passed at the age of 64 years on August 14, 2008 after 34 years on the staff of the school. Prior to his passing, he presented the photographs to Richard Fuka, President of the Rhode Island Fishermen's Alliance. Richard allowed me to use them in memory of Dick and the original members of the staff.

In the discussions of the foreign fishing fleet, I was able to make use of some of the many photographs taken by the late Blair "Moe" McDonough while he was working as the Co-op representative aboard a Japanese processing vessel. Moe passed at the age of 75 on January 1, 2015.

The photographs aboard the *Alliance* were taken by my son-in-law, Timothy Scott, while he was one of my crew members.

The cover of this book was designed by my daughter Wendy McCauley Rifkin.

The proof reading and technical corrections were the work of my daughter Lynn S. Sabina.

The publication of the book has been the assignment of my daughter Pamela J. Scott.

This book was a result of 2 ½ years of converting my notes on yellow legal pads to a readable document by Lisa M. Houle.

Introduction

I decided to write this book about commercial fishing because it is a story that needs to be told by a commercial fisherman who devoted a lifetime in the industry. The title "In My Wake" describes how quickly a wake disappears leaving no evidence of the boats or persons passage unless there is a written description of the event. Most of this book includes sea stories based on my personal experience. Not a typical safe day job. I was either at sea or preparing to go to sea for decades.

The fishermen I have come to know over the years from the Carolinas to Maine belong to a very special brotherhood, their individual stories are not unlike my own. Our purpose, like farmers, has been to catch fresh fish primarily to feed the population of our country. I believe that the vast resource of fish belongs to the people. I was always proud to be a commercial fisherman capable of catching and delivering millions of pounds of fish for the tables of those who would otherwise be unable to access them.

There are a number of chapters that tell the history of the Point Judith Fishermen's Cooperative Association and the many fishermen and shoreside personnel that were involved in its daily operation.

The factual details in the book's contents come from my personal log that I kept during my years at sea and the daily recorded comments on the Co-op activities.

Throughout the narrative, I inject my own view or opinion of events. In the final chapter, I have offered some of my conclusions that are not yet generally recognized by fishery managers. Time will tell. I have included my resume in the Appendix as proof of my qualifications to write "In My Wake."

Chapter 1

My First Try
The Beginning of My Fishing Career – 1953

My wife Joan and I decided to marry in April of 1953. We had been dating for a couple of years while we were students at the University of Rhode Island (URI). Joan graduated a year earlier and was a primary school teacher in nearby Narragansett. I was required to continue my classes through the next fall semester in order to graduate in January of 1954. I had changed courses from Engineering to Business, and I needed additional business courses to complete the graduation requirements. We knew then that I would be going in to the Army soon after graduation in order to fulfill my Reserve Officer Training Corp (ROTC) obligation of at least two years of active duty beginning as a 2nd Lieutenant. We rented a house in Narragansett and began life together.

The summer of 1953 was therefore open. I needed to find employment. My job experience up until that time had been working for the FRAM Company in Central Falls loading the blank filter cartridges on the beginning of an assembly line – hot as hell and at a frantic pace. Also, two summers I spent in a "dye house" in Pawtucket dyeing cotton yarn. One of my neighborhood friend's father ran the operation. That was much hotter than FRAM.

In other years and on college breaks, I worked at Hindley Manufacturing Company in Valley Falls. Another guy and I delivered coils of wire to the different machines throughout the plant. The wire was stored in the basement and my partner showed me how to put each arm through thirty-pound wire spools, hoist them onto your shoulders, and climb the stairs up to the main floor. If the wire was heavy steel (up to 150 lbs.), we would pull them out of the pile and roll them like you would a tire, put it on the elevator, and roll it to the machine. The really tough day would be when we received a shipment by trailer truck, unloaded it, and stored it in the basement. My job experiences up until that time kept me in shape, but had absolutely nothing to do with fishing.

On the other hand, my wife Joan was teaching first grade in Narragansett, and knew most of the fishing families through teaching their kids. Joan's principal at the school was Agnes Stinson, whose husband, Stanley, was a commercial fisherman.

While I was in my third year at URI, I made a day trip on the *Jane Lorraine*. Wendell "Windy" Bray was a crew member on the boat, along with John Champlin. Windy used to come to our annual fraternity bashes and at one of the events, he invited me to go out fishing. I spent a good part of the day with Leon "Bud" Chaplin, the captain/owner of the dragger. While trying to stay out of the way of the setting and hauling of the gear, it was obvious that this was an experienced team of professionals. I really enjoyed talking to Bud. He told me about working ranges, and pointed out specific combinations as the day went on. I remember one time, just after making a turn, he came out and put his hand on the outer tow wire for a few minutes while explaining to me there was a rock right about here, and he was feeling the wire to see if the door had hit it. I think he was putting me on.

At the time, I had no idea that Bud was the best inshore fisherman in the Point. It was a memorable day and thinking back, that was one of the reasons I started looking for a site on a boat. This could be my chance to try out commercial fishing. I found out when I started asking around that it was not like shore jobs.

It so happened, in those years, there were about eight or nine boats in port rigging out for the menhaden seining season. After a week asking around about who might be looking for a crew, I was really fortunate when I was told by someone on the dock at RI Engine to talk to Roger, the captain of the *Mary Ann* which was tied up right at that dock. I found Roger and filled him in that I was at URI, married, and had no commercial fishing experience, but I would work my ass off if he would give me a chance. As I recall, his response was more of a look than a verbal response, but it was not a "no." I hung around while he talked to some other members of the crew, especially Bob Siples who it turns out would be running the seine boat, therefore the seining operation. I believe Roger also checked with Ken Gallup Sr., who owned the *Mary Ann* and also was the owner of RI Engine Co. The rest of the crew of seven were already hired, and Bob needed at least one more man (one with a strong back and arms as it turned out.) I was hired. It never would have happened except that the menhaden seiners, which all went trawling or "dragging" except for the three or four months of summer, usually had a permanent crew of three or four men. In the spring, the crews doubled in size. Fleet-wide, that was an expansion of approximately 30-plus crew men.

The obvious problem as a seiner crew member who was not a permanent crew member was that he would not have a job in the fall when the season ended, and would be competing for work with the other now unemployed crews. That was not my concern in 1953.

The *Mary Ann* was a 60-foot wooden eastern rigged dragger with the wheelhouse and engine aft, and a focsle or crew living area below deck up forward. For purposes of seining, the *Mary Ann* would be the "carry boat" which would be loaded and then take the fish to the processing plant back at the harbor. All that summer, Roger Beaudet, as captain, always stayed with the boat and usually took John Lineham, the permanent crew engineer, and one of the other crew, including me, to unload at Point Judith at the end of the fishing day.

The fishing area for the seiners that summer was the relatively shallow waters of Narragansett Bay. Since most of the boats "steamed" at a top speed of 8 to 10 knots, it took about an hour to get up to the Wickford area north of the Jamestown Bridge. Being more or less landlocked, the waters were calm compared to the open sea, so there was no problem towing the seine boat, then the skiff in line behind the carry boat. The wind invariably picked up from the south-west in the afternoon, and for boats heavily loaded, the trip to the plant at the Point could get pretty hairy.

It was a real education for me rigging out the boat and loading the net into the seine boat, and seeing how the whole seine rig was arranged.

Each member of the crew had a specific job when setting and hauling the net. I couldn't wait to see how this operation was going to work.

As I recall, the first set resulted in only a small catch of a few thousand pounds of fish, but I was absolutely fascinated by the whole process. The net was set and hauled back in such a way that it was all ready to set again in only the time it took to pull the purse-line back through the rings and winding the line back on the purse line spool. I was hooked. This was going to be fun!

Short of seeing the setting and hauling of a seine from a single seine boat on a video, it is hard to explain. Back in the early 1950's, the net was hauled back by hand. The live fish caught in the net always swam hard against the twine especially the first 15' to 20' under the cork line. In our crew, Thad Holberton hauled in and stacked the corks. He was a big man; 6'2", probably 200 lbs., and really strong with big hands. Next in line, "Tex" Lumbert pulled in the twine under the corks. He was also a big guy: probably 6'1", and over 200 lbs. I was next in line, pulling twine next to Tex. I was in good shape back then, 5'10" and 178 lbs. On a good set, it required real pulling power. You pulled so hard it seemed your feet would go through the bottom of the boat; well, maybe that's an exaggeration.

In my sleep some nights, I would start pulling on the sheets and end up with the bed clothes all up around my neck. Not exactly a good beginning for a newlywed. The big negative was how bad my clothes and I smelled at the end of the day's fishing. As soon as I came in the door of the apartment, off came the clothes and they were bagged for washing. Think of the worse smell you ever remember. This was twice as bad.

It was really hot up the Bay, especially early in the day when there was little wind. We all had what we called "seiner's tan." That is, we wore t-shirts most of the time and bib oil clothes bottoms with short boots. Sometimes if it was unbearable, we would haul the seine without the oil clothes bottoms and just got wet, and when the pants, jeans, or whatever dried, they were white with salt stains.

My most important contribution to the fishing operation was that I had the youngest eyes in the crew. These were the days before fish spotters in light planes came on the scene. The crew spent most of the time looking for "flips" – unique little splashes that pogies make. I spent all my days perched up in the crosstree of the mast of the *Mary Ann* looking for a sign. Spotting required total concentration and with two people in the cross tree, it was common not to even speak to each other. My reputation as a fish spotter turned out to be helpful in future employment.

Hauling Twine

During the seining season of 1953, all the boats involved were member boats of the Point Judith Fishermen's Cooperative and unloaded under contract at the Ryan-owned fish rendering plant at the Point. With this many boats seining, the total catch could exceed the capacity of the plant to process a day's catch. They had a system whereby the catches, as they occurred throughout each day, were tracked at the Co-op office, and when the maximum amount was caught, the boats were each notified by radio to stop fishing for the day. The value of the total day's catch was then divided equally among the participating boats, including ours.

Spending as much time in the mast as I did looking for fish, I also kept track of the other seiners I saw during the day. Too often, before we even made a set, some boats would be loaded and heading for the plant. We were not catching our share, and as the season wore on, we were among the worst performers - if not the worst. We still shared in the catch and therefore made a weekly pay-check. There were some boats that were very productive. For some of us in the crew, this situation became very uncomfortable.

There were reasons why we were not successful. Most of the seiners were keeping their seine boats in Wickford, and the seine boats would often leave the harbor even before daylight to meet up with the carry boat coming up the Bay from the Point. Sometimes the seine boats would spot fish in the Quonset area and were ready to set when the rest of the crew arrived on the carry boat. The carry boat, if it had unloaded early the previous day, would already be back in Wickford ready to go.

In our case, we were operating the *Mary Ann* out of East Greenwich, and meeting Bob and part of the crew coming out of the Oaklawn Beach inlet in Warwick where the seine boat was docked. If the *Mary Ann* was coming from unloading at the Point, Roger would have to go up the Bay to Warwick Neck to meet up with the seine boat. In concept, this arrangement should have worked, but in practice, we were invariably late getting out to where the other boats were fishing. Pogies would shoal up during the night in good tight knots, and the first boats on the scene would have the best shot at getting a good set. A good set could be as much as 100,000 lbs., and it was common to have sets of 30,000 to 40,000. One or two sets could load most of the boats in the fleet, which had carrying capacities of 80,000 to 120,000 lbs. I can't recall that we ever had more than 40,000 lbs. for any one day's catch.

To continue, if you did not get a shot at these "untouched" shoals, you would end up chasing around after broken up bodies of fish that were usually on the move and difficult to catch.

Mechanically, the *Mary Ann*, seine boat, and net, were well-suited for the job at hand. I cannot recall that we experienced any mechanical problems throughout the season. Initially, once we located a body of fish, it was Bob who decided how to make the set. We did much better once Thad took over directing where and how to set the fish. His long experience as a beach seiner really paid off, and we gained confidence.

One incident I will never forget. We were hauling in the twine with a decent set when all of a sudden, I can't remember why, Tex started yelling at me and I started yelling right back, both of us red-faced. We were side-by-side in the seine boat with both of our legs locked up in the twine. It's a wonder I didn't get decked, but as suddenly as it started, Tex kind of gave me a half-assed grin and mumbled something or other, and we went back to pulling twine. It sure was quiet on the boat for a while. Thad seemed to get a kick out of the exchange. The rest of the crew seemed to shrink since it was obvious from the beginning of the season that they were afraid of Tex and went out of their way to stay clear of him. Funny, we never mentioned the flurry again, and I remained friendly with Tex throughout my fishing career.

There was one occurrence that clearly went too far for any bride. One night, when I was driving, part of the crew got really drunk. Knowing I was driving, I recall having only one maybe two beers. I drove them home. The first stop went fine. The second passenger, when he was faced with going into his house, said "No Way!" and wanted to go back to the boat in East Greenwich. Minutes later, he was out like a light, snoring loudly. "No way" was I taking him back, so I made a quick decision to take him to my house. I got there, opened the garage, drove inside, got out, closed the garage door, leaving it slightly ajar, and went into the house. It was only about 11:00 pm, and I had called to warn Joan I would be late but did not elaborate. When I told her about our guest in the garage, by the expression on her face, I knew I had gone way out of bounds.

The next day was a planned fishing day. I got going about 5:30 am. My guest was still in place, and we were half way back to the boat when I stopped for coffee and doughnuts and a piss call, and other than him being somewhat confused, we went fishing. Never again.

By mid-summer, the total catch per day dropped to the level where the processing plant was able to process the whole day's catch. As a result, the "sharing" that had been in place was discontinued. We carried on fishing with mixed results. Roger was all for calling it a season. It was evident that his interest had always been to ultimately end up as captain when the *Mary Ann* returned to dragging.

The season ended for me. Classes began in early September. Joan and I had survived as a married couple throughout the fishing season. She had worked as a waitress at the Galilee Beach Club for about a month, then was busy preparing her classroom for the new school year. We had saved a little from fishing and with her salary, we had enough to get by until my graduation in January of 1954.

Fish showing in the net

Chapter 2

My Early Years

The story of my career and association with the sea actually began before I was born. On August 18, 1925, the steamer *Mackinac* was pulling out of Newport Harbor, Rhode Island on its' way back up Narragansett Bay to Pawtucket, Rhode Island. It was a one-day excursion with 672 persons aboard.

At 6:10 pm, 250 yards off Coddington Point, one of the two ship's boilers exploded. The scalding steam immediately rose to the ships two lower decks. Twenty eight vacationing passengers were killed immediately. Twenty seven more received burns which later proved fatal. Many others were maimed for life. More than one hundred were injured. Those on the top deck were spared. Among those on the top deck was my mother, Grace Andrew, celebrating her sixteenth birthday with her grandmother and grandfather. With hot black cinders flying across the upper deck, her grandfather told both women to cover their heads with their multiple skirts.

Captain McVay of the *Mackinac* grounded the vessel on Coddington Point, preventing further loss of life. The *Mackinac* disaster was the second worst disaster in Rhode Island nautical history. The worst one was the loss of the steamer *Larchmont* off Block Island in 1907 with a loss of 181 lives. Captain McVay was captain of both vessels.

My mother died in 2006 at the age of 97. She could still tell her story as though it happened the previous week. Even really close ones don't count.

My earliest memory of the sea, or maybe it was an awareness, was as a toddler going to sleep listening to the constant boom of the waves on Charlestown Beach on the southern coast of Rhode Island. My grandmother and grandfather McCauley owned a house right on the beach, just where the grassy dunes started. My grandmother's sister and brothers owned the two Hindley houses on the adjoining lots to the east. Those two houses were built in 1925. For those reading this story and are familiar with Charlestown Beach, the houses were little more than halfway to the present breachway.

My grandparents' John and Sarah McCauley's house

In those days, the house lots ran from the ocean to the pond. I can remember my father owned a rugged skiff about 16 feet long which he kept alongside my grandfather's house. On calm days, he

The Hindley houses

and his Hindley cousins, Judd (Justin) and Bill, would set rollers under the skiff and push it down the beach to the water. Timing the waves, they would push it into the waves, lifeguard style, and row away towards the breachway. I used to sit on the beach all day until they returned with burlap bags full of hand-lined tautog.

Some time in those early years, my father and his brother, my uncle Ted, and his wife Olive, built a second house directly behind my grandfather's. They had two boys, Donald and Bill McCauley who were older than me. I remember them being allowed to swim in the ocean, and I was not.

I should mention that my dad had a second skiff at our dock on the pond. Dad was a skilled crabber, poling after the blue claw crabs with a long-handled crab net. I was able to go on the pond, sitting in the stern with my mother, with crabs running around the bottom of the boat snapping at us and each other. My mother was an expert crabmeat picker.

June 1937

Enclosed is a picture from 1937 with me at age six, my mother's grandmother Pearson from the *Mackinac*, my grandmother Sarah McCauley, and my dad. Why we dressed up to go to the beach was just what we did. The following summer was to be our last on Charlestown Beach.

The September 21, 1938 hurricane, the worst in Rhode Island history, swept all the houses off Charlestown Beach. About three days after the hurricane, we drove down to see the damage. I remember walking down to the bridge near the beach. All you could see was sand and an odd well pipe here and there.

We had no indoor plumbing at the beach. There was a handpump under the front house for washing. Then there was the outhouse. I remember it well because I became toilet-trained on that two-seater. My grandfather used to supervise digging the hole in the sand each year, then moving the outhouse in place. He made sure that the hole was "limed" every day. At times, there were six grownups and three youngsters making use of the "facilities."

It was hard to believe that the ocean could have caused so much damage. I remembered storms while we were there, that the wash of the waves would come right up to the front door of my grandfather's house. Nothing had ever happened before. On the way out, my dad stopped on the north side of the pond at the beginning of the potato fields. What was left of all the houses was a huge windrow of rubble, unrecognizable as houses, stretching for miles. There had been a few deaths reported, and on the way home, my parents talked about how we could have been at the beach if the hurricane had come earlier in the month or on a weekend.

It turned out that my mother's cousin, whom we called "uncle" Alfred Pearson was at his house on the pond when the hurricane struck. He was able to get to the only high ground around just north of the bridge. He waited among the cluster of homes still standing until the hurricane passed and the water receded. He found his house, completely untouched, sitting about a quarter of a mile away from the foundation. Fortunately, his family was away at home.

The historic specifics of the '38 Hurricane were that it struck the south shore of Rhode Island around 4:00 pm on the 21st. Wind was steady at 120 mph from New Haven to Cape Cod. Since it was a full moon, the storm surge was estimated at 17 to 20 feet above normal high tide. A gust of 186 mph was recorded at the Blue Hill Observatory in Massachusetts. Six hundred died in New England, mostly in Rhode Island.

In my early years, we lived in Valley Falls in the town of Cumberland, Rhode Island. My grandmother and grandfather, Sarah and John McCauley, lived upstairs in their house, and we lived downstairs. The whole Pearson Family lived next door; my uncle Ted and his wife Olive lived up the street with the boys. My

Tom MacItee and the author

grandmother was a Hindley; the three of them worked at the Hindley Manufacturing Company nearby.

During the summer, I used to go fishing with a retired neighbor. Tom MacItee used to take me fishing accompanied by his English setter. With our cane poles, we used to walk along the west side of the nearby reservoir system. The most southern of the two bodies of water was called Happy Hollow, with an overflow dam into the Blackstone River. The northern body of water was called Robin Hollow.

Tom knew all the spots although he preferred Robin Hollow. We caught yellow perch and an occasional pickerel using perch bellies. Sometimes a large-mouth bass would latch on to a night crawler. Tom had worm stashes along the route, and mason jars with a long line attached that he would throw out to get fresh water to drink explaining that the water close along the shore wasn't fit to drink.

"Mac" and I

The setter was the first dog I had come to know and he was a great addition to my summers. One day, we were walking along a narrow path alongside Robin Hollow, when the dog started barking up ahead. Tom went up to see what was going on. Suddenly, there were two loud bangs. Tom had just shot a snake. I was really surprised. I had never heard a gunshot before except in the Tom Mix movies. Also, I never knew Tom carried a revolver in the pants pocket of his bib overalls. We did that for two summers—a memorable experience. Those were my "Huck Finn" days.

When I was in the third grade, age 8, we moved to Saylesville, a small town west of the Valley in the town of Lincoln, Rhode Island. This was a new, one floor ranch style house at the top of a steep hill (Parker Street). One of the first things that happened when we moved was I got a puppy that I named "Mac." He was a mixed breed collie dog. The best dog a boy could have.

Now I could go fishing by myself with Mac as my constant companion. The Lincoln Woods reservation began at the top of "our hill." Most of the area was comprised of a large pond/lake. I got to know every fishing spot along its shore. Often after supper, I would talk my dad in to driving up and making some casts. It didn't take too much persuading.

One day I was fishing by myself, casting a Dare Devil lure for pickerel at an isolated pond near the town. The pond had a dirt road that ran along its southern side. This guy drove up in a car not far from where I was casting. He got out and called to me to come over. I don't remember what he said, but I was on full alert. I yelled back at him to leave me alone when Mac started barking, and he would have gone for the guy if I hadn't told him to stay. I wasn't really worried because I knew we could easily outrun him in a pinch. This pervert didn't know me, but I knew him. He was a garage mechanic at a place my father used to go to back in Valley Falls. He got back in his car and finally turned around and moved out. I never told either of my parents about the incident. For one thing, I didn't want my dad to get in trouble if he tried to deck the guy, and I figured if I told them, they might not let me go fishing by myself again.

When I went swimming at Lincoln Woods, it was always with the guys in the neighborhood. Mac was a great swimmer, and would run down the rocks and jump way out just like we did. One early spring, under my direction, we went along the shore and over a week or so, we collected at least ten wooden skiffs that had broken loose over the winter. We paddled and poled them to a small secluded cove. My first fleet. After a couple of weeks of "ownership," a couple of us went to a guy over near the dam that rented boats and told him we had found these skiffs. He was happy to get them back and actually thanked us.

One summer we stayed at a cottage in Jerusalem, across from the fishing port of Galilee in - Point Judith. We used to fish for fluke in the breachway off the tee dock at Bannister's Wharf, two docks south of Skip's Dock. I was fascinated by the fishing boats coming and going from the port. I remember them tying up to what I found out to be the Fisherman's Co-op. Of course, at the time, I had no way of knowing that I would become involved in that whole scene. There was a lobster boat that tied up to the dock next to Bannisters. The boat was a wide cat-boat style and most days, the fisherman with the long-billed cap would come back to his dock steering by a long rudder handle with his knees. Years later, I found out he was Doug Smith, Bob Smith's father. Bob inherited the dock, and I have rented dock space from him for my 20 foot Boston Whaler since 1994. Some things change over the years, then some don't change much at all.

When I was twelve, my mother had a baby boy. I now had a brother named Jerauld or "Jerry." I couldn't take him fishing, at least not for many years.

In my teens, my father bought another house in Charlestown, Rhode Island. This one was on the main road going to the beach. In fact, it was the nearest one to the beach that had survived the "38" Hurricane. He built a small dock and bought a 15 foot pond skiff. Not long after, he bought a 7 1/2 H.P. Martin outboard. I can't remember if it had a clutch, but the motor would turn 180 degrees in order to back down. It was such a big deal. We were now able to go all the way up to where the breachway came into the pond. The best place for soft shell clams, quahaugs, and oysters. Dad was back crabbing, and I soon became able to catch my share.

My dad and I started striper fishing when I was about 15. The big event for us was going out casting for bass on a charter with Bob Linton. Back then Bob had a boat called the *Fishing Lady* that he had built himself. That was the first big bass that dad had ever caught (picture). Bob Linton went on to be one of the best known charter captains in Rhode Island history. I think he also built the first of

Dad

the Mako boats by himself.

We used to go fishing on a headboat out of Plymouth, Massachusetts. The boat was chartered by Bill Hindley for the employees from Hindley Manufacturing Company; usually a group of about 15 or so would go. I remember meeting at a bar-room in Valley Falls that they managed to get the owner to open at 5:30 a.m. After a few eye openers, they would split up into about five cars and convoy to Plymouth. This was an annual event, so everybody that had a tendency for sea sickness had been weeded out by the time I started going. We used to catch mostly cod with an occasional haddock. The nuisance fish was whiting—nobody took them home. During those outings, my dad would never have a drink. No matter how rough; even in the rain, he would stand at the rail trying to catch the pool winner. I was just as bad. I think I went three times.

The "shop" went fishing out of Point Judith only once. The boat was smaller and not in good shape, and all we caught was scup.

As I got older, we fished the Cape Cod Canal for bass and one trip we fished Race Point. Dad arranged to have a "beach buggy," an old Ford station wagon with big under-inflated tires, drop us off out on the beach with all our gear. It was around 5:30 p.m. We fished all night with only a couple of hours nap, then we were picked up around 6:30 in the morning. I remember we hooked up on bass that night and broke off a few, but never landed any. The buggy went along the beach and picked up some other guys. They had struck out too.

My dad became the first recording secretary of the Blackstone Valley Striper Club. Most of the club members were, you might recall, fanatic fishermen. The competition among them was unreal. As soon as they got out of work on Friday afternoon, they would drive to the Cape, fish all weekend, and get back in time for work on Monday morning.

In college at URI, our fraternity cook Rudy Raitano, was an avid bass fisherman. As soon as supper was over, he and I would often take off and fish the rocks at Narragansett Pier, almost always in the dark. With flashlights around our necks, we would work these "special spots." Rudy was left-handed, so we would often fish off the same rock. I learned a lot, and we caught many nice striped bass which Rudy cooked up for the guys at the house. I was dating my wife at the time, and had she realized that I was going to eventually become a commercial fisherman, well, I don't know!

Through my friendship with Rudy, I became friendly with Dick Lima, a local charter boat fisherman. In those days, Dick was just at the beginning of his career in the business. He later became famous for his line of Lima boats that he designed and had built for the serious fisherman. Many years later, I talked Jerry Abrams, at Freshwater Fish Company in Boston, into buying a Lima boat in the 28-foot class. He liked it so much, he took it to Florida. For years, Jerry was the biggest buyer of fresh fish the Co-op had. The Freshwater fish trailer truck and its driver Mike, waited all day nearly every day for our fish. More importantly, he also paid for fish as soon as he was billed.

Anyway, back to 1953, Dick Lima had a 28 foot lapstrake open boat, and one day he invited me to go striper fishing with him and Jerry Sylvester. That was a big deal for me. Jerry owned a bait shop in downtown Narragansett, when Moy Lee's Chinese Restaurant was still there. Jerry's wife mostly ran the bait shop while he fished the shore. Back then, Jerry was the best known bass fisherman in Narragansett. Dick took us down off Charlestown breachway, I think it was in early October. We were casting from the moving boat with eelskin-covered atom plugs and did we catch fish. The fish, mostly in the 30-pound range, were coming right out of the water after those plugs. With Dick steering, Jerry and I often had doubles. We let them all go. When you go fishing with the "best" you always catch a trip. The same holds true for the commercial fisherman, no matter what port you fish from. Amen.

The McCauley summer home in Charlestown, RI, 1961.   Sketch by my dad.

Chapter 3

The Army

The period of time between the beginning of my fishing experience and the end of studying was a quiet time for Joan and I. My college courses were not too demanding, and she had a full year of teaching experience by then. As a young married couple, we needed to get used to living a normal life.

Upon graduation in January, I received my orders to report to Fort Dix, New Jersey. In March of 1954, as a green second lieutenant, we had to prepare for the move. We had been driving a junk car, a $150 Chevy, since we had been married. I had to show Joan how to pour a gallon of water in the radiator every time she used it.

We decided to buy a new '53 Ford Fairlane. Our first major purchase and the first time we faced being in debt. There was enough room to load it up with everything we owned and started a totally new life together. There were no apartments available on base, and we started looking into local advertisements. Our first encounter was renting rooms in a single family house out in the boonies owned by a lady looking for someone to save her from the bill collectors. We stayed one night and that was too long. I can still smell the strong odor coming from the central oil burner. After that experience, we did a 180 and rented a nice two bedroom house in Mount Holly, New Jersey. It was fully furnished with a garage. Around an army base, it was not cheap, but Joan found it through her connection with the local school department as a substitute teacher. Between my 2nd Lieutenant pay of $400+ a month and her promised salary, we had the feeling of being truly prosperous. Our next door neighbors were "civilians" that worked in the Mt. Holly area and they

Author at Ft. Dix

helped us to settle in.

I reported in to base and was assigned as the Executive Officer, the second in command, of a training company of approximately 220 men. The parent unit was the 271st Regiment, 69th Infantry Division. The company commander was a First Lieutenant who had been in the service for about 15 years. He had been an NCO (noncommissioned officer) in Korea where he received his war-time commission. For him, this assignment was no big deal. As a result, he welcomed me to the company to assist in the "running" of the company, thereby sharing his work load. There was a First Sargeant, an SFC (Sargeant First Class), and four Sargeants and Corporals on the staff as acting platoon leaders for the trainees.

I found out right away that running the company was exactly what I did. One of the goals of a training company was to get the troops in shape. We ran everywhere. For me, that was the easy part after years of running track in high school and in one year of college.

I was given a lot of responsibility, beyond what I had expected, but the CO kept an eye on my performance and made suggestions when warranted.

Generally a new infantry reserve officer coming out of an ROTC program is assigned directly to the Infantry School at Ft. Benning, GA. In my case, I was initially doing a job without that advanced training. Other than being assigned as Battalion OD (Officer of the Day) every couple of weeks, which required being assigned to Batallion HQ overnight, I was home every night. The noncom platoon leaders lived with the trainees in the barracks. Army life was "good." Joan and I were somewhat surprised at how well everything was going.

All that came to an end when I was assigned to Ft. Benning beginning in August 1954. This was a TDY or temporary duty assignment. The infantry training company that I was assigned to was almost all comprised of the 1954 graduating class of West Point. As I remember, there were only about seven reserve officers like myself in the unit. I was lucky to have had the Ft. Dix experience. I thought at the time that these guys were "regular army" elite and will be off the wall - gung ho. The only thing we had in common was that we were all Second Lieutenants and had only the National Defense Ribbon to wear on our uniforms.

We managed to find an apartment off base in Columbus, Georgia. It was okay, and we were again among "civilians" for the most part. We became friends with one couple and that friendship continued for years after our Army days.

As it turned out, the West Pointers had been under the strict discipline of the Point for four years and this was their first assignment after graduating in June, only two months prior. Benning was considered their first true experience of freedom as adults.

Some, as new officers, had married and were adjusting to married life. The single guys initially raised hell after hours, but the hard training that goes with the Ft. Benning assignment soon put an end to their new found "freedom."

A contingent of troops from the 187 Regiment of the 101st Airborne Division was assigned to train our company. They were top-notch in all aspects of infantry operations, and we all recognized the professionalism they exhibited during our sixteen weeks of training.

My indoctrination at Ft. Dix was very helpful in many ways, especially dealing with the physical training. The difference from Ft. Dix was the heat. I thought it was hot back at Ft. Dix in July, but it was like being in Alaska compared to Georgia in August. We were doing pushups, pullups, and - running - everywhere. We would be trucked off to the various weapons ranges on the vast Benning reservation. On the way back to our company area after a long day in the Georgia sun, the trucks would stop, and we would run the last five miles.

We all learned what an infantry officer was all about. Almost without exception, the West Point officers planned on going to the Ft. Benning Jump School after completion of the sixteen weeks. There was an additional incentive in that two weeks would be shaved off the jump school curriculum if we all satisfied the initial jump school physical requirements. Ranger training was also offered at Benning, and most of the officers planned on rounding out their training as infantry officers by including that option. Joan and I seriously discussed me going on to both Jump School and Ranger training. The enthusiasm for going through the two programs was contagious and I was caught up in the whole idea. Choosing Jump School would require me to commit to extending my active duty service for an additional two or more years. We decided not to extend my army career, although I would still have an inactive reserve officer obligation once my two year active duty commitment was completed, which would be in March of 1956. Not an issue at the time.

I will never forget one incident that occurred at Benning. We were on a training night patrol. There were eight of us accompanied by one of the 187 Airborne noncoms (squad size). We had been moving out for about a half hour. I was the point man, first in the inline patrol, with the noncom last and the acting squad leader behind me. It was as dark as can be, and we were following a culvert alongside a dirt road, more or less by feel occasionally checking our progress by compass. Without any warning, there was a loud rattle directly in front of me. I stopped immediately and did not move a muscle, and probably didn't breathe either. The man behind me came up, and I said "stop" then said "listen."

His immediate response was, "Oh Shit!" I said "Back up slow". The rattle gradually faded; the snake was holding in place. We backtracked a damn good distance, and changed our location off to a field on the other side of the road. The guy in back of me was from Florida and was familiar with rattlesnakes; probably in snake farms. His comment was "Wow! That was a big bastard." The noncom with us was the only one with a flashlight, so we never saw it. The noncom was supposed to have a snake bite kit, but I bet he had never used it. Guess who took up the point again — yes, I did — no other volunteers. West Pointers are not dumb. About twenty minutes later, I fell in a hole about four feet deep. I envisioned it was full of snakes and shot out of that hole as if from a gun. Quite a new experience for a guy from Rhode Island.

In September of 1954, the TV and the newspapers in Columbus, GA were full of news about a hurricane that was coming up from Florida. They were hoping the hurricane would come ashore in Georgia and come inland bringing in heavy rain. They were having a serious drought as they often do. Much to their disappointment, Hurricane Carol went right by and headed up the coast. Much to my surprise, I had a call from my Dad a couple of days later. He had gone down to Galilee the day the Hurricane hit to go out on one of the charter boats participating in the Tuna Tournament. I guess he had a tough time getting out of there, then driving back to Lincoln. I couldn't believe it. How the hell could they not get the word up in Rhode Island that the hurricane was coming. I found out much later, that my mother and younger brother Jerry had gone down to Jerusalem, directly across from Galilee, to watch the boats going out for the tournament. They went back home to Lincoln when they heard about the cancellation. Good thing, because most of Jerusalem was underwater at the peak of the hurricane.

I still have the individual pictures of my Benning class. I have never followed through to see how many of those West Point graduates survived through retirement. They used to express a certain amount of concern that the fighting was over in Korea and when they would have another conflict. It sounds strange that they would have those thoughts, but then the army was their chosen career. Already, in 1954, at the conclusion of the Korean War, the services were downgrading, and many of the active duty personnel who had obtained reserve commissioned officer status were being given notice that they would have to revert back to their permanent noncommissioned rank or consider retirement. Wartime was considered a time for fast advancement in rank.

Upon my "graduation" from Benning, I returned to the 271st regiment at Ft. Dix. Joan and I found a small apartment in Mt. Holly and she resumed her status as a substitute teacher. We also acquired a kitten that Joan named "Muffin." This time I was assigned to the Weapons Pool, with my primary duty as a live fire weapons instructor out on the weapon ranges within the Ft. Dix complex.

There was a considerable amount of responsibility directing the operation of the ranges with the strict safety requirements. We ran all the Companies in the Regiment through live fire training to qualify with the M1 Garand Rifle at different distances out to 500 yards. We also taught the BAR (Browning Automatic Rifle) and the light machine gun; all 30 cal. rounds. We also did non-qualifications familiarization with the 50 cal. heavy machine gun, 60 mm and 81 mm mortars, and the 45 caliber handgun.

After a long day on the ranges, we came away with red eyes from all the smoke, and the noise didn't help your hearing much either. In those days we didn't wear ear protectors. The ranges were also the "coldest place on earth" in the winter.

When the range contingent comprised of myself and two other officers and a dozen NCO's were not out on the range, we worked at the Weapons Pool maintaining all the weapons allocated to the Regiment. This included loading the weapons that had been repaired or reconditioned into trucks and test firing each one. A worn out barrel of a 30 gal. light machine gun, for instance, would throw a round through a target leaving an oblong hole as opposed to a clean, round hole.

My superior officer in charge of the Weapons Pool was a 1st Lieutenant and a Korean War veteran. He was a single man and was a dedicated officer and ran a good operation. We were subject to continued inspections by both Regiment and Division. This included the paper-work plus service records of all the major weapons.

Then one day, "just like that," I was notified by the Regimental Adjutant, a Chief Warrant Officer, that the Lieutenant had committed suicide with his own pistol late the night before. It was hard for me to believe. I had been with him every duty day for about four months and had no indication that he was troubled at all. The story was that he had been drinking and been stopped by the MP's on base and had been written up. Apparently, he couldn't cope with the thought of facing a drunk driving charge and the implications such a charge would have on his career. Being "impaired" probably didn't help in deciding to take his own life. Very sad.

The suicide made a long-lasting impression on me. Over the years, I have concluded that only the mentally stable people can have a gun on hand in their home or carry every day. Unusual or unexpected events that can occur gives that person an option to take a life, either their own or someone else's, without the time to think through the ramifications of their action. In the Lieutenant's case, it was the excessive drinking that put him in the classification of an unstable person if only for the period of one night. Just the idea of having any firearms available to an individual with a history of mental illness is incomprehensible. Family and friends responsible for these individuals have an obligation to insure that the temptation to use a weapon is not an option.

A few days later, the CWO notified me that "The Colonel," the Regimental Commander, had appointed me Officer In Charge

(OIC) of the Weapons Pool. The position was the first for me with this level of responsibility.

In early summer I was notified that the 271st Regiment would be phased out as an active training regiment. As each company completed the training of the troops under their command, the officers and noncoms, or staff, of each unit would be reassigned. This was all part of the overall plan to downsize the army after Korea which would also include the end of the active drafting of new recruits.

In my case, the Weapons Pool would have to remain active until the last of the training companies completed range qualifications. I started meetings with the Regimental Adjutant, who was in charge of the details of the phase-out. It would be my responsibility to work out the transfer of all the weapons, parts, and equipment to a Division Headquarters' unit.

With a reduced Weapons Pool staff, we managed to transfer everything without incident. Sounds easy - it wasn't. There were thousands of weapons, for example, over 200 light machine guns alone, each with its own serial number that was listed as having been issued to the 271st over the years.

The adjutant then notified me that the Colonel was putting me in charge of the Motor Pool, since I had successfully closed out the Weapons Pool. The Motor Pool OIC had already been reassigned somewhere off base. Fortunately, there was a very competent Master Sergeant on site who had been there for several years. We were glad to meet each other. He was afraid he was going to have the job of phasing out the Motor Pool by himself.

The Motor Pool was a giant operation compared to the Weapons Pool. It was a couple of fenced-in acres full of vehicles. As I recall, there were about 250 vehicles ranging in size from large trailer trucks, a pile of 2 1/2 ton canvas-covered trucks and jeeps, right down to the Regimental Commander's staff car.

The process of turning in the vehicles was similar to the guns with some notable exceptions. Each vehicle had an inspection file that had been meticulously maintained for years, and in many cases the target of both Regimental and Divisional inspections. I inquired at Division where and how they wanted the files included with each vehicle. The response was: "we don't want the files, just the vehicles as is." We burned files for days in the main coal fire in the Pool maintenance shed. I only authorized "the burning" after getting a signed authorization from Division and an okay from my Adjutant. While I was at the Motor Pool, I qualified to drive all the vehicles; good thing too, since our staff of drivers was being reassigned.

It was toward the end of the Motor Pool phase-out that the Colonel, through his Adjutant, offered me a Regular Army Commission. I had a chance then and there to make the Army a career. Again, a big discussion with Joan at home. The final decision was to complete my two year term then see what kind of career I could settle in to outside of the Army. There was little or no mention of fishing being an option. I was also promoted to 1st Lieutenant about the same time. Finally, a silver bar. The single brass bar, no matter how hard you polished it, was still brass, the insignia of a "learner".

By midsummer, the phase-out was nearly complete. Out of the whole Regiment there were only four officers left. The Colonel, his Adjutant, a Major (who was the supply officer), and myself. It turned out that the Major was reverting back to a Sergeant First Class until he had the time in service to retire. He was another casualty of the downsizing.

During the early spring, Joan and I were waiting for the birth of our first baby. Joan had been going to the base hospital for prenatal care and was seeing a particular doctor whom she really liked. Finally one night, it was time and I took her to the hospital. I was back working the next morning when I got the call. Everything was fine; we had a baby daughter whom we named Lynn, born at Fort Dix, New Jersey. The doctor that signed the birth certificate was a Japanese-American—the first person Joan saw after the birth and also a doctor she had never seen before. This was the Army. Whoever is on duty does whatever is required.

I had a meeting with the Colonel toward the end of the phase- out. The colonel thanked me for the job I had done, then asked me, "Where would you like to go, Mac?" Seeing my puzzled expression, he continued. "We can assign you overseas in Europe, the Caribbean, Hawaii, you name it." My response was, since we have a new baby and only about eight months of active duty remaining, that I would like an assignment somewhere here on the Base.

He and the Adjutant must have anticipated my request because he asked the CWO, "Mr. Cope, what do we have on base for the Lieutenant?" Mr. Cope responded to the Colonel, that there was an opening as Executive Officer at the First Army NCO Academy, and they both agreed that would be a good fit. I said "Yes" without hesitation. My future was assured. I doubt if there were many Army officers or anybody in the service that had an offer like that. I heard the Colonel was planning to retire as well. With the downsizing taking place, it was probably unlikely that he would be offered the opportunity to become a general.

Joan, our new daughter Lynn, and I had a little time before I had to report for duty at the Academy. About that time, we were notified by base housing that there was a two bedroom apartment available on base. Since it was unfurnished, we counted our pennies and bought our first new furniture from Wannamakers in Philadelphia. We bought a high-end light maple bedroom set, which we still have today. The rest of the furniture was adequate for our immediate needs and ended up being used for years.

We were really pleased with the new arrangement, and our neighbors were other officers with young families. Now that we had a family, we also bought a 1954 Ford Country Squire to replace our Fairlane. We assumed the new debt with a smile. We never expected that our Army days would be anything like that. There was one thing. Our apartment was not too far from the end of one of the runways of McGuire Air Force Base that was part of the Ft. Dix complex. On weekends, the Reserve Officers practiced takeoffs and landings. They started about 6:00 am and the first flight of three jets would rattle the building during takeoffs and about one minute later, the fourth jet would climb out. When we were in bed those mornings, especially with a baby, it was a real annoyance to say the least.

It was during this time that I enrolled in a correspondent class. These were available to all military personnel and included a multitude of subjects. I picked one on diesel engines. I don't know why, except the subject was interesting to me since my summer fishing. Studying diesels was more interesting than watching black and white TV all night. The text book was good, and I still have it.

The First Army NCO Academy that I was assigned to was a company-sized unit of approximately 230 men, all of whom were noncoms with ratings of sergeants up to master sergeants. The purpose of the Academy was to run the NCO's through a program to bring them up to speed with all the changes that were envisioned for the now "downsized" Army. All the students of the Academy were on TDY (temporary duty), from Army units located in the First Army area which included the whole Northeast. Most of the noncoms were recently-returned Korean War veterans.

During their stay at the Academy, they were housed in top-notch barracks and took meals at the company-sized mess hall. As part of my new job as the Executive Officer, I was to be responsible for all of the mess hall and supply room. To my surprise, I had two food service-trained Master Sergeants running the mess hall, and the food they prepared was comparable to an upscale restaurant. The supply room was like no other I had seen anywhere. There was a Master Sergeant in charge of that operation as well with a staff of four as I recall. All three of the Master Sergeants I thought of as friends, and in my time there we took care of each other's needs.

When I first came to the Academy, my CO was a Korean War veteran with the rank of Captain. He was also a black man and was the first time I had experienced having a black commanding officer. I can honestly say that in my opinion, he was the finest example of what a career officer should be. I learned from him, what an executive officer of a unit was all about. He had been in charge of the unit since it had been formed, about six months before I was assigned to the Academy. He was then transferred to a command position in a regular army unit at another base.

A Captain who was new to me took over the command. He was a total contrast to my former boss in that he was due to retire soon, and he had been put in charge of our unit in the interim. As a result, he more or less let me run things. At the same time, here I was with a single National Service Ribbon on my dress uniform, and all the rest of the "troops" had "bronze stars" some with a "silver star" and half with "purple heart" ribbons, plus campaign ribbons from all over. Since some had been in service for 10 to 15 years, Captain Albert Sipole put that problem to rest in that he was finishing twenty years of service and had rows of ribbons that he had earned.

We became good friends. During some slow times, usually

in the afternoon, he taught me how to play chess. When a man came in with some story about family problems, he was extremely sensitive about how to help and would go out of his way to offer assistance which sometimes included emergency leave. I would sometimes go into his office after such a meeting, and he would turn the lapel of his uniform over. He had the infantry badge on the outside and a chaplain's badge fixed to the underside. With a groan, he would ask me if I had any problems to discuss? It was his own special brand of humor.

The Captain was scheduled to retire in March, about the same time I was going to complete my two-year stint. We were both short timers. To my surprise, he decided to take a two month leave in order that he and his wife could find a place in Florida for his retirement.

I was notified that I would be the acting Company Commander while he was on leave. Although I was familiar with all aspects of the position, it was still a big responsibility. The Company staff, including the First Sergeant also a Master Sergeant, made sure I didn't mess up.

Those two months went by fast. Things were winding down for me. Our little family made our plans to move back to Rhode Island, so one weekend prior to my discharge, I took Joan and Lynn and our cat Muffin back to my parent's home in Rhode Island. The car was pretty well packed to capacity. Baby Lynn was secure in the back seat with the cat. The cat was surprisingly good around the baby. About the time we crossed from New York in to Connecticut, a car passing us started blowing their horn and pointing to our car. My first thought was a bad tire. Then I glanced in to the rear view mirror, and there was Muffin hanging by the neck on her leash on the outside of the car. I eased over to the breakdown lane and managed to get a hold on the cat. Joan untied the leash from the inside of the car, and we got her back inside. We had always cracked the window for the cat. I never would have believed she could have squeezed through the space. Talk about having "nine lives."

I returned to Ft. Dix to have the Army move our belongings to storage in Rhode Island until we found a place to live. I got back to the base on a Sunday night and when I drove up to park my car, there across the street in a field was a jet that had crashed that morning. The neighbors said it had engine trouble, and it barely cleared the roofs of the apartments. The pilot survived.

I was paid a decent piece of change when I was discharged since I had taken very little time off during my two years of active duty. In those days, we were allocated 30 days off a year with pay, so I had about 50 days coming. It was March 1956, and I was on my way home. Not the same guy that had arrived two years before. The value of my Army experience was hard to measure, but in my opinion, it was to help me through my lifetime more than my college education. What did all this Army experience have to do with commercial fishing? Not much.

The author with Jack Blease, my wife's cousin,
at Fort Dix, N.J.

Chapter 4

Trying Again

We found a second floor apartment in Wakefield, Rhode Island adjacent to the Larchwood Inn, our favorite restaurant. Now to find a job. Joan wasn't all that thrilled when I suggested that I would try fishing, but that was one of the reasons we chose Wakefield for our first residence.

By the time we were settled in it was early April. I started hitting the docks. One of my former neighbors in Narragansett was a day boat fisherman. I knew Bill Rose quite well since he had helped me with the "work" to become a Mason. He didn't need a man, but he knew another day boat captain/owner who needed someone.

Based on Bill's recommendation, I got the job. A two-man boat. In other words, I was going to do everything but run the boat. Sounded like a good place to learn, and I did. I used to get to the boat early, start the engine, drop the net that was hanging up drying from the previous trip, and laid it on the rail ready to set out. Everything worked on the boat and I was able to assist setting and hauling, and we did catch a mix of fish.

The problem was, we didn't go out very often, and when we did, it was a short day. I hated to go home after getting up early and then not going out. When we did, the money wasn't there. One thing I noticed was that we always made our tows in about the same place, a couple of miles east of the Point Judith Lighthouse then towing north to the mansions in Narragansett. I remember one of the best weeks we had, the captain told me he had to buy new tow wires with that week's landings, so the paycheck was less than usual. He never showed me a trip/week settlement slip. I seemed to be paid a "random" amount.

It was a good thing I had come out of the Army with some cash, but that was being consumed quite fast with these meager paychecks. I talked to Bill, but he didn't want to comment, and I didn't know how we were doing compared to him, although I kept track, and he seemed to go out on a regular basis.

I became very frustrated with the situation and with no other prospects, I decided to give up on the whole idea of fishing. I had my hopes, but I had a family to support, I had the education and my Army experience, there was no need to put my family through this kind of insecurity.

I started looking for positions through the job placement at the University of Rhode Island (URI) and diligently searched the newspapers looking for a fit. The very first job that I came across that was really interesting was at Electric Boat, the major builder of submarines located at Groton, Connecticut. Groton was about an hour away driving down Route 1—not bad.

I made an appointment for a job interview and I remember my first impression of the place. I presented myself at the gate that I had been told to go to, was given a temporary badge, and a guide took me to my interview. This was a high-security, super busy facility with safety-helmeted workers that were visible everywhere, involved in all the jobs related to building a submarine.

I was introduced to my new boss, a veteran engineer in charge of Inventory Control. He gave me an overview of what he had in mind for me to do. This was a new job, so there were no specific guidelines at this point. I was given a tour of the immediate Inventory Control area. My desk would be in the main work area where about 35 or so women were posting entries on inventory cards. My first impression was that it was a busy place and somewhat noisy with all the machines being used at once.

I decided to take the job. My new title was Administrative Assistant, Inventory Control, Electric Boat Division, General Dynamics Corporation, Groton, CT. My wife was pleased that I had a "real" job with a regular salary. In 1956, Electric Boat (EB) had completed the *Nautilus* except for additional sea trials. The second "nuclear" boat named *Sea Wolf* was in the water, but had another year of work before being readied for sea. I had no problem getting the necessary security clearance to work at EB, so I had opportunities to go aboard the *Sea Wolf*.

If you have walked in to a marine store like West Marine, you notice the price of the strictly marine items are costly. The real value of inventory at EB was in the "beyond belief" category.

Late that summer, I attended an in-house submarine familiarization course for new employees. Most of the classes were held at a small college across the river in New London and the Navy Submarine Base located north of EB. The course gave us an overview of every general system in the subs, much of which was considered classified.

During my time at EB, I had a ride with a driver who used his car as a mini-business. This was a good deal for me because he always did the driving. It was about an hour each way in those days on the old Route 1. There were four of us besides the driver. They worked in the electrical field, drafting and testing of vessel components. Gordon Napier, one of the regular passengers and I used to sit in the back seat and talk about boats, and fishing. One day he brought a plan from a magazine to show me. It was called a Pemaquid Dory, about 20 feet long. In the early spring I started cutting the oak for the bow, keel, and stern of the boat at the Wakefield Branch Woodworking Mill on Robinson Street in Wakefield. I assembled the pieces, adding oak frames. All this was done in the back yard of my father's summer house in Charlestown. Since I had a regular job at EB, this would be a good project. It was many years later when I finally finished the boat in my own back yard.

On our daily trips, we would leave in the dark and come home in the dark except during daylight saving time. I was sitting at my desk most of the day, then in a car. I started jogging around the neighborhood after dinner at night. I never saw any other runners back in those days.

My work at EB was complicated and interesting at first, but over time, it became tedious. I really couldn't see where this choice of a career was leading. Without an additional engineering degree or a Master's Degree, I could not see how there would be opportunities for significant advancement within the company.

In the late spring of 1957 I was contacted by Harold Loftes, one of the top seiner captain/owners in Point Judith, who asked me if I would be interested in being a member of his crew for the upcoming season. I believe it was Tex from the *Mary Ann* days that had recommended me to Harold.

It didn't take me long to decide, like seconds, and I convinced Joan that this was a chance to try fishing again only with much brighter prospects.

I gave my notice at EB and that was the end of my ten-month stay. No regrets, but I was thankful for the job, since I was again financially in decent shape.

The "trash plant"

Chapter 5

Seining—Spring of 1957

I was 25 years old, late in years to be starting out "again" in the fishing business. Many of the fishermen in the port of Point Judith, back then, had grown up as members of fishing families and by my age had years of valuable experience.

In my haste to leave EB, I ended up having to wait two months until June to begin work with Harold on the *Menco*. I managed to land a site on a three-man dragger called *The North Star* with Captain/Owner John Sisson, who was also a well-known marine artist. The other crew member was Bob Smith, who was much younger than me; this was the beginning of a lifelong friendship with Bob.

We went "trash fishing" that spring, which was used primarily for fish meal and not for human consumption, delivering most of the catch to the rendering plant. We saved whatever "good fish" we caught, such as blackback flounder, for sale at the Co-op. This was my first experience working on a dragger and it gave me beginner's knowledge of bottom trawling.

June came and I started my summer seining with Harold and Warren Loftes. The *Menco* was a 65 ft. Chesapeake Bay-built wooden boat with a combined wheelhouse and deckhouse well forward, leaving a generous open deck aft over the fish hold. The remaining crew of Linwood "Lin" Rathbone, the cook, and George "Eggy" Gamache worked on the boat year round and had been together for years. Tom Sanders, like me, was the additional crew necessary for seining.

They were used to having fun together. There was a lot of good natured kidding around, so to speak, and Captain Harold was an active participant, if not the target of many of the jibes. There had already been considerable work done in preparation for the beginning of the season, so it didn't take long to get started.

Harold and Warren, after a lifetime working Narragansett Bay, started catching fish right away. One of my assignments was as a fish spotter up in the mast. I often wondered if that was one of the

Lin Rathbone and Eggy setting the net

main reasons for being hired—a pair of eyes.

The big difference this time around was we started early and went fishing every day. Even on the windy or foggy days we would give it a try. There were few days that we didn't catch fish. By the end of June, we had landed, nearly 1 million pounds of pogies (Menhaden).

In all my years of fishing, those years with Harold catching fish with a seine, especially that crew, was the most fun I ever had. I couldn't wait to get out on the Bay every morning. The whole crew shared my enthusiasm. We were even making money! I suppose that was our goal, but we just liked working together, and yes, having fun catching fish. There were many important lessons learned that summer. A crew that is making money will never bitch about anything. No matter how hard things get, how bad the weather is, or even when a crewmember is physically hurting, the work gets done. Not once did I ever hear a member of the crew say anything derogatory about anyone else on the boat. Most important, the captain has to lead and create a positive attitude. We all had the utmost respect for Harold and Warren. In Harold's case, he could do every job on the boat including major engine and electrical repairs. Harold had even built the 44 ft. seine boat we used in his back yard in addition to five or six small draggers over the years.

Early in the season, we worked the upper Bay, especially the Providence River. We caught a lot of fish in the river, but it was dirty work. The net, when pursed, would act like a dredge and the whole lower section of netting and the rings would come up covered with mud. When we hauled in the net by hand, we also got covered in mud. It's a wonder we didn't get infected with something.

We did some crazy things sometimes. About the time each of the crew pulling twine on the rail had twine piled up as high as their knees, someone pulling twine by the rings, usually Eggy, would push the man next to him, and like dominoes, one after the other, fell over into the twine. Anything for a laugh—a good time was had by all.

I recall one day off Bristol, two of us up on the mast were looking for fish, when a friend of Harold's down on deck visiting for

Hauling the seine (author second from the top)

the day said "That looks like a body right there" and he was pointing at an object not more than fifty feet away. He was right. We had all been looking for flips much farther away and completely missed seeing it.

Tom Sanders and I went out in the skiff, the two volunteers, to retrieve the body. The body turned out to be a woman dressed in a long night-gown. Tom and I carefully lifted her into the skiff. I remember that she had a few bruises, but looked like she hadn't been in the water too long. Meanwhile, Harold had called the Coast Guard and before long a small cutter came out from Bristol Harbor to take possession of the body. The Coast Guard crew lowered a long rescue-type basket down to us, we lifted her in and they began pulling the basket up while we steadied it from below. At the point it was beyond our reach, for whatever reason, the basket tipped and down she came back into our arms. The next try, Tom and I strapped the body securely to the basket and the second lift went fine.

After the Coast Guard filled out their report, we resumed fishing. We found out the next day that the woman had jumped from the Mount Hope Bridge.

We used to tease Harold about Jack Westcott catching fish

Hardening up the "bunt" end

up the Providence River. No matter how early we would start in the morning, the *Joyce Ann* was always there ahead of us. Those of us spotting fish from the mast and Lin Rathbone looking for fish with his binoculars from the wheelhouse, would say that we saw Jack set out—or it looked like he had a big set out, or even that he looked loaded and probably was heading for the Point.

We knew that Harold couldn't stand missing out on catching fish, and Jack was the main competitor. We also knew Harold would much rather catch fish anywhere else than chase after Jack. Just busting him up!

We had two big sets one day and loaded the boat with fish still in the net alongside. Harold decided to keep on brailing the fish aboard, to transfer it from the net to the hold, loading the deck evenly. When we finally emptied the net, the deck of the *Menco* was nearly awash. Warren, who usually took the boat to the Point, said "Cap, I don't want to take the boat loaded like this." Harold said he would take it and with Eggy and I aboard, we started for the Point while Warren and the rest of the crew went to Wickford. It was a hairy trip. The sea was very calm and we made it without incident. It

Ready to brail

Brailing the pogies

seemed that while the boat was moving ahead, there was a little more freeboard. When we were inside the harbor, Harold very slowly throttled back and we eased into the pump dock. There was a lot of shoveling to clean up the deck. We weighed out 150,000 lbs., about 30,000 more than we usually carried.

We had caught millions of pounds of fish by the end of August, but the fish were becoming hard to find in the Bay. Warren had started spotting fish from the air using a chartered plane and pilot. Once he found a decent shoal, Warren would direct Harold just how to set the seine. This was to be the future of seining operations, including tuna and harpooning swordfish.

Warren's replacement on the boat was "Thad" Holberton, whom I had fished with back on the *Mary Ann* years earlier. He took over hauling the floats next to me. Thad was a good friend of both Lin and Tom.

In September, Harold and Warren invited me to go with them on a larger plane to look for fish outside the Bay. We checked out the waters around Martha's Vineyard and Nantucket Sound without seeing anything of interest. We then checked out the north

150,000 lbs.

side of Long Island. We saw fish being caught by the big pogie boats operating from the Smith meal plant at Promiseland, west of Greenport.

As I recall, there were at least 8 of these 120-foot carry boats fishing the two seine boat system, which is very effective encircling the shoals of fish. The Smith boats could lift their seine boats and steam at 15-18 knots compared to the 7+ knots by the *Menco* towing our seine boat. If we were going to fish along the north side of Long Island, we would have some serious competition. At times during the summer, as many as three Smith boats fished in Narragansett Bay, so Harold knew their capabilities.

That day we did see bodies of fish in Great Peconic Bay. According to Harold, the big seiners had agreed not to fish in that area. This was where we went. With Warren spotting, we were able to load up with one or two sets each day. Tom, Lin and Thad took the seine boat and skiff into Greenport and found a place to board. Harold, Eggy and I took the boat back and forth to Point Judith with the fish. Warren and his pilot were flying out of a grass field on Long Island.

Later that month, we moved the operation farther west and operated out of Mattituck Inlet, where the guys found another rooming house. We were far enough west so that we could get in a few sets before the Smith boats from Promiseland arrived. We followed fish down the coast until the fishing dried up. None of us were home that much, if at all that month.

The last set of the season was just east of the Green Fairway Buoy outside of Old Harbor, Block Island. Warren said it looked like we got around the fish when we set. There is about 60 feet of water there and we often missed fish because they could sound and go under the net before we could get it pursed.

Not this time. We must have caught them all. However many "all" was. As soon as the rings came out of the water, the seine boat heeled way over almost taking water over the rail. The fish, as a body, were driving down against the netting unlike any set that I had ever seen. Harold lowered the rings back in the water that brought the boat back some. The fish, finally realizing they were caught, started breaking water all over the surface. They drove the floats under water and fish poured over the top of the net along the outer edge opposite the seine boat. Normally Eggy, in the skiff, would pull up some corks and tie them off to the skiff. This time Harold yelled to Eggy to push the corks down with the oar to let more out. More fish were pouring out under the seine boat through the opening in the net where Harold had lowered the rings. We had one tough pull hauling the seine allowing fish to spill out the whole time.

The set turned out to give us a load of 120,000 lbs. and we let some go at the end. How many fish were in the net initially, we could only guess—200,000 more or less. The whole crew realized this had been a close call. What an end to the season that would have been had we sunk the boat. Warren, flying up above, witnessed the whole scene.

The season ended on October 23rd according to my records. 1957 was a great season and our total catch was around 7 million pounds. Our crew shares were beyond any of our expectations. I heard that all the boats from the Point did well. The difference with us was the use of the plane. With Warren in the air, we were able to fish off Long Island, thereby extending the season. There would be no place for me on the *Menco* when the boat went dragging through the winter and spring. One long lasting benefit of that season was that Joan and I went looking for a house lot. We found an acre lot on property that was being developed. The price = $2,100. A dollar went a long way in those days.

Chapter 6

Gaining Experience

Knowing that it was a common practice, at least in Point Judith, that the new crew member on a boat was given the job as cook, I needed some serious help before I stepped aboard a boat. Before leaving the *Menco*, I asked "Lin" Rathbone, our amazing cook, for some recipes. He wrote down ten dinners including the preparation and how much to buy for a crew of four.

The fall of 1957 went by working on different draggers as a "transit", filling in for regular crew members who were taking trips off for various reasons. Most of the trips were dragging for yellow eels with a mix of blackback flounders.

Back then we unloaded the boat loads of eels at the trash plant by hand. That means by 100 lb. basketfuls, one at a time, with a winch lifting and swinging the basket up onto the dock and dumping the fish onto a conveyor belt. This process took three crew members. One on the winch, usually the captain or mate, one on the deck at the hatch, and one grabbing the swinging basket and dumping the fish. Usually, I was on the dock doing the dumping. There were some cold hours during the winter. Quite a contrast compared to unloading pogies with a pump. I wasn't making a lot of money, but I didn't go behind. The one thing I didn't like was the insecurity of not having a steady job.

Early in the winter of 1958, I landed a site as cook with Captain Sam Cottle on the *F/V Dorothy & Betty*. In addition to Sam, who also owned the boat, there was Norman Gilbert as mate and Paul Champlin as engineer.

Fishing offshore in 50-80 fathoms south of Block Island, we made three or four day trips catching butterfish, squid and some fluke. I remember Sam saying how there were not many fluke along the "edge" compared to past years.

We would spend our days on deck sorting the catch on our hands and knees. Each tow, we washed the fish and iced them down in the fish hold which was divided into pens to keep the different species separated. It would be another 30 years before the use of conveyor belts was implemented for sorting fish standing up.

Later in the winter, we had some good tows of scup more to the west, south of Long Island. In early spring, we went trash fishing for hake and whiting. Before noon, most every day, we would fill the boat with about 75,000 lbs. as I recall and head for the Point to pump out the fish. We could make up to five trips a week, and it was fun loading up every day.

At least in the beginning, I was the worst cook Sam had ever had. Sam enjoyed his meals, and here I was with Rathbone's recipes as my only resource. Most of the dinners could be cooked in the oven which allowed me maximum time to work on deck.

As summer came on, Sam worked the *Dorothy & Betty* off toward the "fingers" and the "dump" catching a mix of fish. I remember Sam blasting away with his pistol at the sharks as we pulled the net in. Sometimes a blue shark would be hanging on to the cod end while we were hoisting it aboard. Because of the sharks we had to pull in the wings each time we hauled back. We would then dump a basket of floating trash fish overboard and steam far enough away from the feeding sharks to be able to set out again without them chewing up the cod end.

During one of those moves, in my haste, I flipped a metal float that hit me in the mouth, breaking off two of my front teeth. At home the next morning when I turned over in bed and Joan got her first view of my new look, she was somewhat horrified. I had some "glue-ins" made up and they are still there. I just have to eat corn and apples backwards. The only way I know how.

Sam rigged the boat out for swordfishing including a short stand at the bow. On nice days, Paul and I used to sit up in the mast while Norm steered with Sam out on the stand when we went on fish. He was pretty accurate and we caught enough to make it worthwhile. We had a small dory up on the forward deck that we could easily put over the side to tend the fish. I always volunteered to go in the dory. Some of my best memories from my years of fishing was out on my own tending a fish. Once you picked up the ball and pulled in enough line to put a few turns on a thole pin, you would be off on a mini sleigh ride,—not nearly that fast– but fun. Once away from the boat, it was always so quiet. The only noise was the ripples of the water against the bow of the dory. You could clearly hear the voices of the crew as they continued looking for another fish. One peculiarity of the small dory compared to the larger ones I used in later years was that you could easily pull the dory up to the fish. If you did that while the fish were green you could look down and see it swimming along maybe 8 ft. below the dory. Often, they seemed to look up at you and flick their sword up toward the bottom of the boat. Over the years, I never got "punched." In this smaller version dory, there wouldn't be anywhere to go if one managed to get you.

Almost all "strikers" will tell you to tend them lightly so as not to pull the dart. Often when the fish came up the dart would have gone through the fish and lay flat, "toggled" and the fish was finished. Gaffing the tail and pulling the tail up to get a loup around it was a trick and a half, and you usually ended up getting soaked. Once the tail was tied down to the cleat and midships of the dory you were done, although there was still a lot of thumping until the fish quieted down. It was then time to raise the oar vertically indicating to the crew that you had the fish. The boat would then come alongside and hoist the fish aboard. If they had another fish, they would tow me over to the ball and I would repeat the drill.

That summer, I contracted for a new house with a well-known local builder. We were expecting our second child in the fall and the house was part of our plan for the future. Joan and I had our second daughter, named Pamela, in October. While Joan was in the hospital, I moved everything from our apartment into the new house. All was in place when I brought Joan, Lynn and Pam to our family home. We lived in that house for forty years.

In early spring of 1959, Sam decided to go seining for pogies. He bought a seine boat from someone in Gloucester. The whole crew steamed to Gloucester to tow the seine boat back to the Point. We went through the Cape Cod Canal on the way. My first time through the Canal. It was a nice, calm day and we worked on nets we used for dragging on the way. Somewhere off Boston, I was mending the heavy twine of a cod end when my jackknife slipped and I drove the point into my left inside forearm. What a way to screw up a nice day. When we reached Gloucester, Sam took me to an accident room where I got stitched up. It was a deep cut, but missed any vital parts. After all these years, I can still see the five stitches.

We took on three additional crew members when we went seining. After rigging a new seine we were ready to start the season. Paul and I had seining experience and, as I recall, so did the new crew. We caught fish right away and loaded the boat including the deck with about 85,000 lbs.

That summer, with all the pogie seiners working, the Point Judith Plant would exceed its capacity, and we often had to sail to a rendering plant in New Bedford.

The highlight of the summer was a set we made south of the Old Jamestown Bridge. We filled the *Dorothy & Betty* to capacity, then Sam and Paul sailed for New Bedford. We still had a net full, so we eased the net out to give the fish some swimming room.

Since we were just off the north end of Dutch Island and we had plenty of time until Sam got back, a couple of us went ashore on the island. It turned out to be an adventure. At the time of World War I, the government built Fort Wetherill and Fort Getty on Jamestown to protect Newport and the Navy facilities. They also built Fort Greble on Dutch Island to protect the west passage to Narragansett Bay. The forts were reactivated during World War II.

Never having been on the island, we were amazed at how extensive the concrete fortifications and gun mounts were. There were a couple of buildings on the east side and other than the automatic lighthouse on the south end, the island was not only unoccupied, but kind of desolate. The only life on the island were some king-sized rats.

When the *Dorothy & Betty* returned it was dark, and by that time most of the fish were dead, making them very heavy to raise up so we could brail them aboard. We filled the boat a second time. The total came to around 150,000 lbs. Not quite as many as the *Menco* had set on a few years earlier off Block Island.

That fall I had an opportunity to join the crew of the *Whitestone* as the engineer. I really enjoyed my time on the *Dorothy & Betty*, a good crew and captain to work with. I knew that I would not have a chance to do anything but cook if I stayed. Norman and Paul had found a home there.

Silas "Dub" Barrows, (his dad was also nicknamed Dub), was the captain and owner of the *Whitestone*. The crew was comprised of Fred Rose the mate, and Bob Conley the cook. Dub and the crew were all brought up on Block Island. Dub taught me everything about the engine room and deck gear, such as the main winch. This would be my area of responsibility. I have to say I was more comfortable being engineer than my previous job as cook.

The *Whitestone*, a 65 ft. eastern rig side trawler was a good heavy built "sea" boat. We fished off-shore through the winter and experienced heavy weather on many trips. As with the *Dorothy & Betty*, we fished with 4 1/2" twine in the wings and body of the net and 3 1/2" back end including the cod end.

Again, we spent most of our time on deck sorting through the fish. Even when we were buried in fish, Bob was able to cook exceptional meals. Having recently been a cook, I appreciated how good he was and also how inept I was by comparison.

Regardless of the time of year, day or night, Fred Rose was always ready to play cribbage. He and I played countless games during my time on the *Whitestone*. In addition, Fred entertained us by telling jokes, one right after another, never telling the same one twice. I could not figure out how or when he had heard or learned these jokes. They were good too. Since he was at sea with us most of the time and Fred didn't hang out in bars when ashore, it was an unsolved mystery.

We caught many trips of hake and whiting in the spring. During that summer, Dub rigged out for swordfishing and we fished in more or less the same area as we had on the *Dorothy & Betty* two years before. This time, we were using a full-sized dory.

One day they dropped me off on the ball of a struck fish and I was able to tie the fish up alongside, when I saw a ball nearby leading to another fish they had struck, I decided to bring the fish into the dory and row over to the other ball. I pulled up the head of the fish so that it laid parallel to the dory. Sitting on the center seat I got my arms around the fish and rolled it aboard right across my legs. The only problem, the dory tipped the other way,—far enough to get my back wet before I was able to steady the 175 lb. fish. Not such a good idea. I secured the fish and picked up the other ball, brought up the swordfish and secured it alongside. The crew on the boat was unaware that I had picked up the second fish and were circling around looking for the other ball. They got a good laugh when they came alongside to hoist the two fish aboard. They didn't say so, but I think they thought I was nuts.

Another day I had my hands in the water securing the strap around the tail of a swordfish when I realized the head of a good sized blue shark was inches from my hands. Close one; never realized it was there.

That summer one of the swords dove straight down into the mud. Pulling by hand, I couldn't budge it in the dory. We took the line aboard the *Whitestone* and carefully hauled on the line using the winch head for power. We saved the fish; it came up dead with mud up to the side fins.

My limited experience with swordfishing can't compare with the stories the different crews of the *Ocean Clipper* could tell. Some days they had as many as 30 fish all harpooned by Gerry Adams. Now that's swordfishing. Many years later when I was President of the Co-op, swordfish gillnet boats landed well over a hundred fish a trip valued at $150,000.

While working on the *Whitestone*, I became reasonably proficient using the surplus Lorans, double or single units. Loran, short for long range navigation, was a hyperbolic radio navigation system developed in the US during World War II. Young fishermen today probably have no idea what I'm talking about as it's no longer in use, but it took practice to take a quick reading. Over the years, I also learned to splice wire and mend nets.

Dub had bought the *Whitestone* from a fisherman working out of Hampton, Virginia. He now owned a fish unloading and processing facility in Hampton. Dub decided to take the boat to Virginia for a couple of months during the winter black sea bass fishery season.

In January of 1961 we sailed for Virginia. I remember the night we left home. It was difficult to leave my wife and young family, even though they were comfortably settled in our new house. The plan was to fly home a couple of times during the time we were fishing in Virginia, and that was what we did.

The couple of months that we were in Hampton, we lived aboard the boat, taking our meals and a shower in town. Not ideal, but the winter weather was much warmer than Rhode Island and we knew we were there for a relatively short time.

The Virginia and North Carolina boats, in turn, fished up in New England during the summer, using Newport, RI as their base. Over my years of fishing, I talked to them frequently on the ship to ship channels without ever meeting them face to face. The few I did meet in Newport looked nothing like what I had envisioned based on their voice.

Many of the Hampton and other Chesapeake Bay and North Carolina boats were working on fluke (summer flounder) during the winter. We made one trip on fluke, fishing with a fleet of boats down near the Virginia / North Carolina border. In a couple of days we caught a trip. To us, the fish every boat was working on were really small averaging about 10 inches. They were so thin you could "see through them". I can't recall the exact dock price paid to the boats but I think it was 12-15 cents per pound.

We just ran the fish down the fish hold as they came aboard. We had a trip of about 50,000 lbs., which was typical for the small Hampton draggers. After that trip, Dub said "that was it" for fluke fishing.

The unloading was done by an all black crew under the supervision of the dock foreman. We didn't have to do anything. They dumped the mixed fish on to a big culling table where eight or more workers sorted the fish by size including other species. The fish were washed and iced in wooden boxes ready for shipment to market. I remember Dub asking the owner how big the sea bass had to be. His answer was classic. "If you cut the head and tail off without putting the knife in the same place, the fish is big enough". That's small.

However, we came to realize that the black population, in particular throughout the coastal south, counted on the smaller less expensive scup and sea bass as the primary source of protein in their diet. By the time the unloading was completed, the foreman allowed each member of the unloading crew to take home a small bag of fish, most of which would have been thrown overboard back at the Point.

Since Dub had fished out of Hampton a few years earlier, he knew the fishing grounds off Virginia and had the Loran numbers for most of the known hangs. As a result, we were able to start catching the black sea bass right away. It was easy fishing. Unlike Point Judith, using the same mesh size, instead of picking and sorting our way through a deck load of fish, we just opened the deck plates and ran the fish down into the pens in the fish hold. We took turns icing the catch as the fish rained down.

In a couple of days we would have a trip. We would lay to at night and set in again before first light. On the way into Hampton, we sailed through the entrance to Chesapeake Bay north of Cape Henry into Hampton Roads, then up the Hampton River to the dock located just south of the Booker T. Washington Bridge.

The boats in that area caught scup the same way at different times of the year. We heard of trips on larger boats of 100,000 lbs., sometimes with fish on deck. The fish were landed and sold regardless of size because they had a market.

Years later, when the quota for each state was divided up, the quota was based on the landings of these boats. Not surprising, to this day, the lion's share of scup, black sea bass, and fluke are given to North Carolina primarily. Also, the federally legal minimum size agreed to by the Atlantic States Marine Fisheries Commission (ASMFC) for fluke is only 14 inches because the Southern states maintain that fluke in their region seldom reach large sizes like those that migrate north. In my opinion, it is the fluke that survive that migrate north. It is what it is! It is very hard to explain to a recreational fisherman up north when their minimum size is 17 inches.

One trip, fishing east of the entrance to Chesapeake, the net was exceptionally heavy when we hauled back. We finally fleeted the twine in using a combination of the falls and the whip. A torpedo had worked its way all the way down into the cod end tail first. We first saw the business end right at the waterline when all of a sudden, there was a lot of bubbling coming up. Dub hollered to cut the bag off quick and using a couple of dexters, we cut the bull rope and the back end of the net, and down it went. Dub ran into the wheel house and we got the hell away from the area at full speed. We all half expected that the damn thing was going to go off, but—nothing happened. We never got to find out if it was World War II German Ordinance, but there was a lot of shipping sunk in that area during the war. Dub took a Loran bearing of where we had let it go, and we repaired the net and continued the trip. Again, close ones don't count.

A scalloper named *Snoopy* hauled up some kind of live ordinance in the same general area that did explode, sinking the vessel with no survivors.

I couldn't speak for Dub, but the rest of the crew and I were happy to go home and resume fishing out of the Point. Being away at sea is hard on the family when we are fishing from our home port for three to six days. Fishing like we were in Virginia was, for lack of a better word, "unfair" to them.

It is interesting to note that in those times, boats could fish for any species wherever they wanted to go and unload their trip to any buyer anywhere, including the Gulf of Mexico if the fisherman was so inclined.

We started our spring fishing on the *Whitestone*, picking up pretty much where we were the previous year. The weather down off Virginia had been more moderate than back home and that had been a plus. We hadn't iced up all winter. Back in the 1960's, we always experienced cold winters. Not only would the harbors freeze up with a heavy crust of ice, but at times, the ocean outside would freeze, especially south of Nantucket. Nantucket Sound froze over most winters requiring Coast Guard ice breakers to clear a passage to Nantucket in order to supply the island.

Buying a boat of my own was always one of my goals. As I got older, I was beginning to doubt whether I could ever accumulate enough money to even come up with a down payment. I needed a big hit. I decided to ask Harold Loftes about going seining with him that summer. Harold said that he could use me, so I decided to make the change.

I let Dub know of my intention to go with Harold. It was difficult for me to leave. It had been beneficial experience working on the *Whitestone*. Captain Barrows and the crew had been great to work with, the money was good, and the boat was one of the best sea boats in the Point.

Heading to the fishing grounds on a moonlit night

Chapter 7

The Really Close One

Three summers had gone by since the last time I had worked for Harold Loftes on the *Menco*. Since then he and his brother Warren had built a new boat named the *Miss Point Judith* the year before in St. Augustine, Florida. She was modified by Harold from the traditional shrimp boat configuration. At 72 ft., she was larger and faster than the *Menco*. In her first season, the vessel had proven to be an ideal carry boat with a capacity of 150,000 lbs. in the fish hold.

Warren had taken flying lessons and he was our fish spotter with the *Menco's* own Piper Cub. The *Miss Point Judith* had added two experienced crewmen since I had last fished with Harold. They were Larry "Jazz" Weinrich and Edgar "Junior" Clark, Jr. I hadn't met them before, but I knew Larry's brother Frank along with "Junior" Clark's father, Edgar Clark Sr., who were "lumpers" at the Point. Jake Dykstra's brother Bill Dykstra, Sr. was also one of the "Big Three" lumpers that pumped out or unloaded the trips in baskets by hand.

The seine was also new and different in that it was all made of treated synthetic twine that was much stronger than the tarred cotton twine we used to use.

Starting back seining with the old crew of Thad Holberton, Tom Sanders, Linwood Rathbone and George "Eggy" Gamache was as though I hadn't been away at all. Hauling back during this season, Harold no longer handled the rings, relieving him from the hard physical work, so he could observe and supervise the operation. With the additional two crewmen, we could haul back faster even with a heavy set. Remember, this was before the hydraulic power block.

The seining was good right from the start of the season. As it was with the *Dorothy & Betty*, most of the trips were unloaded in New Bedford or the Point, usually with three other crewmen. We took turns which crew members would make the trip or go back to Wickford with the seine boat and skiff.

One Friday afternoon in mid-June, I was part of the crew going to unload in New Bedford along with Jazz Weinrich and Junior Clark. By this time in the season, the New Bedford trips had become routine. We went out through Newport, once clear of the outer buoys, I relieved Harold at the wheel so he could have a nap. It was thick fog with the usual traffic showing on the radar. I liked the new boat and that day, with only about 7580,000 lbs. aboard, she handled almost the same as when she was empty. Everyone turned in and I woke Harold after an hour and a half, and then I hit one of the upper bunks.

I was out like a light when Junior Clark woke me up telling me to get up right away. "Harold needs you—there is a ship close by." I flew out of the bunk landing in my loafers and was standing next to Harold in an instant. He said he had lost the ship in the radar and I took a look and all it showed was a dark ring all around the center of the screen. We were stopped at the same time. I stepped out on deck, on the port side, with the other two guys, when I heard the ship's horn blow. The horn was not only very loud, but it seemed to come from up above us. Seconds later a high bow wave appeared out of the fog and what appeared to be a dark mass extending above us, less than 100 ft away. We all yelled at once. Then, first Junior with Jazz on his heels took off for the stern. There was absolutely no way the ship wasn't going to hit us. Their action caused me to run aft too. I could tell Harold had thrown the engine in gear and jammed the throttle wide open because as I was running that 40 feet to the stern, the ships bow seemed to be tracking me. I fell over a pile of gear stored back aft and scrambled over the stern. I was always a strong swimmer and I swam full out under water. I could sense the hull of the ship as it was passing by, then I heard the sound of the engine and the propeller. In that second or two, I knew I was going to get chopped with the blades. The water around me was all bubbles and froth, then like the miracle it was, the sound diminished. I surfaced seeing the high stern nearly overhead, then it disappeared into the fog.

It's impossible to describe how elated I was to have survived. I felt like I could jump up and run all the way to shore. The reality was that the ship was gone and I was in the very cold water. I spotted Junior right away. He was nearby hanging on to the cover of the Coke cooler. Harold was not far either, standing on the bow of the *Miss Point Judith*. I seemed to recall that the engine was still running wide open, then abruptly stopped as the boat sunk. In seconds, the bow of the boat settled away under Harold and was gone. Junior and I yelled to Harold to grab something to keep himself afloat. We could see that he was trying to survive while coping with the violence of the sinking when he grabbed ahold of a piece of wreckage. We kept calling for Larry and finally we heard him calling out in a weak voice. We were able to gather together in a close knot.

In the distance we could hear loud noises and what seemed forever, we could hear the engine of a small boat. I gave out a series of loud shouts and suddenly out of the fog came one of the ship's motor lifeboats with about 6 crewmembers on board. They pulled us out of the water and after assuring them that our whole crew was accounted for, we headed back to the ship. We were saved. We estimated that we were in the water for twenty minutes. The lifeboat crew were all young Norwegians and they wrapped us in blankets. By then, our teeth were chattering from the cold water and probably shock. We came alongside the anchored ship and I vaguely remember climbing up the metal stairway they had lowered over the side.

Larry and Harold were being treated by the onboard medics while Junior and I were given a glass of schnapps, then we took a hot shower. It took a long hot soaking to stop the shaking. We did get one laugh in the shower. Our balls had pulled right up into our groin and there wasn't much left of the penis either. We assumed it wasn't a permanent condition.

As I recall, we were given some clothes to wear while ours were dried and then we joined Larry and Harold about an hour later. They seemed to have recovered as much as could be expected considering their ordeal. The Captain of the ship came down to see how we were and I believe he apologized to Harold for running us down.

At some point, the Coast Guard came alongside in a 36 foot motor lifeboat that came out of Martha's Vineyard. After a recap of what had happened with the coxswain of the 36 footer, we carefully walked back down the outboard stairway and were helped aboard the lifeboat tied alongside the ship.

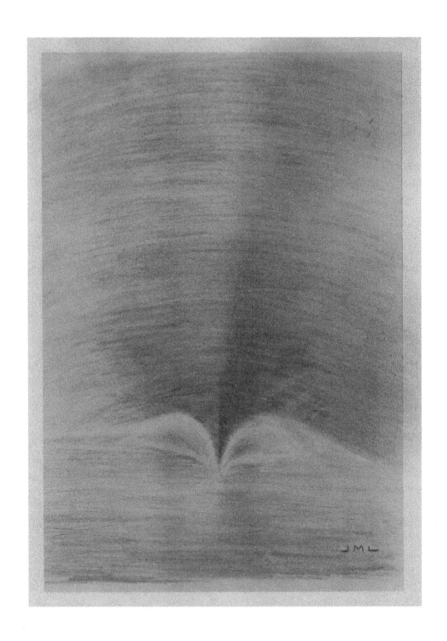

The bow wave of the *Montevideo*

We were seated in a small enclosed cabin and we all thought we were heading back to another equally dangerous situation if we had to go to the Vineyard Co-op aboard this boat. The fog was just as thick as ever.

The coxswain assured us that we would remain tied alongside the ship until the Coast Guard 83 footer arrived to take us to Point Judith—good news! After a relatively short time, the cutter arrived and we transferred aboard.

On the trip back to the Point, we sat around the mess table and talked about the incident. We heard, for the first time, what had happened to Jazz. He told us when he reached the stern of the *Menco* he jumped in the water feet first. Unknown to the rest of us, he couldn't swim worth a damn. As a result, he was not that far away from the point of impact. He floated right beside the hull of the ship for the full length before it passed and he was clear. How or why he missed that prop remains a mystery. No wonder he was the last one we finally heard from when we were in the water. Of the four of us, in my opinion, he had the worst experience.

On the way back, we crewmembers made it clear to Harold that he did everything he could to avoid the collision. He had a lot to think about after losing his "new" boat and all. I think by the time we approached Point Judith, he came to realize that the most important thing was we had all survived without injury. We could just as easily died together that night. Even really close ones don't count.

We were landed at the Coast Guard dock back in Point Judith around 1am on Saturday morning. The press was on hand, ready to take pictures of the survivors. I got the impression that when they found out we were not injured and no one was lost, they quickly called it a night.

In the meantime, as soon as we were recovered by the ship and the Coast Guard was notified, a Coast Guard representative arrived at the door of our house to tell my wife what had happened and that none of us were injured. Warren had also called Joan and assured her that I was fine. I drove home in the early morning. Joan was more than happy to see me and see for herself that I really was not hurt.

After daylight, I drove to my mother and father's summer house in nearby Charlestown to tell them what had happened before they heard about the sinking on the radio. They had never given me a hard time about fishing for a living after paying for my college education at URI. My mother however, did speak to Joan about it quite often over the years.

The facts of the sinking needs to be examined. We were hit by the 3,240 ton Norwegian freighter *Montevideo*. The 350 ft. long freighter had come through the Cape Cod Canal going in a Westerly direction for the East Coast ports of Norfolk, Philadelphia, Baltimore, then New York.

The vessel was under the control of a coastal pilot at the time. We were hit just west of the Wilkes Ledge Buoy at the west entrance to the Cape Cod Canal. Although unconfirmed, the speed of the ship at the time of impact was estimated at 15 knots. The *Miss Point Judith* was hit just aft of the wheelhouse/deckhouse at the position of the mast. The impact cut the *Miss Point Judith* in half. While in the water, we had observed hull planking as small as a foot in length.

All four of us were required to testify at the Federal building in Providence shortly after the incident. A key factor in the Coast Guard investigation that followed was the *Miss Point Judith* was stopped prior to the collision. Harold told how he had pushed the throttle full forward, turned the rudder hard over in an attempt to avoid the collision. Testimony was taken on the *Montevideo* after docking in New York.

The conclusion reached from the testimony of all involved was that both vessels contributed to the accident. For insurance purposes, the owners of the *Montevideo* were not responsible and the cost of the loss of the *Miss Point Judith* was assumed by Harold's insurer. As crewmembers, we were paid for the loss of any fishing gear and other personal belongings that were lost due to the sinking. This included gear lost by the rest of the crew that were not on board at the time.

Harold needed a boat. He still had the seine boat with everything ready to catch fish and a full crew. Soon after the incident, Harold, Warren, Eggy, and I drove south to the Chesapeake Bay region, the home of the East Coast Menhanden fleet, in search of a suitable boat to carry fish. We searched all over the region without seeing any boat that would work for us. We saw fields of discarded wooden seine boats just rotting away. Apparently the big companies chose not to sell any of their older vessels in that they would probably end up at sea competing with their active fleets. I remember going to one shore side plant where we were directed to the main office that appeared to be painted gray. When we got close to the entrance, we realized that the building was actually painted white, but every inch was covered with flies. What a smell! Of course, this was a very isolated area, not like Point Judith where the smell from the plant was always a problem.

We returned home. Meanwhile, Harold arranged to lease the *Menco* for the remainder of the season. We were back in business. We had lost a few weeks of fishing, but that was no big deal.

A few weeks after we started back fishing, we were running in thick fog east of Prudence Island up in the Bay. Since that is the main channel running up into Providence, there were big ships sounding their fog horns as usual. Apparently that was enough for Jazz, his nerves were shot after the collision, and he quit that week. As I recall Junior Clark also ended his fishing days at the end of the season. Both ended up working at shore side jobs—who could blame them?

Considering the way the season started, we caught plenty of fish throughout the summer. The places we worked followed a similar pattern as in 1957. There was a big difference with Warren flying the plane. He and Harold would plan where the boat should be located each morning based on what Warren was seeing from the plane. After he would set us on fish, he would fly around the bay as far east as the Sakonnet River. In fact, although a long steam, the river became one of our favorite spots.

The season ended and overall we had a prosperous result. My goal of accumulating savings to consider looking for my own boat was realistic. Of course, you could never have enough.

It may be of interest to recreational or sport fishermen that after three seasons of seining, two on the *Menco* with Harold, and one on the *Dorothy & Betty* with Sam, I believe the total catch that I took part in came to approximately 15 million pounds. In that total catch, we never caught a single striped bass. Since bass feed on pogies/menhanden, not catching any at all sounds like a lie, but somehow they must have evaded that type of seine.

I was back in a familiar situation. With the end of the sein-ing season, I had to find a site while I thought more about going on my own. I can't remember the circumstances of how it came about, but I ended up as a crewmember on the *Nyanza*.

In early October of 1961 Joan and I had our third daughter named Wendy. Thinking back, thank God I survived the sinking of the *Miss Point Judith*. We never really talked about it at the time, but the thought was always there.

At the time, Danny Silvia was running the *Nyanza*. It had been his father's boat and now was owned by his mother. Lenny Page was the cook and Pete Laurie was the engineer. The boat was a sixty foot eastern rigged dragger. Dan never ran a watch since we were fishing days, so my job was, more or less, another deckhand.

Fishing on the *Nyanza* followed a routine. Beginning that fall, we fished for yellowtail flounder primarily and black back flounder with a mix of codfish once in a while. Throughout the time I fished with Dan, we worked the area south of Block Island.

We would fish all the daylight hours of the first day, then go into the dock in Old Harbor on Block Island. We were away from the dock shortly after day break, and eat a good breakfast on the way out to the first tow. Depending on the weather or how much fish we had aboard, we might go back to the Island for a second night. I ne-glected to mention, that on the way back from our last tow while heading for the Island, Lenny would prepare supper so that we could eat while we tied peacefully at the dock.

Dan seemed to have a handle on all the tows in the "south of the Island" area. I assume he had learned the area while fishing with his father. Thinking back, I believe that Dan's uncle was Henry Mello, a well-known, experienced Point fisherman who owned the *Lucy M.* Following what I called our routine, we spent many winter nights in Block Island. As soon as we hit the dock, we would hoist up the net cleaning out all the dead fish and leave it hanging to dry overnight. That way, the net would be dry and ready to set instead of frozen in a heap on the rail or worse, covered in snow.

Those winter nights on Block Island, living on a dragger de-fied description. Back then, I think every business that was operating in the winter closed at 5 o'clock. There were only a few lights around the docks, that was it. There is also something about an island that increases how hard the wind blows. I think it's like an airplane wing effect. But some nights, lying in your bunk, it sounds like the wind is blowing 50 mph. We would get up in the morning and the wind would still be whipping. Dan would call some of the boats to see how bad the seas were and more often than not, it wasn't rough at all. We would, with some reluctance, throw off the lines and head out. Sure enough, the wind was much less only miles from the island. Years later, I would be fishing offshore south of Nantucket and hear boats talking about the weather and how hard it was blowing in the Harbor.

It must have been one night sometime in January of that winter that we were steaming into Point Judith heading for the west gap. I was in the wheelhouse with Dan. We had about a half mile to go and Dan turned to me and said something about going down to the engine room. I didn't get what he said, but before I could ask him again, he fell to the wheelhouse floor and began a series of violent convulsions. I immediately slowed the boat and disengaged the clutch, then sounded the horn to get some help. Lenny and Pete were in the wheelhouse in seconds. Lenny knew right away what had happened when he saw Dan's condition. Unknown to Pete and me, Dan was epileptic. Lenny helped Dan until the seizures calmed. Pete took the boat to the dock and we tied up. Lenny took Dan home. He had been through these attacks with Dan before and he assured us that Dan would be fine after a good night's sleep.

Pete and I had a talk with Lenny the next morning stressing the danger we were in not knowing about Dan's affliction. We pointed out to Lenny how easy it would be for one of us to be with Dan during similar situations and that was what we did all the rest of my time aboard. Lenny said Dan did not want us to know he had the condition.

Thinking back, Dan did remarkably well keeping his epilepsy under control. The "routine" made sense to me now. As long as Dan got ample amount of rest while fishing, he was able to avoid the episodes. I never knew if Dan was taking medication for the problem, but these days, a number of prominent people including a well-known NBA star has been reported to have epilepsy but keeps it under control with medication.

I fished with Dan through the spring and to my knowledge,

he never had another incident on the boat, I thought Dan was an exceptional skipper considering all the demands that come with running a dragger.

Pete Laurie, not long after we sailed together, started Point Judith Welding Co. on Point Judith Road with his three sons. Over the years, I spent a good chunk of my boat share on welding projects. They always had a better way to do the work.

My time on the *Nyanza* was well spent. I learned something about the grounds "south of the Island" and catching yellowtails. It was time to make my move.

An 83 ft. U.S. Coast Guard cutter

Chapter 8

The *Jerry & Jimmy*

In the Spring of 1962, I began seriously looking for a boat to buy. I was thirty in the fall. I had made up my mind years before, that if I didn't have a boat by the time I was thirty, I should give up the idea of fishing. What I would do as an alternative, I had no idea.

I had been looking at charts for years and there was one hell of a lot of ground where you could fish. What I wanted was a boat that I could take fishing anywhere. I had pretty much decided there was nothing in Point Judith at least that I could afford. I looked at all kinds of boats in New Bedford and talked to a lot of people: every shipyard, marine supply houses and engine dealers. I remember meeting one of the many prominent captains at the Caterpillar dealership. His advise to me was: "Remember young fella, new is good enough." Well that was good advice but not applicable to me just starting out.

I finally narrowed my search down to two boats. One was a 75 ft. hard-bottom dragger, rigged both sides that I might be able to swing. The other was the scalloper *Jerry & Jimmy* owned by Bob Brieze, who owned two or three other scallopers. Bob was originally from Latvia with an amazing story of how he came to New Bedford and became a boat owner.

There were many reasons for making my choice. Gerry Adams on the first *Ocean Clipper* was dragging for lobsters in deep water, 200 fathoms or more. He was the only one able to do it out of the Point. The *Jerry & Jimmy* was no *Ocean Clipper*, but it had a big Hathaway winch that could hold plenty of wire. The boat itself had been built in Thomaston, Maine; not at Neubert and Wallace, but a yard nearby. The boat was 80 foot long and was built in 1946, soon after the war when the Maine yards had plenty of select wood left over from their government work. I remembered even EB had built three steel draggers after the war (I saw the plans when I worked there).

Although the boat looked like hell with all the rusty steel sheathing on the sides, it had two additional things going for it that sold me. The *Jerry & Jimmy* had ridden out Hurricane Carol in "54" down by the Nantucket lightship with eleven men aboard. The other thing was, the boat was making eleven day trips one after the other with three day layovers. The engine was a 240 HP Waukesha, the second engine that had been installed in the boat. By the size of the engine room, the first one must have been a big direct reversible engine. At the time, Hathaways carried all the engine parts and had installed the Waukesha. It was air starting with an air activated clutch. Nothing like anything I had shipped with.

As far as the rest of the boat, it had eight bunks forward, two aft of the engine room, and one in the wheelhouse. By coincidence, the boat had always been the *Jerry & Jimmy* named after the original owners two sons.

My brother's name was Jerry and my mother always called me Jimmy although she spelled it Jimmie. Based on the name alone I had to own it. I'm not superstitious but it seemed to be a good omen (I can say that now because it was a good safe boat right up to 1974, when I sold it to Frank Lamy).

The plan was to take possession of the *Jerry & Jimmy* after the boat completed its last scallop trip. Bob was going to let me know when it came in, then he was going to take off the scallop gear. He owned a number of scallopers that could use the gear which included the dredges, booms, tow wire plus all the repair parts stored all over the boat. Since I had no interest in scalloping, getting the gear off was just that much less I would have to do to convert the boat to dragging.

I really had some time on my hands and went fishing that May with Jim White on the *Lucky*. The very first day, fishing out front off Green Hill, we took one bag aboard of whiting leaving the split overboard. We "H & G'd" (headed and gutted), a couple of bags, set in and barely cleared the deck, then hauled back with the same results. As I recall, we stayed on our knees cutting all day until late afternoon. We had been washing the fish and icing them down in boxes. I have no memory of actual poundage we landed. I think I stayed with Jim a couple of weeks, pretty much catching the same each day we fished. It was a work out for sure compared to other fishing I had done. Jim told me that Bill Rice was experimenting with a machine to cut whiting. I wonder why?

I finally got a call from Bob Brieze that the boat was ready. You might know after cutting my knuckle on my left hand so many times that I contracted fish poisoning that travelled up my arm. It was the only time in my fishing years that ever happened. No big deal, I had a lot of work ahead.

Financing my first boat was an exercise and a half. Because the boat was from New Bedford, I started with the banks in New Bedford and found out right away, that they financed the man borrowing and could care less about the boat. I had better luck in downtown Wakefield. Between a note with my dad, a note with his aunt, a sizeable note with Bob Brieze, my own money, and a bank loan using my house as collateral, I pulled it off.

I had estimates for everything I would need to go fishing beginning with the shipyard. I chose to have the work done at Norlantic in Fairhaven. The boat was hauled and inspected, as I recall by someone Sam Snow had picked. Sam Snow was the Agency for the Home Insurance Company that insured the Co-op boats. There were no problems at all. The inspector stated that there was no evidence that the boat had ever been aground. To my inexperienced eye, the hull shape was amazing, especially around the stern and it looked so dam big out of water. The *Jerry & Jimmy* drew about 11 feet.

The only formal paperwork involved was to document the change of ownership. The vessels official number went with the boat. At that time, there were no state or federal permits required. That would soon change.

I had gone over the work the yard was going to do with the manager. This was before Ave Strand became manager. Once they started, things went fast. Norlantic had a big experienced crew including a complete machine shop. That was when I started to make out a daily "to do" list, a practice that I continued throughout my working days.

I had hired a crew by this time with Clarke "Chappy" Chapelle as engineer, Pierce Chappell as cook and over all handyman, and Dave Champlin as mate. I had Chappy in New Bedford right away so that he and I could become familiar with the engine and Bob Brieze was still around to answer the ton of questions we had. None of us had fished on a boat this big. It was the near the end of June and we headed for the Point.

I have a confession to make and this is as good a time as any. Up until this time in my fishing career, I had never been mate on a boat. I had never docked a boat, had never set a net or doors, and obviously never made a trip on my own. To make matters worse, I had all the charts but hardly a single hang on them. My ass was really hanging out there, but I had more confidence in what I could do with the boat based solely on what experience I had as crew on a number of good boats.

I had discussed buying the boat with the President of the Co-op, Jake Dykstra, and I assume the Board of Directors was on board. I had become a member in 1958 when I was fishing with Sam Cottle. I have no idea what anybody thought when we showed up at the Point. At least the crew were all members of the Co-op. I don't remember where we tied up but at some point, because of its size, the *Jerry & Jimmy* was assigned to the west end on the south side of the main ferry dock in Galilee, where we tied up for years.

In preparation for fitting out, I had ordered my tow wire through the family company, Hindley Manufacturing of Valley Falls. Their whole business was in hardware made from wire of every description. My dad ran the shipping and receiving end of the business. The order was for two spools, each held 525 fathom of 5/8 inch wire marked every 50 fathom at the factory. No fooling around. The Hathaway winches took all the wire with room to spare for the ground cables and legs. I had been to see Alfred Wilcox down in Mystic, CT and he built two nets for me. One, a 52x72 fine twine net including the liner and cod end for trash fishing. Then a 60x80 with 4 1/2" twine for everything else. Both nets were hung on wire rope top and bottom. While I was in New Bedford, I had bought a 60x80 Levine net, right there in Fairhaven. Most of the New Bedford boats my size were using them at the time. It also had a heavy nylon 4" bag, plus a spare belly. Wilcox had sections on hand for these nets at the Co-op marine store.

In mid-July, I was ready to begin fishing. We started our first trip on yellowtail flounder around the "outside hole" south of Block Island. Using our new Wilcox 60x80, we caught good right away. Everything worked as planned and with an experienced crew, we caught about 30,000 lbs all yellowtails in two daylight days. I ran a watch at night. In all my years of fishing, if I "laid to" at night,

I always ran a watch. After seeing how fast a boat could get run down, once is enough.

We unloaded at the Co-op and iced up and got groceries, and were ready to go again with one day off. After about four trips, we landed about 40,000 one day. Jake Dykstra came down on the boat and watched us unload. We were shelving the fish with plenty of ice and, to me, the fish looked as good as the fish coming off the other boats. In those days, the Co-op was selling most of the yellow-tails to New Bedford. I was told that same day by the fish salesman, that if I was going to continue catching yellowtails, I would have to sell them probably in New Bedford. Since I was a big boat, I could make the trip, etc. He said to keep in touch and if landings of yel-lowtails at the Co-op dropped off, I could come back.

I recall that Jimmy Mello, who had the *Princess* at the time, gave me the scoop about the New Bedford auction and what to ex-pect. By the end of the week, I landed my first trip in New Bedford. As I recall, Tichon's bought the first trip of about 45,000. The fish were all "small" by New Bedford standards which was all the Block Island fish were considered to be. Also, the bottom of each fish pen was considered "seconds". As new and kind of frustrating as the ex-perience was, we were paid about the same for the trip as we would have at the Point. We were also paid within an hour after unloading. While we were waiting, I iced up the boat then sailed back to the Point. Since we were fishing south of the Island, I preferred sailing from the Point each trip. This was to be our routine throughout the summer into the fall. I think we did take out a few trips at the Point in October.

In mid-October, we made our first lobster trip in deep wa-ter. We set out on the west side of the Fishtail, or Black Canyon in about 125 fathoms. By the time we set out 450 fathoms of wire we were close to 200 fathom. We hooked up the wires, then let out an-other 50 fathom. I made a slow turn heading WSW until the fathometer showed we were shoaling. At one point during the turn we hit 250 fm. A ratio of 2/1 towing in deep water was ideal so that was ok. I settled on 190 fathom and towed off about WSW follow-ing the bank for a total of a two hour tow. We hauled back, no problems at all. The crew was at the rail taking in the twine while I was taking the weight with the bull rope. We could see pretty far down and all we could see was red. I think we all thought we were going to be rich. When we hardened the bag with the whip, we saw we had a strapping bag of red crab. We sorted the catch and had about 1 1/2 take out baskets of lobsters. I don't remember that any-one else was fishing there that day, so I set back on the opposite course. I managed to land in about the 180 fm. where we wanted to be. We towed longer this time to get back to where we had set out on the west side of the fishtail. We spent the whole trip right there, only varying the depth from 170-200 fm. As I recall, after four days and nights, we caught about 4500 lbs. We unloaded at the Point, selling the trip to Wickford Shellfish. The *Ocean Clipper* had been selling there for a few years, so there was an established market for dragged lobsters. The price was 60 cents/lb. for selects and 40 cents for culls and large. We had a good run, averaging about 55 cents, $2,500 gross. In 1961 that was a decent trip considering fuel price was about 28 cents/gallon and we didn't use any ice.

BLACK BACK FLOUNDERS

During the summer, we had built two lobster tanks using full 8 ft. sheets of plywood, so, doing that math, the tanks were 16 ft. long by 4 ft. wide and 4 ft. high. We had added a couple of Jabsco pumps and the circulation seemed to be adequate since we had few losses.

Our first trip, as I mentioned was in mid-October and we fished the whole winter for lobsters until mid-April when the water warmed up. We were limited to about 4,000 lbs. with the boxes we had. During the winter when the water was cold, like fifty degrees or less, the lobsters were in good enough shape to lay them on their backs in the ice down in the hold. We soaked burlap bags to cover them. Every four hours or so, we sprayed them with the deck hose. In theory, putting them upright on fresh water ice allowed them to suck in fresh water which might cause them to croak. By icing them, we could add another day or two of fishing bringing the total catch to 5,600 lbs.

I remember one January night, we started unloading at the state pier at the Point around nine o'clock. We were unloading into wooden boxes and putting them on the Wickford Shellfish truck. It was so cold, the lobsters were dropping their claws unless you handled them very carefully when placing them in the box. We made a few hundred pounds of "selects" into "culls" before we caught on.

Gerry Adams almost always unloaded the *Ocean Clipper* in Wickford, so I never knew what he was catching for a trip and I never once asked him. All I know was with the *Clipper*'s power, he was catching a lot more than I was. Gerry was always known as the best in the swordfish business. To me though, he was known for starting the deep water trawl fishery for lobsters at the Point, and he must have made a pile of money over the many years he worked out there.

We fished in some bad weather that winter. Setting back into the wind sometimes was just not doable with the old Waukesha. I often set down wind then turned around, always on the deep side, running the wires in a wide arc at full speed. Most of the time it worked out fine. In the beginning we used to have foul sets mainly because of not having enough power to hold a strain on the doors

BUTTERFISH

while running out 475 fathom of wire. No fun, but we got good at sorting it all out. By the way, it took the *Jerry & Jimmy* about an hour to haul and set with that much wire.

When I bought the boat, Bob Brieze told me not to exceed a certain exhaust temperature. There was a gauge right where the exhaust was bolted to the engine and although it was a maximum 1000 RPM engine the exhaust temperature was what you had to tow by. I made many trips to the engine room each day even after I figured it out. The first year, we pulled the heads on the engine more than once.

A side story: The floor in the front of the big cast iron oil-fired stove in the forecastle of the *Jerry & Jimmy* was almost worn through. Pearce's comment was that he sure wasn't the first cook to stand in front of that stove. The original floor was 2 1/2" thick hardwood. He cut it out and fitted the pieces just like new.

In mid-March of 1963, we were lobster fishing the deep water west of the fishtail when it got too windy to fish. The weather report I recall gave up to 30 mph NE, so we started in. By morning, the wind had picked up from the Northeast and we were barely making headway. We got to 40 fathom south of Block Island before we stopped. I laid the boat with the wind on the starboard side. By then the wind had picked up to maybe 70 mph.

We buttoned up the boat, tying the net along the starboard rail. We made sure the doors were secure. All the deck pen boards had already been secured under the drums of the winch. We had drained the lobster tanks about halfway and maintained the water level partly to make them heavy enough so they would not ride up on the heavy cables holding them to the portside.

We had a new heavy duty riding sail with all new fittings. A damn good thing we did. Through the morning, the wind just kept getting worse. Gale warnings had been issued, but this was more than a gale. None of us had been out in these conditions. The *Jerry & Jimmy* was laying over to port and moving sideways at a good clip. Every time a wave looked like it was going to break on board, the boat would just slide way from it. Because of the sail, there was no rocking at all. The starboard rail was well up almost acting like a breakwater. Once in a while we would get clipped by a breaking wave, but always in the bow.

We had a safety line running from the main mast aft to the wheelhouse, so when necessary we could move around the boat. I could access the engine room through the wheelhouse and we kept an eye on the engine room. Needless to say, I never shut the engine off.

By the time it got dark, the seas were running 30 to 40 ft. high comparing them with the height of the main mast. Down in the focsle, the wind was so strong it hurt your ears. We kidded that it was better if you kept your mouth open. Night-time was the worst part. With the deck lights on, the seas looked higher than ever. I remember standing by the starboard wheelhouse door, looking up at the seas, for hours on end. We didn't get much sleep, but nothing happened. By morning we were still whistling down wind.

Late in the morning of the second day, we saw a large ship heading west toward New York. The ship was having a tough time of it with seas breaking over the whole deck. I checked our radar and was able to pick out the ship even with the whole screen cluttered with sea return. Up until that point, I had given up on seeing anything on the radar—good to know.

During that day, with no rain, the deck actually dried out. An amazing thing with the wind blowing up to 100 mph by then. The other crazy thing, we had heavy steel hatch covers on both wooden hatches with a lip of about six inches that extended down over the sides. It took two men to place them over the hatch. Well, the covers would lift straight up off the hatch and drop on deck. Apparently the compression on the boats hull when hit by a big wave would cause them to lift. I decided not to tie them down and after it happened a half a dozen times, we secured them to the rail. I supposed with the boat working like that, if we stopped the air from escaping the hold, we could cause damage of some kind.

By the end of that day, we were in the deep water near Hudson Canyon. I could hear boats from New Jersey talking on the radio and they were having a bad time. They had been drifting like we were, but now, they were running out of drifting room as they approached the Jersey shore. They probably were unable to do anything other than drift. I had tried running ahead slow that afternoon and within five minutes I buried about three quarters of the port rail under water. Assuming most of those boats were smaller than the

Jerry & Jimmy, they would be unable to move but had no choice but to try. I had been in Cape May with Dub on the *Whitestone* and no way could a boat make it in there with these conditions. During that night and into early morning there was no further communications among those boats.

We put in three days of this weather before the wind and seas dropped off and we were able to begin to work our way toward home. We had drifted about 100 miles and ended up about 50 miles off southern New Jersey in 40 ft of water. We had been fortunate, more than that really, since we had not sustained any damage or injuries. We were just beat. The weather improved as we headed for the Point about 175 miles away.

There was one thing I learned from that trip. Having survived Hurricane Carol back in '54, the *Jerry & Jimmy* proved once again just how good a sea boat it was. As long as I had the patience to let it just drift everything was fine. I managed to get a call into the Co-op sales office once we got in range so they could let the families know we were safe. That was when I first heard that Art Reposa on the *Priscilla* was out there too. I had not heard him on the radio during the storm and it was not until were back at the dock, as I recall, when we heard that he had made his way into Cape May. That was good news. The bad news was that five of the Jersey boats that we had heard talking on the radio were lost.

We continued fishing the deep water into April moving farther east up to Veatch Canyon. In May, we worked up the bank to 75 fathom. The water was getting too warm to consider lobster dragging and the catch per tow dropped off. We did catch fluke inside that helped "the cause".

Chapter 9

F/V *Jerry & Jimmy* Part II

The boat had made money since buying it the previous summer. I had thought about seining pogies in the summer like Harold Loftes and a number of other boats were doing. It would be a lot of work to put the whole seining package together plus the lost time. Then I found out that Art Reposa had his whole rig for sale. It was too good to pass up, so I bought it from Art. Seine boat, skiff, net, the whole works. Art said seining wasn't his thing. In fact, he said it got to the time when he hated to go. Well, at the time I couldn't wait to go.

Dave Champlin and I were the only ones in our crew that had been seining. Dave had worked on the *Charles H.,* one of the Champlin boats. We managed to fill out the crew with two other men with some experience and my cousin, Bill McCauley. Bill had come aboard in time to make the last lobster trip of the spring.

At that time, I had paid off a good chunk of the note to Bob Brieze and thought, with a decent seining season, I would be in great financial shape. After three successful seasons seining pogies on other boats, I should have enough "know how." If I had nothing else, I never lacked confidence.

There were few fish up the bay that summer. The sets we made sometimes looked pretty good but we caught few fish. What fish were around were usually caught by the boats working with planes. Finally, in desperation, I hired a pilot with limited experience but by that time it was slim going. One day, I went flying with my pilot to see if there were fish anywhere that we might have overlooked. After that excursion, I decided to call it quits.

The crew wasn't making money and neither was I. Financially, I was back to square one where I started a year earlier. There was no market for the seining equipment; and to make sure I wouldn't go down the seining road again, I sold the net to a farmer to cover his blueberry bushes to keep out the birds, sold the seine boat to a guy in Connecticut who was going to convert it for whatever, and I gave all the floats to my friend and college roommate

John Avedesian, who was the Waterfront Director at Camp Fuller in Wakefield. John used them to designate the swimming area and for years the kids called them the "lemon lines."

It was almost August, so for the rest of the summer we went fishing for yellowtail flounder south of Block Island. My cousin Bill McCauley stayed on board as our fifth man. He had been renting a cottage in Snug Harbor all summer and toward the end of the season, the owner, a native of that area, offered to sell the property to Bill. Bill told me he paid $3,500. As the weather started to turn cold, the house was no longer practical to live in and it was impossible for Bill to commute from his permanent home in Cumberland, so he decided to "call it a day". With the boat unloading our yellowtail trips in New Bedford, it was tough on the crew making two or three trips a week. Up until about 2011, Bill and a fishing buddy could be found in his Amesbury skiff fishing for fluke east of the channel buoys going into the harbor of Point Judith.

In the fall, we were making good trips on a mix of greysole, blackback flounder, yellowtails and lobsters south of the "corner buoy" about 30 miles south of Nantucket and unloading the trips at the Point. It was during one of those trips, that I had the first accident on the boat. Dave Champlin had fractured his wrist, but still wanted to go fishing. He really didn't want to miss a trip, and he seemed to being doing fine using one hand. He usually ran the winch hauling back, but couldn't manage the winch with one hand, so

Dave Champlin

Dave took over unhooking the forward door, which he was able to do. One haulback, the boat rolled and the operator on the winch let the drum engage. Dave was about to unhook the door, when the strain came back on the wire, lifting the door, and taking his hand up into the block cutting off one of his fingers. I was on deck unhooking the aft door. We got Dave down in the focsle and bandaged his hand. I don't recall that we needed a tourniquet to stop the bleeding but we got that under control. In those days, the Point boats carried morphine aboard and I gave Dave a shot. It did help. We bagged the severed finger and put it on ice. We headed for the port and called in the accident to the Co-op. On the way back, I gave Dave a second shot. I believe one of Dave's brothers met us at the dock and took him to the hospital. The doctors did reattach the finger. Whenever I saw Dave over the years, I always asked him about the injury. The finger was of use, but bothered him especially in cold weather. Over the years, there were very few injuries on either of my boats, but this was the worst one and I remember it like it happened yesterday.

A Wakefield doctor had arranged to provide morphine for use on the boats in the event of an emergency. The Co-op was responsible for handing out the morphine by request. I think I signed for my supply. Twenty four years later in 1986 when I was President of the Co-op, we hired a specialist to open our large safe in our then upstairs office. The safe hadn't been opened in many years and we wanted to get rid of it. When it was opened, instead of the million bucks we hoped for, all we found was some old corporate papers and cartons of morphine ampules. Each ampule contained enough for one hypodermic needle. Altogether there were 2 1/2 cartons x 24 ampules or 60 doses. It was about 11:00 in the morning and I took the cartons to the Narragansett Police Department. Talk about a surprised look when I presented my "gift". Probably the first time in station history.

The doctor also prescribed a big bottle of penicillin for each of us. From then on if anyone on the boat had a symptom of anything they took a pill. We made sure the boat had a large can of Bag Balm for everything else—hemorrhoids, skin disease, etc.

I recall my first trip on the Southwest part of Georges. We fished about five days and caught mostly large black back flounder. Jimmy Mello, on the *Princess,* had given me some tips on where to try so we weren't fishing blind. We took the trip to New Bedford and a new buyer for me bought the trip. Taking out the trip, there must have been 1,500 lbs. of fish that wouldn't fit in a fish box. They called them all large along with the rest of the trip of large. I came back later in the day and the dock crew were repacking the whole trip separating the big fish as "lemon sole." I was pissed, but being an "outsider", my complaints were ignored. It was a good trip but should have been better. Next time I went on the board at the auction, I went up and told that buyer never to bid on my trips again.

With Bob Brieze as my sponsor, I was accepted as a member of the Seafood Producers Association. If I was going to be directed by our Co-op fish salesman to go to New Bedford, this turned out to be a good move. Over the years, I got to meet many of the boat captains. It was a great experience for a new captain such as myself.

Since Jimmy Mello was one of the Point captains that had experience fishing around the Lightship area out to Georges, I ended up fishing with him quite often. First when he had the *Princess* then later when he bought the *Northern Lights*.

I had hoped when Dave Champlin recovered from his accident, that he would come back on board. Dave called me that fall to tell me he was going back fishing but with his older brother Ken. He didn't say, but I think the family put him under pressure to make the change. After the accident, which could have easily been much worse, I couldn't fault them for looking out for Dave's future.

In thinking about a mate, I decided to ask Bob Smith, from the *North Star* days, if he would be interested in going trip fishing. At the time, I think it was early winter, we were making three or four day mixed fish trips in order to work around the weather.

Bob made the trip and it turned out to be a rough one for a first trip. Bob's memory of the trip was that it blew northeast with snow and we ended up with 50,000 butterfish, 2,000 fluke and 2,000 lobsters. I do remember the trip back to the Point only because Fred Jones' boat the *Baby II* sunk that night. As I recall Fred and his crew had been rescued by the time we got up in the vicinity of the sinking. Bob had some other issues with a furnace at home while we were out. All in all he decided trip fishing was not for him. Recently, he told me that was the only trip offshore that he ever made during his many years of fishing that continue to this day.

If I remember correctly, we continued the mixed trips through January of 1964. Then in February, the weather really took a turn from occasional gale warnings to almost continuous gales with "storm" warnings mixed in. I never made a single trip during the whole month. At times, the inner harbor at the Point froze up. The *Jerry & Jimmy* had 1" oak sheathing a foot above the waterline and a stainless steel plate bent to fit around the bow. This feature had been done when the boat was owned in New Bedford where the inner harbor was frequently frozen over.

Later that winter, I believe it was April of 1964, the lobsters in deep water had thinned out so we decided to try inshore around 80 fathom. I passed Gerry Adams on the *Ocean Clipper* working south of the 71 fathom hole around 14400 and moved east and set in around 80 fathom south east of the 63 fathom shoal (NNW of Atlantis Canyon). I made about a 2 hour tow along that edge. When we hauled back, the cod end came floating up full of tile fish. We probably had 5,000 lbs. We were just taking back our second tow by the time the *Clipper* got there. It must have been around ten in the morning. The two of us worked there the rest of the day. The crew never got off the deck—just zipping the gut. The fish were all 20-30 lbs. too. I started out with five ton of ice, Gerry said he had three ton. We decided we both had to get to the Co-op by morning. I remember we took out, me on the north side and Gerry on the south side. The *Ocean Clipper* took out 53,000 and the *Jerry & Jimmy* had 51,000 lbs. I don't remember the price, but the price never recovered that spring. Years later that whole area was full of the tile fish long lines. Back in 1964, there were no longlines or lobster pots. You could fish anywhere for whatever came up in the net and we did.

In May, we started trash fishing for hake southeast of Nomans island. Our fine twine net (52x72) worked well and the fish were thick. The *Jerry & Jimmy* held about 100,000 lbs. in the hold with one bag of about 4,000 lbs. sitting on deck. The area was only 40 miles from the Point. We could leave the dock around 11:30 at night and be set in by daylight. We could make seven or eight one hour tows catching 12 thousand to 20 thousand lbs. each tow, and be heading back to the Point by two or three pm. Depending on the number of boats unloading, we could finish pumping out the fish, wash down the hold, and be ready to head back to the grounds. We could catch a nap while steaming back and forth. Depending on the weather, we made four or five trips per week. As I recall, the price was twelve or thirteen dollars per ton, so for 250 tons we grossed around 3,000 dollars per week. The expenses for a week with thirty cent fuel probably came to six hundred dollars. Doing the math, with 40% for the boat and 60% for the crew after expenses with a crew of four would be $1,440 divided by four or a crew share of $360, the boat share would be $960. You might think as the captain/owner I would make $1,320 per week. On paper that might look great. In reality, any boat eats money.

We usually hung on fishing for trash until mid-July. In June, there was a mix of hake and whiting. Toward the end of the season, it took a day and a half to fill up, but we could pick up enough butterfish, squid, etc. to fill make it worthwhile.

It was always fun catching hake. My cousin Ralph Pearson was on the *Jerry & Jimmy* around then. Ralph had been in the Coast Guard until around 1959, then at my suggestion, he started fishing out of the Point. He fished on several boats before joining my crew in 1963, as I remember. Ralph used to stand by the rail when a "split" of 3,000 lbs. or so would come aboard. He would trip the bag, then tie the tripline knot while the empty bag was suspended off the deck, then flip the bag back over the rail. Too bad I can't provide a DVD of that whole procedure. Splitting hake aboard was quite a show.

Back then, we nailed pen boards in the individual pens so that there was about a two foot space below the boards. This baffle type of arrangement allowed the fish to flow throughout the hold. We usually left all the deck plates off on the portside while we took the fish aboard on the starboard side. That way, the load stayed more or less level until the hold was near full, then we would open all the deck plates in order to fill all the pens. Once full, we would tighten all the deck plates, then dump a bag or more down the hatch until the hatch overflowed. By loading this way, there was no "free" surface in the hold, making a solid mass with no movement of the catch.

I can tell the story about the one day when we had only about 80,000 lbs. aboard. The wind picked up from the west as we headed for the Point, right into the building sea. The hake in the hold stayed in place for an hour or so, then broke some of the pen boards that went across the center section of the hold. Soon after, the surging hake broke the remaining boards. (The oak boards were 1 1/2 inches thick by 8 inches wide by 4 foot long). Once the boards broke the fish would surge forward as we hit each wave. Down in the focsle, the kitchen closets and work counter that were fastened to the boats bulkhead were groaning and working with each surge. The boat was never built with the intention of carrying anything but iced fish. I was sure the forward bulkhead was going to let go. Even slowed down, the sloshing of the fish was just as bad. We stayed out of the focsle until we made it to the Point. Not good.

Before we went again, we pulled out all the cabinets including the ice chest. Once the whole bulkhead was exposed, we bolted 4x4's vertically tying in the hull ribs on the bottom and the deck beams on the top. By the time we completed the job, you could see it was an "overkill". Our carpenter crew got to work with some ready-made kitchen cabinets from the Wakefield branch and we were ready to go. We missed three days of fishing.

According to my records, the Ryan Fish Plant closed down sometime in 1963, primarily because of the strong odors emanating from the liquid dehydration process. There had been a series of modifications to try to control the smell but they were never enough. The Co-op, realizing the importance of the plant to its members, bought the plant and put up another building on the property that housed a large drum style drier. This new fish meal process allowed the plant to reopen with considerably less odor problem. This new operation continued until 1973.

There were several years that we sold our "industrial" fish to the Smith Meal Plant over in Amagansett, Long Island. One night going into the "Promised Land" plant (that's what they called it) I ran aground on the edge of the channel. I had a deck load making the total about 120,000 lbs. It was a soft landing, but since I was laying alongside the channel, I couldn't back off. We sat there a couple of hours until the tide rose enough to swing the boat so we could back off. I think I made that trip only about three times. It was a long run from south of Nomans.

Most of the time, we were able to pump into one of the Smith's pogie carry boats. In the early spring, they often anchored off Oak Bluffs in Vineyard Sound. They had enough compartments in the fish hold so that each of our boats had their own sections and were paid by the exact weight. Once the Point boats had all unloaded, the Smith boat would steam back to Long Island during the night and be back the next afternoon. They could carry about 800,000 lbs., as I recall. There was an even larger Smith carrier that anchored inside the breakwater at the Point. That one worked well because the day boats out of the Point could get into the "act."

Late summer and early fall was always productive for catching yellowtail and blackback flounder, grey sole and lobsters. My favorite spot was the south corner of the Corner Buoy or the "banana" in the Nantucket to Ambrose traffic lane. I always called it the Nantucket Lightship area. I had some reliable Loran numbers for the *Andrea Doria* wreck and I worked around there for years. Sometimes when I cut it close, I would pick up some big cod and pollack. One night, the inevitable happened. I hung up the net just as solid as could be. I never saw the actual wreck on the depth recorder, and the Loran numbers didn't match up, although I was close. The depth there is only 40 fathom and with the tide running hard, I was afraid to knock the wires out. I lined the wires up so they were running dead astern and shoved the throttle all the way forward. Not much happened except a lot of turbulence under the stern. A couple of minutes went by when the boat jumped once then again. I looked astern and both doors were way off to the side. We hauled back and all that was left was a ground cable on one side and a ground cable and leg on the other side. That was my contribution to the *Andrea Doria* wreckage.

Another night I was towing east in the same general area when I saw this big target on the radar coming towards me at a good clip. I could see a lot of lights on the ship. I put on my deck lights then made a call on channel 16 on the VHF. I announced that I was a fishing vessel towing east, etc. The response was immediate. "This is the *Queen Elizabeth Two* heading west for New York. We have you in sight and will pass north of your vessel". He then added "We have three captains aboard the vessel if you have any concern". It was quite a sight seeing the *Queen Elizabeth II* all lights blazing going about a mile and half away doing probably 25 knots.

It always seemed like it was at night when things happened. One particular night, we were farther east near the south end of Boston Harbor traffic lane. The tide was running hard and I had the rudder over to port to compensate when I suddenly lost steerage. I quickly checked below with Harlan Stanley, Sr., my engineer in those days. Everything was intact, the steering cables, chains to the quadrant, nothing wrong. We were standing on the stern looking down with all the deck lights on, when Dave Conley, our cook, volunteered to dive down and take a look. About that time a big blue shark swam by under the stern followed by many more, attracted by the lights. Scratch that idea. I called the Coast Guard and reported our position and our loss of steering. We hauled the gear back and awaited a tow. As I recall, about five hours later, a 110 ft. Coast Guard vessel stationed at Woods Hole that was on patrol in the area showed up. We hooked up the tow and started for New Bedford. The Coast Guard captain called me about a half hour later and told me he was going to pick up a New Bedford dragger and hook him up astern of us. We made up a heavy bridle so we could tow off our two after bits and the hook up with the other boat was pretty easy, and the three of us inline proceeded to New Bedford.

As a side note, this incident happened around 1964. In the years 2009-2011, my grandson, James Scott, was a seaman in the Coast Guard stationed on a 110 ft. cutter out of Woods Hole.

The *Jerry & Jimmy* had a broken wooden rudder when we hauled it out at Norlantic. The yard made a new wedge shaped steel rudder that followed the contour of the stern. The leading edge was 3" pipe and the back was about 6". The rudder was hollow and they filled it with a thick oil so it wouldn't be buoyant. The new rudder was a huge difference from the original. It was extremely effective turning in deep water.

There was a memorable lobster trip we made, again in that area, in 45 fathom north of Hydrographer Canyon. It was not a place that I had ever tried before, but the lobsters were really thick. The best tow was six takeout baskets or 500 lbs. in two hours. The lobsters were as hard as a rock and felt like they were "humming" or vibrating when you picked them up. There must have been another 200 lbs. of egg lobsters as well. We filled the circulating water boxes on deck and put another batch down the hold on ice covered with wet burlap bags. In two and a half days, fishing around the clock, we had close to 7,000 lbs.

The only thing wrong with this trip was that I went right back a few days later and it was slim picking. Over the years, I went back there at least six times and caught zip.

One trip I will never forget. I was towing for lobsters near Gerry Adams on the *Ocean Clipper* in late November of 1964 when it started to blow northeast. All I could think of was "not again".

Around 6 am, Gerry called and suggested we get out of there, being west of the "fishtail", and go to New York City. It was over one hundred miles, but closer than the Point and the seas would be nearly broadside rather than bucking into them. We sure did some rolling with the seas getting bigger by the hour.

We were probably making six or seven knots. After about four hours the *Ocean Clipper* was out of sight. By the time we got up to "Ambrose Buoy", it was dark and raining hard. Now began the "experience". Fortunately, there was a New York Harbor chart on board from the *Jerry & Jimmy* scalloping days. The radar was working well enough to pick out the large sized buoys so we started in. About every other buoy, I went alongside to check the buoy number with the spotlight. I talked to Gerry and he was already tied up at one of the Fulton Market docks. He said he would be standing by on the radio until I got in. We passed Fort Hamilton then under the Veranzano Bridge, which was completed in 1964.

In "Upper New York Bay", there were multiple freighters anchored off our portside. After what seemed like ten years, we got up to Governor's Island, then turned up into the East River. Visibility sucked and there were at least five tugs and barges that went down by us heading down river. I had just talked to Gerry and he told me to look for a flashlight waving at the end of the dock where he was. We moved slowly along the west side of the river when one of the crew spotted the light. Best sight I ever saw. We could just make out the Brooklyn Bridge.

The constant rolling had pulled loose the steel sheathing on both sides that extended about a foot below the water line. The steel was still on there since the *Jerry & Jimmy's* scalloping days. The steel ran about 25 feet along the rail, then down the side about seven feet. Once the seas got under the steel, it curled up and stood out like giant water wings on both sides. I expected the whole mess to tear off but it was firmly welded over the cap rail.

We had a tough time tying up so we could pull the stern in to get on the dock. As I recall, it was about 11pm on a Saturday night. Welcome to New York City.

Sunday morning, I called the salesman at the Co-op office, told him our problem plus we had next to no money. He said he would make some calls. I remember about eleven Sunday morning, the owner of the Blue Ribbon Fish Co in Fulton Market came down. He saw the mess we were in and said he knew a welder that could fix us up. He gave us around three hundred bucks and I think he gave Gerry some too. The next morning, a welder with a helper came down, parking on the dock. They cut and hammered away at the steel all day while we pulled the pieces up on deck with a whip. He took it all off, renailed and sanded the oak underneath. It was better than it had been. Blue Ribbon sent the bill on to the Co-op. We were good to go. Gerry had sailed earlier in the day. Next morning we sailed to go back fishing. It was a clear shinning day as we took in the sights on the way out of the Harbor. Thanks to Gerry, we made it.

I was home one night in September of 1963, when I had a call from Fred Rose, one of the former crewmembers from my time on the *Whitestone*. Fred said he was wondering if I might have a site for him on the *Jerry & Jimmy* this coming winter. As it turned out, that was at the time when Enoch Steadman was going with me during the winter, and I had already confirmed that Enoch had the job. I explained the situation to Fred, who knew Enoch of course. We talked about families and that was it. I remember that I was pleased that Fred considered working for me. He was always good company and an experienced crewman.

Later, during the winter of 1964, I was shocked and truly heartbroken to learn that Fred had died as the result of a bad accident aboard the *Menco*. Tex Lumbert, from my original seining days, was the captain and owner of the boat back then. They were "trash" fishing for yellow eels at the time. There is no tow of fish heavier than eels and apparently while fleeting in the net, Fred and Stanley Stinson, the third crewmember aboard, were unable to hold the twine against the rail. The weight of the tow pulled the net back overboard taking both Fred and Stanley with it leaving Tex the only one left aboard. Tex managed to pull Stanley back aboard. There was no sign of Fred. Somehow Tex with help from Stan, managed to pull the net back aboard and found Fred still tangled in the net. Fred had been in the water far too long to revive him. Stinson was in rough shape himself having been overboard in the winter.

That was a sad time for the Point. Fred's wife and family were devastated by his loss. Tex had a real hard time after losing a crewmember, especially the way it happened. Most accidents on fishing boats like this one, happen so fast and are so unexpected that the survivors spend a lifetime reliving the event, and thinking of how it could have been prevented.

A number of us went over on the ferry to attend Fred's burial on Block Island. After all these years, I still remember Fred's phone call.

This reverse negative photograph was presented to me by URI Fisheries School graduate Joe Upton

Chapter 10

The New *Jerry & Jimmy*

Over the years, I learned how to fish the deep water from as shallow as 100 fathom out to 225 fathom. On the east end, it was good until about half way between Hydrographer and Veatch Canyon. From there we could tow west right up into Veatch Canyon and down the west side then all the way to Hudson Canyon including up into the north end of the Canyon. We tried the west side of Hudson, but the doors buried in soft mud.

In my "hang" book, I had drawn out how the bank turned using Loran bearings at each turn. Without that very specific information, it would be impossible to set out 500 fathom of wire without ending up too deep or too shallow. If by mistake we ended up too shallow, it was better to haul back some of the wire rather than try to turn say with 500 fathom out in 120 fathom of water. If we did that, the tow wires ahead of the doors would come back all shiny. We often towed for lobsters south of Hudson Canyon beginning at the southwest corner (15025). We fished as deep as 300 fathom with good results and no red crabs. Carteret Canyon was our south end, not that we couldn't have gone farther, but we just didn't.

I remember one trip we made in that area south of Hudson. We had a good trip on board when the wind picked up from the northwest. We were near a boat from Atlantic City and the boat captain suggested we go in there. We stayed pretty much together running in. I called Wickford Shellfish through the Boston Marine Operator and they agreed to send a truck to Atlantic City to pick up our trip. If I had not been following the other boat, I would never have gone in. The channel ran parallel to the beach at one stretch and it looked like we were running through the white water inside the breakers. I was damn glad to get to the dock.

We had to wait about three hours for the Wickford truck. In the meantime, a local buyer came aboard and wanted to buy our trip. At the time his going price was about 10 cents less than what we were being paid, but anyway I told him I had a truck coming from Rhode Island to buy them. When our truck arrived so did the State of

New Jersey game wardens. They checked every single lobster we took out for size and signs that the lobster eggs had been "scrubbed" off. We had no violations, but the time it took to unload didn't help the condition of the lobsters once we dropped the water. Later that day, I talked to a few Atlantic City captains about the "inspection". They said they couldn't remember seeing any State people checking one of their boats over the years. Now each state requires a boat to have that state's license to land fish or fish in the state's waters. I got the message.

When I started fishing the deep water in 1962, there had been no formal trawl surveys of that whole region that I am aware of. When I started we didn't keep the monkfish we caught because there was no market for them and there were some slammers. In some places there were sea anemone and other unusual bottom plants. The only fish we kept was the big silver hake. When hauling back with the side trawler, it was necessary to steam around on the gear as soon as the doors came up otherwise the hake would blow out the mouth of the net. Coming up from as much as 200 fathom, they became instant "floaters". We would gaff the ones that got free of the net. The fish were 10-12 lbs. and we usually ended up with about five thousand lbs. each trip. Dave Sterling was in my crew for a couple of winters and he went to extremes with a long gaff to get every last one. Ralph Pearson nicknamed Dave "the gaffer".

The other "by catches" were glass bottles and odd colored rocks. We had a milk carton on deck for the bottles—they were for me. Pierce Chappel took the rocks and threw them in with the bottles. Some tows, especially up into the canyons we would catch quite a few bottles. When the cod end was tripped you could hear the bottles hitting the deck.

The main reason for the bottles was that we were fishing more or less in the trade route from Europe to New York City and back. The bottles once on the bottom eventually ended up in the many small crevices that our net would reach.

I wrote a story that was published in *Yankee Magazine* of June 1968 entitled "Bottles from the Sea". I have since sold my bottles or given them away.

Over the years, I made a practice of leaving the house around 9:30 pm after the girls had gone to bed. Sometimes I would pick up a crewmember on the way and try to be heading out around 10:30. One particular night we were under way on schedule. The weather was clear and calm with little or no wind. I always took the first watch until we were out almost to the MoA Buoy southeast of Block Island. I went forward and woke up the next crewman on watch, checked the engine room and turned in after he came up, coffee in hand. We had done this uncountable times. I always posted the watch list and what time to wake me on a clip in front of the wheel.

A good night to sleep and I was out like a light in no time because it was so quiet in the focsle. It seemed like no time later when the *Jerry & Jimmy*'s keel hit hard then hit again in successive bumps. I was out of my bunk, down the deck and in the wheelhouse in seconds and killed the throttle and punched the clutch out. My crewman was still fast asleep and had no idea what had happened. We were sitting in rocks that was for sure, but where the hell were we? The other three crewmembers were now on deck and I turned on the deck lights. I yelled to them to check down the fish hold to see if we were leaking and the same with the focsle. I ran down the engine room half expecting to see water rushing in, but nothing was wrong. The same report from the fish hold and focsle. I looked around and could see the lights on the end of the breakwater at Old Harbor, on the east side of Block Island. Just a guess, but it didn't make much difference at the time. Our compass heading was northwest. Since we were not sinking and I could only feel an occasional bump with what little swell there was, I decided to try backing off. Since the *Jerry & Jimmy* had an air clutch, it was going to be engaged or not. I pressed the clutch button and the propeller turned then I put it back in neutral. The boat appeared to move back. I kept doing that and each time we edged out. After about 6 or 7 tries, I didn't feel any bumping. I had the sounding machine on, but it was showing little or nothing under the keel. I thought maybe the transducer had sheared off.

Eventually I could see 10 ft. under the keel and I kept going astern. Once every few minutes the sounder showed big rocks, but we still had five to six feet of clearance. Just to be sure, I backed out to forty feet, then put it in gear ahead and turned until we were facing east. I could see the Island on the radar and the fairway buoy north east of us. Apparently, we had gone ashore just south of Clay

Head. Later on, I checked the chart of Block Island and they called that "Jerry's Point". That is really a coincidence.

I steamed around at different speeds and everything was normal, no vibrations, nothing at all. By now it was about 3 am. We must have made a big turn to the east for two hours in order to come all the way into the Clay Head area. Somebody "up there" must have been watching out for us.

I was convinced that the boat was sound. The *Jerry & Jimmy* was a well-built boat and now I knew just how rugged it was. I decided to continue with the trip. We had lost a little time, but once again close ones don't count. By the way, I never knew for sure which way the boat really turned. It seemed logical that it turned east. Had the boat turned west, I believe we would have ended up on the south side of the island which would have not been as forgiving.

As expected, next time we hauled out the only sign that the *Jerry & Jimmy* had been aground was a scuffed up worm shoe. The worm shoe was a substantial piece of oak about four inches thick that was lagged to the bottom of the keel.

There was another story to tell that is somewhat in the same category as the grounding of the *Jerry & Jimmy*. During the winter, we often fished for a combination of fish species. Using a tailpiece and cod end of 3 1/2" mesh, we caught trips of butterfish, squid, fluke and some lobsters mixed in. These trips lasted about three days and nights with most of the butterfish caught at night. If we got on the butterfish, the trip only lasted one night. We often caught a total weight of 40-50,000 lbs. These fish species had a limited "shelf life" and flake ice was preferred for best results. In the winter, I always took an extra or fifth man to work on the deck. Enoch Stedman, a lobsterman in summer, went with us as the fifth man for many winters. Enoch was fun to have on board and fit right in with the crew.

One night, I was on watch making a tow. It was the second night of the trip and I fell asleep sitting in the chair alongside the wheel. All of a sudden, the wheelhouse door was slammed shut and I woke up nearly jumping out of the chair. There stood Enoch by the door and he said "Having a little nap cap?" I checked the time and took a Loran bearing. We were towing along just fine. I didn't ask but I assume he told the crew I was sleeping on the job.

We finished the trip, unloaded, and tied the boat up on the

south side of the State pier. Next morning, I got down to the dock and the crew was on deck working on the net. Enoch said he hoped I had a good night's sleep with a grin on his face. I went in the wheelhouse and there were five big calendar girl pictures from the Police Gazette nailed to the walls with six inch nails. Enoch was looking in the door and said "Maybe the girls will keep you awake, Cap". That was Enoch at his best.

In the early years that I owned the *Jerry & Jimmy*, I used to haul out and paint the boat in July. This was a slow time after the hake trash fishing was over. Some of the workers at Norlantic in New Bedford would work after the yard closed for the day. They would sand wash the whole topside, spray paint the primer and the finish coat. I usually stayed over for one or two nights. The yard did all the steel work and the outside hull and bottom painting. By doing the work this way, I could complete the annual haul out and paint up in three or four days unlike the weeks it used to take on other boats I had worked on.

One year in 1965 or there about, I had Point Judith Welding build a new steel main mast with a four foot radar reflector extending above. Norlantic had the whole assembly galvanized and ready to install when I hauled out that summer. I cut out the six foot long cross tree out of oak using the yard's big band saw. They allowed us to use their equipment in those days. Same thing at home at the Wakefield branch mill on Robinson St. in Wakefield (pre-OSHA). While the boat was hauled out, we rigged out a single block and hoisted the crosstree in place on a predrilled plate about five feet from the top of the mast. There were two of us up there and it was a precarious position drilling and bolting it in place. It wouldn't have seemed so high if we hadn't been hauled out. The hell with this. I decided to paint the top of the mast and the crosstree back at my dock.

As I recall, I decided to paint the top of the mast and cross-tree white leaving the radar reflector and the rest of the main mast unpainted since it was galvanized. We were tied up on the south side of the main pier and Block Island ferry dock. I started early one quiet Friday morning. It took me about two hours to complete the job and finish painting.

I was standing on deck talking to my brother Jerry who was

helping me paint up. He was in college at URI and living with me that summer while working in the kitchen at the Larchwood Inn in Wakefield. Anyway, I looked up to see this well-dressed man walking across the state pier toward the boat. He asked me if I was the captain of the boat. That was the one time when my response should have been "that depends". I acknowledged that, yes I was the captain and owner. "Well", he said "my car is parked on the other side of the pier and there's some paint on it." I said we would take care of it and sent my brother back with him with some clean rags. About fifteen minutes later, Jerry hadn't come back so I walked over to see how he was doing. This was one of those "oh shit" moments. Jerry was rubbing away on the hood of the car in a hopeless attempt to clean it. Here was a new maroon Cadillac convertible with the top down, completely covered inside and out with these tiny white paint dots about twice the size of a head of a pin. Worse than that, because it was hot and sunny, the dots had dried on contact, even on the leather seats. Obviously, there was nothing we could do and I walked over to the guy who was talking to one of the crew of the Block Island Ferry. I apologized and gave him my name and telephone number. He gave me his card. Can you believe, I never heard from him. Maybe he thought he shouldn't have parked on the State pier— who knows. I didn't recognize the name on his card but I found out from the ferry crew that he was "Junior Payne", the owner of Payne's dock in New Harbor on the island. At the time I couldn't have picked a more prominent Block Island landowner. To tell you the truth, I thought he would end up owning half of the *Jerry & Jimmy*.

I believe it was fall of 1964, Joan said we need to talk about the girls. "Lynn, Pam and Wendy are at an age when they need you around more, especially on weekends", Joan explained. "You are on the boat so much now, it would be a good break for you as well," she said to back her point. Right then and there, I said I would give it a try and so the fishing schedule changed. I still left home to go fishing around 9:30 pm, but now it was on Sunday night.

The crew liked the idea of being home on the weekends too, but what we went through to do it. I didn't exactly ignore the weather reports, but I did fish in a different way. In the winter, we concentrated on butterfish, squid and fluke. We pretty much gave up the directed lobster trips. Spring was trash fishing, summer was yellowtail flounder, then in the fall, we chased scup and sea bass. The only problem was the schedule had us landing fish on Thursday or Friday which were not usually the best market days back then.

I would say it worked. It was the first time I could actually make plans ahead of time like "normal" people do. It was of course good for a young family. While the girls were in school, Joan often worked as a substitute teacher and would be home by the time the girls got off the bus.

Around that time, Nelson Bourret, a fraternity brother at URI, built a house diagonally across the street from us. The family, one son and two daughters were about the same age as ours. One year Nelson made a trip on the *Jerry & Jimmy* just for fun. A couple of years later, he was commuting to Connecticut. Anyway, I asked him if he would be interested in going fishing. He gave his notice and that began our long association at sea.

Late that fall of 1965, I decided to finally have a hemorrhoid operation. It was either that or bleed to death. In those days, it was necessary to take about a month before I could go back fishing. I hired Russ Blaney, an experienced captain, to run the boat. Russ took the boat lobster dragging and made good trips. Christmas was coming, so he made a long trip. This was Nelson's first year and his whole family was waiting for him all that week. Russ finally came in the day before Christmas. Quite different than being home on weekends.

The engine in a boat, any boat, is the key to being safe out on the water and with fishing vessels it's the whole show. The Waukesha in the *Jerry & Jimmy* had seen better days when I bought the boat, but it did the job with a lot of TLC. I mentioned earlier how the exhaust temperature was critical when towing. We did blow a few head gaskets over time which caused blow by that "grooved" the block. The engine was an inline six cylinder and the first time or two, the cooling water supplied by an overhead large fresh water "day" tank, would flood the cylinder on top of the head with the blown gasket. Not knowing there was a problem, we tried to start the engine, a compressed air starter, and after about a half of one revolution, the piston came up against the water with a thump that shook the whole engine.

In the beginning, we took off the heads to find the damaged culprit. As long as the engine was running, there was no problem. We never shut the engine off on a trip except to check the oil level but then we knew how much lube oil it took each day, so we would run it for a week or more without shutting it down.

Of course we marked the water level in the day tank. If the level was down, we would bar the engine over using a crowbar against the gear of the flywheel. If we came up on a cylinder with water, we learned to remove the injectors to find the cylinder that pumped water. We changed the oil in the engine that was contaminated with fresh water each time it happened. The dipstick for the oil would show overfull which was another indicator.

All of these "actions" were when the engine was cold. At times, we came down at night to go out on a trip only to find the "problem". Instead of cancelling the trip, we would pull the head that was damaged and put on a new head gasket or a rebuilt head. We carried all kinds of spare parts for just about everything on the boat. Things got to the point where I had to come up with a system that would solve the problem. Every time we shut the engine off for more than an hour, we would pump all the water out of the engine into the day tank using a small electric pump (a water puppy). We shut off the day tank valve until we were ready to start the engine, then open the valve and flood the engine. We ran the engine for years that way without a problem.

By the fall of 1965, I had paid off all the debt on the boat and had set aside enough to consider a new engine. There was no point in thinking about selling the boat with the existing engine. The more I thought about the installation of an engine, the project became more extensive.

I started out by talking with Ken Sr. and Barry Gallup at Rhode Island Engine, a GM Dealership. Based on the performance of the 220 HP, 900 RPM Waukesha with a 4 to 1 reduction gear performance, I decided on a GM v12-71, rated 350 HP at 1800 RPM. With a 6 to 1 reduction gear, I could use the existing propeller and shaft. That would give at least 75 more turns per minute when steaming. Because of the age and condition of the Waukesha, I steamed at 850 RPM and towed at 700 or 175 turns of the shaft per minute. With the v12-71, I was told towing at 1700 was reasonable with a 6 to 1 gear which could give me 283 turns of the shaft. I was satisfied with that much of an increase in power since the v12 with gear was considerably shorter than the Waukesha especially with the long auxiliary power shaft that extended out in front of the engine to drive the pumps and air compressor. Now that the v12 was an electric start, I could get rid of that. I decided there was enough room gained to construct another whole row of fish pens. By making that new compartment water tight, I decided instead on a below deck lobster tank that could hold about 7,000 lbs. of lobsters.

I then had a series of planning sessions with Don Holgate of Holgate's Shipyard in Snug Harbor on the west side of the channel. Dale Chappell, Pierce's brother, was the foreman of the shipyard and was a master craftsman. With their input, I decided to remove the existing wheelhouse, trunk, aftermast and replace the structure with a steel trunk. A new wooden wheelhouse and new steel aftermast went in as well. The main mast had already been replaced with a galvanized steel mast. I also decided to pull out the four fuel tanks and refurbish them as necessary. I further decided on a new 3' inch pump, powered by a Lister Diesel, to supply circulating water to the new proposed lobster tank.

Sounds expensive and yes it was. My initial plan for financing with a local bank was not possible with my expanded plan. With an introduction from Jake Dykstra, the President of the Co-op at the time, I was able to get National Marine Fisheries Service (NMFS) financing though the Boston office. That office consisted of primarily one executive, whose principle job was to administer government loans to fishermen. How things change.

In order to limit the downtime for the project, I signed the contracts for the engine work and the shipyard. Dale Chappell laid out the outline of the wheelhouse on a space inside the main building at the yard and fabricated the trunk and wheelhouse ready for installation. During those three months or so, we continued fishing. When every component was ready, we hauled out. It was in January 1966 and a time when the railway at the yard could be devoted to the project.

When everything was removed, it was downright scary. There was nothing on deck except the winch. Down below you could see the forward fish hold bulkhead from the aft end of the engine room with only the fish hold stanchions still in place. Dale decided the forward engine room bulkhead should be removed based on its condition of being exposed to the heat from the engine room.

Since this was going to be a three or four month project, I had the shipyard put me on the payroll along with Nelson Bourret. I needed to work with someone and since Nelson had just started fishing, it was unlikely that he could find a site on a boat for the winter based on my own experience. It was a hard, cold winter working in the shipyard. One particular job we did was to remove tons of iron bars that were wedged between the hull frames in the bilge of the engine room. Apparently, these had been installed as ballast to make up the weight difference between the Waukesha and the original engine. We had to use crowbars and hammers to get them out since they were rusted in place. Don Holgate threw them all in the cement of a new foundation he was pouring for the yard haul out winch.

My main job was to be on hand to make sure we were in agreement on all aspects of the project. We also brought Bob Merriam in on the planning to insure that all the electronics would be given space in the wheelhouse and would be easily accessible for maintenance. Over the years that I owned boats, if it wasn't for Bob's guidance on selecting new equipment and prompt servicing of everything related to electronics, I would have been lucky to get away from the dock. I am sure every boat owner in the Point and beyond would say the same thing.

There were few hold ups over the winter with only two that I was involved in. Once the existing four fuel tanks that held about 1,200 gallons each had been sand blasted and replated where necessary, principally on the bottoms of each, Nelson and I painted them with a thick black epoxy type paint. Well, with the cold weather, we were hoping they would dry before they had to be reinstalled. The tanks, of course, were the last pieces of the "puzzle" to come out and the first to go back in. They were a little "sticky" but we managed. The same happened to the paint we used for the inside of the hull including the engine rooms. We used heat lamps everywhere until the paint dried. Each coat was equally "difficult". Everything inside the hull was white. It sure looked like a brand new boat. Nobody paints behind and under the fuel tanks except us.

The job was finally completed in late March. It was worth

it. The boat looked and ran like a brand new rig. RI Engine's people did a perfect job. I can't recall one single problem either mechanical or electrical that we experienced when we went back fishing. The weight of the engine being further aft did not change the original water line after removing the ballast. The only "new thing" was the engine noise. The GM was a real screamer compared to the old Waukesha, but we learned to live with it. I once called the Boston Marine Operator on my radio and she specifically asked me what all the noise was since she could barely hear me. I told her it was the engine. She came back with some "sympathetic comment".

The *Jerry & Jimmy* increased its speed by about one knot from 7 1/2 to 9—big deal. With these trawler hulls, the increased horsepower just digs a deeper hole in the water. Towing was another matter. Using the same gear, we could tow, for example, 3 knots before and now, up to 4 1/2 or more. It was a big improvement for all aspects of fishing in deep water. Now I was in debt again. It was time to start pushing the boat.

The F/V *Jerry & Jimmy*

Pen and ink sketch of the *Jerry & Jimmy*
by the author

Chapter 11

The Change

In the late fall of 1966, the College of Resource Development, formally Agriculture, of the University of Rhode Island began exploring the idea of a School of Fisheries. Because of my involvement with the red crab study, I had become friendly with Dr. Andreas Holmsen, who was the principal investigator for the red crab study.

Dr. Holmsen was one of the professors assigned to look into the Fisheries School proposal and he asked me to become involved in the early discussions along with Jake Dykstra from the Co-op, and I think Jack Westcott, and several other captain/boat owners from the Point.

One of the reasons I was interested in a School was I saw it as direct way of getting into fishing without going through the slow process of working on a succession of boats in order to learn the basics just to become an average crewmember, which was more or less what I had to do. In my case, I did have some good breaks where I was able to make money and learn.

The early vision for the Fisheries School was that it would be a two year program offering an Associate's Degree. This in itself was a significant departure for a university. The push for the program was the strong belief by the staff of professors in the College of Resource Development that a School of Fisheries would be a beneficial addition to the College and provide a source of trained fishermen for the industry. During this time frame, the late '60's, there was a noticeable expansion of the fleet throughout New England.

The captains and boat owners present during those early meetings at URI were cautiously optimistic that our own fleet at Point Judith could absorb a limited number of graduates each year. Little did we know the positive impact the graduates would have on our fleet.

The target date for the first year opening became the fall semester of 1967. At the time of our first discussions that did not seem doable, but as the year went on the timetable became more re-alistic when the School selected three members of the staff of the Fisheries School at St. John's, New Foundland to be the initial cadre of professors.

Over the winter and spring of 1967, I was kept abreast of the School's progress more as a courtesy for having been minimally involved in the beginning.

In the winter of 1967, Howard "Howie" Holt asked me if he could make a trip. I told him yes, but not in the winter, maybe in the spring. Howie was a friend from college and a fraternity brother. He was a funeral director from Woonsocket, RI. No way I was going to have him get beat up by going lobster dragging in the winter. In mid-April I called him to see if he was still interested, and he sure was. At that time, Harlan Stanley, Sr. was the engineer, Harlan Stanley, Jr. was the cook, and Nelson Bourret was the mate. Barry Weinrich was the deckhand. We started the trip in the Hudson Canyon area and worked our way south of the Canyon. Fortunately the weather was fine and Howie was enjoying the trip. The weather report was "reasonable" for the next two or three days. About the third night, the wind picked up from the northeast. We stopped fishing and jogged up into the wind. By morning, the wind was screeching.

Believe it or not, in no time, we had an identical storm as the one in March of '62. Well, this was my second one, I knew what we were in for. There was one big difference. Young Harlan had cooked a leg of lamb the night before and we all enjoyed a big din-ner as we jogged along. Howie surprisingly ate a small share even with the violent conditions. By morning, I began to feel lousy. It felt like my eyes were bugging out of my head. I felt like throwing up but couldn't. Nelson and the other three crewmembers were having the same symptoms. Howie was only slightly better off. Harlan said that the leg of lamb was frozen and was at the bottom of the freezer when it was being cleaned out at the store. Here we are in a brutal storm with a case of food poisoning.

We had worked our way up into 40 fathom before we could go no further. About the same as last time. The wind hit a hundred plus again and we drifted for three days, but fortunately nothing happened. We took turns running to the head until we finally straightened out at the end of the second day. I had called home through Boston to let everyone know we were alright, especially Howie's wife. When it finally let up, the wind just quit and by nightfall it was good enough to steam at full speed.

I made the decision to resume fishing once we got back up to where we left off. I just told the crew that if we steamed back to the dock it would take twelve hours, then we would have to come back another twelve hours. Since we didn't have a trip, that's what we did. No problem except for Howie, he naturally assumed we would go to the dock after that ordeal. Although he had known me for so many years, he didn't know I was a borderline nut. We did get a good trip in the end. I gave Howie a certificate stating that he was a survivor of the storm of 1967. By the way, I have not had a meal of lamb since.

The new *Jerry & Jimmy* with all the changes we had made, especially with the weight and trim of the boat, was equally as good in this storm. We did have a plywood door in the new "turtleback" aft of the wheelhouse that let go when a sea hit it and Howie managed to get soaked while visiting the head located at the stern.

Everything on the *Jerry & Jimmy* was working like a new boat in the spring of 1967. Nelson Bourret, my neighbor was a fast learner and was doing a good job as mate. Harlan Stanley, Sr. was the engineer and stayed on top of all the maintenance. Harlan was always washing down the engine room and it was one of those "eat off the floor" compartments.

I spent most of my shore time working on gear, making sure we wouldn't lose fishing time when we were on the fish. Harlan Stanley, Jr. was the cook and the four of us would work together by learning to do every job on the boat.

One day, I was helping "Stan" in the engine room. We were working on the lobster well pump and there was limited space for your feet because of the inside curvature of the hull. I was lifting with all the weight on my right leg with just enough room for my foot. We were in that position off and on for about an hour. When we finally got things back together I could sense that my back was "not right".

This was what I think was the beginning of what turned out to be a chronic back ailment. Sometimes mending nets, I would be half bent over the twine and would have a tough time straightening up. I tried as best I could to hoist the twine up with the whip so I wouldn't be bending over. In time, I learned to do every job on the boat keeping the weight on both feet and as near to an erect position as possible.

About twice a month, I would have back spasms and have to go to my chiropractor to get straightened out. Not fun, but I had to keep fishing and just plain put up with the condition. I knew other fishermen that were dealing with the same issue. It was almost a "fishermen's thing".

We had been fishing for yellowtails with a mix of grey sole and flounders on the southwest part of George's bank during the late summer into September, unloading our trips in New Bedford. We had consistently been landing some good trips and we were fishing five handed. As I recall, it was during that fall that Ted Foley started fishing with us. Ted was an experienced fisherman and a welcome addition to the crew.

In the beginning of September, the tail end of a hurricane was passing to the southeast of us and we ran for New Bedford. The rolling around on the way in did a number on my back. I developed a case of sciatica, which is a continuous pain that runs down the back of your leg. By the time we unloaded our trip in New Bedford, I was damned glad to get home. I had to take a life jacket and couple of pillows to chock myself in the bunk so I could get some sleep, but the pain down my leg kept me awake until I got so tired, I would finally nod off.

My chiropractor gave me some pills to quiet things down, and I stayed in bed for a day. That helped, so I went fishing again. I did this three trips of six days each in a row. I ended up staying in bed laying on my back taking the pills for two days or more each time, until early October. By then, I just wasn't coming out of it. After that last trip, I was in bed for a week. In discussions with my chiropractor, who was also a medical doctor, I was advised to give up fishing. In his opinion, all I was doing was aggravating my condition. They had no firm idea how long it might take for the condition to improve. I then went to see a top surgeon about a back operation even fusion, but he advised against it since he thought I would end up far less "flexible" than I was then.

So, what to do? The boat had been doing well, but I had no

illusions that I could live off the boat share when I still had payments for all the renovations; and also, I was not sure the boat would continue to produce at anywhere near the current level if I wasn't there running it.

The decision was made for me. Dr. Holmsen from URI called to ask me if I was at all interested in teaching at the Fisheries School. My name had come up as a candidate, and the staff of the school along with the Dean of Resource Development had agreed to offer me the position. Although I had never thought about such a career change, it sounded like winning the lottery after what I had been through the past month. I had a meeting with Dr. John Sainsbury, the new school department chairman, and his staff, where we talked about the courses they needed me to teach. I agreed to take the position. The really big problem was the classes would start in the second semester beginning in late January. The content for each course would be up to me.

I was appointed by the State of Rhode Island as an Assistant Professor Equivalent at URI, dated November 2, 1967. When I graduated from URI back in the class of 1953, I had no idea that one day I would be on the staff. I am sure the degree from the University was one of the main reasons I was offered the position. There were certainly other captain/boat owners fishing out of Point Judith that had far more knowledge and years of experience that would have been great teachers.

Original gate at University of Rhode Island,
Upper College Road

Chapter 12

The University of Rhode Island Fisheries School

Lying in bed dosed with muscle relaxant drugs is hardly the way to start a new career no matter what field that might be in. There was so much to do. My first course beginning in mid-January of 1968 was Marine Propulsion, principally diesel engines. Since the school was new with the first semester having started in 1967, there was no existing course material or lab equipment available. That was my job.

Fortunately I had taken a correspondent course on diesels when I was in the army and I still had the book. I called the publisher and the book was still in print. Dr. Sainsbury, the department chairman, approved my choice and the URI Bookstore ordered twenty copies. As I recall, there were about eighteen students in that first class.

The lab was going to be a much greater challenge. The Dean of the College of Agriculture, then Dr. James W. Cobble, had made a small industrial steel building located among other agriculture buildings in West Kingston available for the engine and twine/net labs. My budget to set up was generous enough

Dr. John Sainsbury,
Department Chairman

to be able to buy a rebuilt 6-71 GM Diesel from Rhode Island Engine Co. including an exhaust system installed in the building. I was able to acquire a six cylinder Cummins diesel through their New England Distributor. The Caterpillar Dealership supplied us with a cut-away 4 cylinder engine that had been used in trade shows that ran on an electric motor. All the cylinders, valves, gears, etc. were visible and was a good teaching aid for a four cycle engine. The College of Agriculture contributed a four cylinder Waukesha generator unit. All three engines were able to be started and run using adapters to the single exhaust system. I was allowed to buy two complete sets of tools. We built a work bench and were ready to go for the start of the second semester. No small accomplishment considering my back problem, but as my doctor had predicted, getting off the *Jerry & Jimmy* was the only sure way to recovery.

Captain Joseph "Chic" Krawiec, a fish boat captain/owner from Stonington, CT was already on the staff teaching Introduction to Small Boat Equipment and Operation. Chic was a big help in getting me set up in the lab and over the following years.

Rather than hold the lectures for diesels in one of the class rooms on the main campus, I chose to do my teaching in a room within the lab building that had once been a large office. In order to give the students ample exposure to the engines, I split the class into two groups with a 3 hour hands-on session for each group. I had been thinking about my qualifications for teaching the diesel class. At the time, although I was no diesel mechanic, I had spent years in the engine rooms of a number of boats plus the experience with the *Jerry & Jimmy*. At least I certainly had more knowledge and experience than the young students I was about to teach. My goal was to familiarize the workings of an engine room to the extent where each member of the class might have an opportunity to become the engineer. Regardless, every fisherman should have a good idea of the engine room systems of the boat he is working on. In the event that they captain a boat, they should not leave the dock until they are thoroughly familiar with the engine room along with a competent engineer.

The first semester that I taught was a learning experience for me. Right away I could see a difference in these Fisheries School students compared to what I had expected. This group was highly motivated—they wanted to go to sea. There was always a full class under any circumstances such as weather or even sickness. There were many times when some were really sick. Unfortunately I had never been exposed to anything like it. As a result, that first year, I caught whatever was going around. I survived—barely.

Teaching was always a top subject in our home. My wife,

Joan, was an elementary school teacher and the three girls were all into school as their main focus. When I had to leave fishing and become a teacher and college professor no less, it was quite a revelation—like, how was this possible? Over the years when asked what their father did? I would tell them to answer that I was a fisherman or in later years the captain of a fishing boat. Now I was teaching, studying for class, correcting test papers, etc. The big difference was that I was home all the time.

During my first semester, which was in the winter/spring period, I talked to the staff about the students going to sea during that summer. Since this was an associate degree 2 year program, this would be their only opportunity for them to get some first-hand experience as a deckhand. I also pointed out that they might find out that fishing was not for them and in fairness maybe they should choose another career rather than taking a second year. As I recall, there were something like eighteen in that first class and there were minor concerns that we could lose a few, but on the plus side, the sea time would go a long way to further their acceptance to the industry upon graduation.

Well, it was my idea, so it was my job to place them all on reliable boats where there would be a good chance that they would be safe. Between Chic and I, we managed to find jobs for all of them between Point Judith, Stonington, and New Bedford.

One of my main jobs that summer was to keep track of the "guys at sea". In most cases, they worked on a half share as an extra deckhand. I made sure they were covered as crew under each boat's insurance since the University had no way to provide insurance. As the summer went on, a few of the guys did get up to a full share at times when the regular crew members took trips off. I think overall, they made more money than they would have working normal summer jobs.

I recall being at the dock in Fairhaven when one of the boats with a student aboard returned to its dock after unloading a trip. I walked right by one of our guys until he spoke up. He looked like he had lost a lot of weight and was totally wiped out. To his credit he stayed with it until it was time to begin the fall semester. In only a few cases, the assignments didn't work out and I had to find another boat. The *Jerry & Jimmy* was part of the program of course.

Bob Merriam,
Electronics and Electricity Professor

The summer of 1968 was my one and only summer at the University. I did have to plan the courses that I would teach during the second year of the program. But it was still a long summer being away from fishing the boat. On the plus side, my back situation was less of a problem as time went on.

In the fall semester of 1968, I was responsible for teaching a class in hydraulics. At the time, there were little or no hydraulic installations on the boats in Point Judith. Even pot haulers were scarce. My source of information came primarily from Jens at Scandia in Fairhaven. I came across

Dick Wing,
Engineering Professor

a handbook on hydraulic systems that became the textbook for the class. We constructed a heavy table with a lip all around to contain the hydraulic oil that spilled when setting up systems that included motors and hydraulic rams. The system ran on an electric driven hydraulic pump. Much like the engine class, we had a split class for the labs.

There was a need for someone to teach electricity and electronics in the second semester of the second year, and I suggested Bob Merriam, if we could get him to do it. Bob not only took the job, but taught there for many years.

I remember being in Rhode Island Engine one day when Ken Gallup, Sr. asked me how I had ever landed a job teaching engines at URI, implying that I didn't know enough about it to speak of. He was right of course, and as a result, I began talking to one of the Rhode Island Engine mechanics about working at URI in the engine and hydraulic labs as an instructor. At the time, Dick Wing was going to night school working on a degree in education. Once I got approval from the school, Dick was on board. Probably the smartest move I ever made. I often thought though, if Ken Gallup would have considered teaching part time like Bob Merriam did. Once Dick Wing was hired, the option was no longer reasonable. I

Captain Geoffery Motte, Navigation Professor,
and the author

regret not asking Ken though.

During the fall of 1968, I opened discussions with Wickford Shipyard about locating the Fisheries School labs and classrooms in a building located on the water at the north end of the yard.

Wickford Fisheries School

At the time, Jack McGeogh and his partner Tom were managing a popular restaurant located on the Wickford Shipyard property. They were now also owners of Wickford Shellfish, where I had been selling the lobster catches from the *Jerry & Jimmy* for many years. Since I had an inside track to the owners of the yard, John Sainsbury and Geoff Motte, the navigation professor and I were able to negotiate a favorable lease for the buildings which, as I recall, was being used as a yacht brokerage. Sainsbury was able to convince the Dean that this would be a good move locating the Fisheries School on the waterfront instead of our building in West Kingston. I think the move to Wickford assured the future success of the School.

Dick Wing was assigned the job of relocating the engine and hydraulics lab to Wickford and he made a very impressive layout. Dick, as I had expected, made a great lab instructor.

Prior to my involvement, the fisheries school had purchased a 45 foot cabin boat which Chic Krawiec and the staff had converted to a small stern dragger named the *Gail Ann*. During the first semester of the school, Chic had taught the students boat handling, use of electronics, and introduced them to setting and towing a net. That first year, the *Gail Ann* was docked at the bay campus of the Graduate School of Oceanography. Once we moved to the Wickford school, the boat was docked at the bulkhead right in front of the

Dick Wing with the Engine class; Net class in the background

school. John Sainsbury and the secretarial staff led by Gladice Coggshell was still located in the Agriculture building at the main URI campus where each of the staff including me was assigned a desk.

In early January of 1969, I took the *Jerry & Jimmy* on a short trip to the deep water in the area of the fishtail to catch "red crab". This was the last trip scheduled in the multiyear series of a contract with the University through Dr. Andreas Holmsen. By the way, Dr. Tom Meade, also a School professor, had participated in this red crab project to determine the best approach to process the red crab meat for introduction into the marketplace. Tom made at least one red crab trip on the *Jerry & Jimmy*.

My crew for this trip included my engineer and one regular crewmember. I also had two of our students aboard to handle the gear. In addition was my daughter Lynn, who was in the 8th grade at the time and had written a class paper on red crab, our school secretary, Gladice Coggshell and Dr. Candice Oviatt of the Graduate School of Oceanography completed our three "lady" members of the team. Richard Sisson representing the RI Fish and Wildlife, who had been on a number of red crab trips over the years, decided to make this "final" trip as well.

At daylight, we set out in 200 fathom of water and needed only two hour and a half tows to catch a significant quantity of crab, about 10,000 lbs., for further processing studies. It was an uneventful trip up until then. On the way back to the Point, the wind picked up from the southeast; and by the time we reached the dock, the wind was blowing about 35 mph. Just a little rolling around so that all my "shipmates" were able to experience going to sea in January. I can report that none of the crew became uneasy.

The author Jim McCauley with Bert Hillier in the background on the *Gail Ann*

In January of my second year, 1969, I began teaching "Fishing Operations" to the second year students. Again, this was a new class with only a minimal outline of what Dr. Sainsbury would like to see covered. Dr. Sainsbury wrote a book on the introduction to commercial fishing which he used in a class during the first semester. The course that I came up with covered the handling of all gear types from trawling, seining, trapping and the use of electronics in actual fishing situations. I also included vessel accounting, financing and insurance. The course included a day at sea each week using the "split" class. Since I was teaching diesel engines to the first year students, which included split labs and one hour classes three times a week, I ended up teaching a three hour class on "Fishing Operations" on Friday afternoons. Needless to say, this gave me a full week of contact with students. Assuming two five to six hours for each of the split classes in Fishing Operations, I was with the students 22 to 24 hours a week during my second year. You know, it was fun. Compared to going to sea for six or seven days, fishing around the clock, this was easy once I got the hang of teaching. By the way, most "normal" professors at the University did not have nearly that many student contact hours, although many were involved with graduate students or working on research involving specific grants that they had been able to bring to the University.

In the first year that I taught "Fishing Operations", I took the students out on the *Gail Ann*. Depending on the weather, we fished outside Narragansett Bay. As I recall, we did get out to Block Island on a few occasions. I had to give them a "touch" of weather. On one

Gail Ann seining

trip, we had to slow down considerably so as not to blow out the windows.

On each trip, I would designate the area and tow we would make on the chart. Each of the guys were assigned a job—captain, engineer, cook and deck boss, who would decide which crewmembers remaining would run the winches setting out and hauling back. I just kept an eye on the whole operation. The class was responsible for starting the engine, navigation, etc. from the time we left the dock until we tied up at the end of the day. The cooks often cheated, especially the married guys, who would have their wives cook something "special". Cooking onboard was a learning experience especially on the *Gail Ann* that was inclined to roll most days.

That first year teaching Fishing Operations was the only time I used the *Gail Ann* for the "at sea" part of the class. We were able to work out a schedule with Fish and Wildlife of the State of Rhode Island to use their 57 foot dragger located in Jerusalem, the west side of the Point Judith Harbor Channel. It so happened that Captain John Sisson from my *North Star* fishing days was Captain of this boat which was used for fish surveys, etc. We used our own nets and at the end of each day, put everything back in place.

This was a larger and more seafriendly boat, and we fished along Narragansett Pier and "out front" of the South Beaches. We unloaded our daily "trips" at the Co-op, and as I recall, there was only one time when the captain for the day ran into the end of the Co-op dock.

Over the years we did have some arguments among the crew. In most cases, it was because the captain for the day, either set out in the wrong place or got off the tow, and we were hung up. I would not point out we were in the wrong place. Part of the learning process. If we hung up two or three times in a row, I had to intervene before the captain got his "ears boxed".

We did add a power block on the *Gail Ann* and a cage around the propeller so we could go seining. We had a skiff and outboard allowing us to make a typical single boat menhaden set. I made sure we didn't set an obvious bunch of fish since we were not in a position to load bulk fish on the boat.

During the spring of that year, I gave notice that I wanted to be off for three months during the summer. My contract was changed to a nine month contract without difficulty and I began planning a summer fishing on the *Jerry & Jimmy*.

Early in 1971, acting Dean of Agriculture, Everett Christopher, requested a meeting with me to go over all the courses being taught in the Associate two year Fisheries School program to determine which specific courses should be recognized by the University for credits toward any of the four year bachelor degrees. Apparently the Dean wanted my opinion since I was a URI graduate and familiar with the basics of what compromises a three credit course for example. My recommendations ended up being accepted. Over the years, the significance of being able to apply the credits benefited may of our graduates as they went on to obtain advanced degrees. Also, by that time, Dick Wing had earned his bachelor degree in education.

In the spring of 1971, David Thomson, our net specialist on the staff, decided to take a teaching position in a country in the western Pacific region. I had an idea who could fill his job. Years ago when I was looking for a dragger, I met Captain Albert "Bert" Hillier, the owner of a "hard bottom" side trawler. Since that time, Bert had sold the boat and come ashore. In 1971, Bert had been teaching everything a "green" man needed to know to ship out as a deck hand in the New Bedford fleet. The school was designed as a rehabilitation program financed by the city of New Bedford. Bert's specialty was net construction and repair. He could do more with a twine needle than anyone I had ever met. He had the strong hands and thick wrists that develop only from decades at the trade.

When I proposed the URI Fisheries School job to Bert, his eyes lit up and he was ready to sign up. I cleared the hiring with Dr. Sainsbury and Jeff Motte, both recognized that Bert was a real likeable New Foundlander or "New Fie", that would fit right in. I scheduled a meeting with Dean Christopher and filled him in our Bert's credentials. Bert showed up for the interview with the Dean dressed in a dark gray suit, white shirt and neat tie with a bright shine on his black shoes. The Dean may have been taken by surprise by Bert's character and enthusiasm. Bert got the job. Not an easy sell since Bert's formal education consisted of a high school equivalent certificate from the British Navy.

The Dean went along with my recommendation, and I am

sure it was a first hire as an Assistant Professor Equivalent in the history, past to the present, of the University. From that day on, no one ever questioned Bert's amazing abilities. As a matter of interest, the University still has a 65 foot trawler/research vessel named the "Captain Bert" designed by Dick Wing.

Now that David Thomson had vacated his position there was a need to carry on with a course that David taught on advanced fishing gear which included the large mesh wing trawl and midwater single boat and pair trawling designs. Since Bert Hillier was not acquainted with this category of gear at the time, I was assigned to teach the course. The course would be in the fall semester for the

Captain Albert "Bert" Hillier

second year students.

The three credit course called for two lectures and one laboratory each week. As it turned out, I was able to expand on the material presented during that first semester teaching the subject. David had the students construct scale models of the various designs which helped the class visualize what the gear would look like when towed. I think the most important outcome of the class was to instill the idea that there is room for development of fishing gear beyond where we were back then and today, especially with the introduction of new twine material, increased towing power, trawl door configurations, etc. Equally important was and is, the development of fixed gear, especially with the increasing cost of fuel.

During the school year, the staff of the Fisheries School started getting feedback from the first graduating class. Most of the "stories" came from visiting graduates and it was not a surprise that they had landed jobs on boats in ports throughout New England. Our goal at the School was to turn out viable candidates and achieve recognition from boat owners and captains. From what we were hearing, we could make adjustments to our classes. Bert Hillier's net classes were especially important to promote since entry level deckhands in the past usually had little or no knowledge of twine work. I had several students and graduates on my own boats and they were welcome additions to my crews.

I have deliberately avoided naming our graduates in that I would not care to offend any of them by excluding them, since I was and still am maintaining a friendly relationship with quite a few of them after all these years.

The Fisheries School was apparently beginning to gain recognition throughout the industry and government, when in May 1972, Albert "Bert" Hillier was awarded a contract to design and construct a net for "Groundfish Sampling in the Northwest Atlantic". The net contract was with the Northeast Fisheries Center, Woods Hole, Massachusetts. The net Bert designed was based on a standard "Yankee 41" bottom trawl net. The net had a 100 ft. sweep comprised of 16 ft. of 18" rollers in the center with standard roller spaces in between. The next section on each side was 8 ft. of 14" rollers. Out in the wings, there was a graduated sweep comprised of 16 ft. of 6" diameter roller spaces then 18 ft. of 4" rubber discs at the wing ends. At the time, I told Bert of my concern for how the net would catch on smooth bottom like we have south of Block Island. As a result, Bert suggested and constructed a 96 ft. "Tickler" arrangement for the net. The tickler had 45 ft. of 1/2" chain in the center and 3/4" wire on the wing ends. There was a 3 ft. connector chain from each

Captain Hillier with a scale model net

end of the 1/2" chain to the sweep to keep the "tickler" centered when towing making turns.

I do not recall any feedback from Woods Hole as to how the net performed. I was especially interested in how it caught yellowtail flounder south of New England compared to boats working out of New Bedford and Point Judith. The net designed by Bert in 1972 was probably well-received by the captain and crew of the survey vessels because the product was, in my opinion, indestructible.

I was asked to make a presentation at the "Fish Exposition" in Seattle in late October of 1972. By then, I had built the *Alliance* covered in later chapters. While we were there, Chic Krawiec and I would have a booth advertising the School in the northwest. My subject was lobster trawls in deep water. In preparation for the "talk", I prepared a series of slides of the pots and gear with diagrams showing the arrangement of a typical pot field along an 80-90 fathom curve similar to Hudson Canyon. I then took many reels of "super eight" film on board the *Alliance* showing the whole operation. It took me many hours to edit and splice the film, and then I had four copies made.

The site of the Expo was in the main hall where the Seattle World's Fair had taken place. Picture this: I was the first speaker for the day on the first day of the Expo. The hall was full to capacity. I think every fisherman from Alaska to California was there. If you have ever been to Seattle, you know that it rains every day in the fall. Not this day! The sun was shining brightly and the room had windows on one whole side "and" there was not a single shade on any of those windows. Here I was with an hour of slides and movies that couldn't be seen by the audience although the management made a half-assed attempt to cover the windows. Well, here I am trying to describe in words alone how the gear was rigged and handled as the slides and movie was projected on the screen that most of the audience except those in the first two rows could see. The longest hour of my life.

While in Seattle, I spent time with the Marco people. I gave them a copy of the film on lobster trawling featuring the Marco pot hauler. I also did another film with the *Alliance* dragging which featured the twin winches and the net drum over the stern ramp. They had no "daylight" problems at their offices.

As I recall, it was early winter of 1973 that we found out that Joe Chic Krawiec had developed cancer. Mornings he used to drive his Cadillac up to Rhode Island Hospital in Providence for chemo treatments, then come back to the Wickford facility pretty well wiped out and sit on a pile of twine in the lab to get himself together enough to work with the students in the afternoon.

Chic's condition was stable throughout the winter and early spring. Then in late spring he had a setback and went into the hospital in Westerly. At different times the staff visited him in the hospital and he maintained his usual humorous outlook. One day, Geoff Motte and I went to visit him, the bed was empty and we learned that he had passed. We all enjoyed working with Chic over the years. I thought it was important to include this segment as a reminder of our memorable colleague.

The Fisheries School was an interesting and important part of my career in the fishing business. But during the last few years at URI, I had built a new 85 foot stern trawler named the *Alliance;* its planning and construction is described in the following chapters.

I notified the Dean of the College that I would resign at the completion of the spring semester. I turned over all my teaching materials for my courses. I knew Dick Wing had the engineering courses covered. I think by then that Bob Taber, who later founded Trawlworks in Narragansett, had taken over the fisheries extension projects for the University. The school hired George "Eggy" Gamache from my seining days with Harold Loftes, to take Chic's place in small boat operations and he took over the sea time part of the course that I used to teach. Teaching at the University would have been a good job for someone going into their retirement years, but it was not my time. The bills were no longer current. I remember Barry Gallup at Rhode Island Engine telling me that he knew I would be back. I don't know that he was worried about my account, let's say he was concerned.

As for the Fisheries School, it would continue to graduate "Fishermen" for many years. I was at least able to make a contribution at its beginning, especially bringing Dick Wing and Bert Hillier aboard. By the way Dick Wing earned two Master's degrees during his years at the University.

Chapter 13

URI and Fisheries School Projects

During the approximate same time period as the previous chapter about the Fisheries School, there were a number of significant contributions to the fishing industry made by URI and Fisheries School staff.

During the fall of 1968, David Thomson, the professor on the staff responsible for teaching nets and gear, introduced the wing trawl to the local fleet based on a publication "The Use of European Wing Trawl for Herring" by David Thomson. As I recall, David acquired two nets from Britain. The net was able to achieve a headline height of up to 22 feet. Beginning in late fall, some large catches of herring were landed at the plant in Point Judith. By the end of the 1969 herring season, there were eight Point Judith boats fishing with the "wing trawls".

The herring were caught in the inshore area around Point Judith and off Narragansett. The Point Judith fleet had caught significant quantities of herring back in 1946-1950 in the same area using whiting nets. It is interesting that the large freezer boats caught significant quantities of herring in the same general area during the winter months in 2011/2012.

Single boat midwater trawls were tested during the summer of 1967, prior to my appointment to URI. These tests were carried out by small boats of 60 feet with 300 HP. The University worked with the Co-op on the project and the results were published under the title "Comparative testing of Midwater Rigs for Small Draggers" by Dr. Andreas Holmsen. Few commercial quantities of fish were caught. It was probably more a matter of the time of year when the tests took place than any other factors. As I recall, that was the conclusion that was reached. The *Jerry & Jimmy*, even while I was captain, never participated in the herring fishery because of offshore winter fisheries.

I had mentioned in the previous chapter that I had asked the Dean of the School of Agriculture/Resource Development, if I could change my contract to nine months so that I could go back fishing the *Jerry & Jimmy* in the summer. The following story of that summer of 1969 was significant to Point Judith fishermen and I could also pass on the information in my classes.

During the spring the *Jerry & Jimmy* was dragging for lobsters and were finding at least a thousand pounds in a twenty four hour fishing day. Nelson Bourret, as captain, was doing a good job of keeping the boat operation financially sound. By April, they were working from 75-85 fathom of water catching a fair amount of fluke with the lobsters during each trip. In past years, we had to give up dragging lobsters as the surface water warmed, and we could not keep the lobsters alive even with a strong flow of water through the below deck holding tank.

I had been talking to Barry Gallup at Rhode Island Engine about a refrigerated sea water system. Although untried, I committed to building a diesel driven compressor unit that I could bolt to the deck in an enclosed box to protect the unit from the weather. By the time I completed my class work at the end of May, the unit was ready. I was going back to sea for the summer with a new "toy" to work with. It did work as planned.

The unit was started when we got to the "clean" water off Block Island where we filled the below deck tank. This was a closed system recirculating the water in the tank. It took all of the eight hours of steaming time to the grounds to bring the water temperature down to 48-50 degrees F. There was still a lobster box that could hold 800 to 1,000 lbs. on deck and the cold water coming out of the refrigeration unit was piped directly to the deck box, then would over flow into the main tank below. Dragging for lobsters causes far more stress that potting them. They have to be hosed off well and placed not thrown into the cold water of the holding tank. Any "soft" or "weak" lobsters went back overboard. During the cooler hours of the night, we would remove the lobsters in the holding tank to make sure they were in good condition before putting them below in the main tank.

The system worked well and we were able to tow for lobsters all summer, primarily in the "Fishtail" to Veatch Canyon area. Needless to say, we were alone on the grounds. The fluke were long gone. It did seem that the main body of lobsters were slowly moving east along the bank almost like cattle feeding. We tried anticipating where they might be on the next trip, about three days later, by moving about twenty miles farther east. That tactic seemed to work. Being out there by ourselves that summer was a disadvantage trying to find and stay on the "bugs".

During the spring of that year, I had a 30'x40' inground pool installed in the back yard. I hired one of the students in the class, Cyrus "Cy" Lauriat from Mt. Desert, Maine to lug fill by hand using a wheelbarrow. It was a big job, but he was able to grade the back yard just the way I wanted it.

I had Cy work for me on the *Jerry & Jimmy* after he graduated the following summer. One day in late July, we were sitting by the pool when I asked him what he knew about lobster pots. Being from Maine, he had a working knowledge of the pot fishery. I told him of my interest in setting some pots off the *Jerry & Jimmy*.

Back at that time, the Prelude Corporation founded by Bill Whipple was running a deep water lobster pot operation out of Westport, Mass. Not much was known locally about how successful the operation was. I knew the captain of the largest of the boats was formerly dragging for lobsters out of New Bedford, so I knew that he had the knowledge to locate their pots in the right places. I believe in the early days of the Prelude fishing, they were concentrating on the area east of Veatches. On occasion, I would drag up one of their pots. They used a heavy cast clip device to attach the pots to the ground line and apparently, on occasion, a clip would fail and a pot would fall free. I never was close to their sets when I was dragging but over the last year or more, I had caught ten of their "bear traps". These traps were roughly 4 ft. long by 2 ½ ft high, and at the time had an oak frame with twine laced on the sides in place of lathes. The pots had entrance heads on each side of the center with a large "parlor" on each end. The pot had a common top with a bait bag hanging in front of each parlor entrance.

With these 10 pots as a start, I ordered 100 inshore single funnel on one end wooden pots from Wilcox Marine and so began our lobster operation. I remember setting the pots in 72 fathoms west of Veatches. I towed for lobsters all around and right inside of the Canyon, therefore I set the pots so that they wouldn't be in the way although I had never caught too many lobsters in that location. We set the pots with up and down lines with rope ground lines and hauled them on the winch drum on top of the wire. It was a slow process.

The first time I hauled the three trawls was after four days of dragging. To my surprise, we caught about 500 lbs. The bear traps, acting as anchors on the ends of each trawl caught half of the lobsters with only 10 pots. That was my first experience trapping offshore. I have to say I felt absolutely stupid for not trying this much sooner.

For the rest of the summer, we would haul the pots when we started each trip, then again at the end of the trip. We baited the traps with whatever "trash" fish we caught. We could count on a thousand pounds extra each trip by hauling them twice. I could only speculate how many lobsters the Prelude boats were catching, I knew it was time to build a new boat designed for the offshore lobster trap fishery.

During that past spring, my father had come down with Hodgkin's Disease, a cancer of the lymph nodes. Dad's doctor at the time was primarily a heart specialist and had more or less given up on any treatment for the disease. By the end of summer my dad was covered with small black spots and was clearly in big trouble. I asked my own doctor what could be done. He recommended a chemotherapy program that was located at Rhode Island Hospital in Providence, RI. It didn't take much to convince my mom and dad to start the therapy which my doctor arranged. Throughout the fall and early winter, I would meet them at the hospital and sit with Dad during the treatment. In time, the black spots disappeared and the doctors were encouraged with his progress. The chemo treatments did cause Dad to lose his appetite and he was tired and had to rest after each treatment, but overall he had a good outlook.

Since I had only the one class in hydraulics in the fall of 1969, it was decided by those "in charge" that I would take on additional duties working with the fishing fleet in Point Judith. The first assignment was to investigate the potential for single boat midwater trawling for herring, similar to Dr. Holmsen's project.

At the time, there was an ongoing program in experimental phase, under the direction of "Wes" W. Johnson, Industrial Development Service of the Department of Fisheries of Canada based in Ottowa. There had been extensive testing of the gear by Captain

James Calder, captain and owner of the fishing vessel *Mary and Jay* based at Campobello Island, New Brunswick, Canada.

Wes Johnson arranged for "us" to go out with Captain Calder to see the operation. Chic Krawiec, Ken Gallup, Jr., captain/owner of the *Big Dipper*, John Dystkra, captain/owner of the *Two Brothers*, and I made the trip to Campobello. On November 4th, we were able to observe a full day's fishing with James and his two brothers.

The operation was totally new to us beginning with the net which was designated as a No. 5 B Canadian Diamond MidWater Trawl (21" mesh). This was a four panel net with a top and bottom head rope of 142 ft. and side headropes of 132 ft. The sides were v-shaped (66 ft. to the center of the side panel). There was a 60 lb. weight attached to the bottom leg where it attached to the bottom of the side panel. The doors were 3 square meter "suber krub" otter boards. The *Mary & Jay* was an eastern style trawler, (wheelhouse aft), but was arranged with frames on either side of the stern, so was in effect, a stern trawler. To complete the rig, there was a Furuno FNR 200 Net Recorder attached to a "float board" mounted in the center of the headrope. The net recorder was wireless and required a transducer unit to be towed at a depth of 10 ft. off the side boom.

We made three 1 ½ hr. tows that day, two of the tows resulted in 25,000 lbs. of saleable herring, and the third tow was undersized fish. The fish were pumped aboard and there was a fine screen located at the outflow of the dewaterer that collected the herring scales that were also sold for something to do with the jewelry industry. The tows were made over rocky bottom with significant depth changes. Depending on where the fish were located in the water column, the net depth was controlled by a combination of adjusting the trawl wire length and the towing speed.

While we were in Campobello, we stayed at a small hotel (the only one). We were the only guests. The owner was also the cook and always offered us a glass of beer with breakfast. It seemed a "little" strange until he told us he was heading to Florida for the winter as soon as we checked out. I guess the beer on tap would not last until spring. On the way driving back to Rhode Island it began raining so hard that we decided to hold up at an old inn in Thomaston, Maine. After dinner and a "few" drinks, we went up to our rooms. I was with Ken and Chic was with John D. The next morning at breakfast, Ken and I heard that Chic's room was leaking pretty badly, so he called down to the desk to send up a row boat if they had one handy.

Upon our return, the Fisheries School authorized the purchase of a No. 5 Canadian Diamond Trawl through Captain Calder. A second net was ordered by one of the captains. A set of 3 square meter "surber krub" doors were also purchased. The Bureau of Commercial Fisheries in Gloucester, MA purchased a second set of doors. The University Graduate School of Oceanography purchased a Furono FNR 200 Net Sounder. A Wesmar sonar unit was purchased and installed aboard the *Big Dipper*.

Since none of the participating vessels were under charter, the trials were carried out at times of their own choosing. All of the gear was made available by mid-December. Chic and I published a report entitled "Single Boat MidWater Trawling for Herring in Rhode Island Waters". The report included all the net, doors, and rigging details.

Along with my teaching duties, I managed to make several trips on the *Big Dipper* with Ken. Everything worked as planned, but as I recall, there were mixed results as to the catch. In later years the Rhode Island fleet would benefit from these early trials.

There was another project that I initiated in early fall of 1969. This was a study between URI and Oregon State University. I had met Bill Wicks from the State of Oregon Fish and Wildlife at a fisheries meeting in Boston. I remember Bill well because his bags were lost during the flight from Portland. He showed up wearing a bright sport shirt among a crowd of "suits". My idea was to introduce "deep water lobsters" to the deep water off Oregon. They had tried some Maine lobsters in some rocky coastal areas that were unsuccessful in that the seals or sea lions cleaned them right out. By going deep, 80-100 fathoms, that problem would be solved.

Bill worked with the Oregon State Marine Science Center at Newport, OR and we made the arrangements. With the agreement of the RI Fish and Wildlife, I was able to land 90 large egg-bearing lobsters, normally illegal, 30 large males and shipped them overnight to Oregon. Every one arrived in good condition. I took a flight to Oregon a day or so later, paid for by the University. When I arrived, I found the lobsters stored outside in a large cement tank. The water was well circulated and cold, 60 degrees or so. I suggested that we cover part of the tank with black plastic to get them out of the light. Within a half hour the lobsters were out of sight under the plastic.

If you have seen a three to five pound female "egger" there are a great many eggs attached. With the lobsters being in good condition, my job was basically over. In return, OSU was going to ship live salmon fry to Rhode Island to begin a program of introducing west coast salmon in Rhode Island waters or raise them as an aquaculture project. The Science Center in Oregon was located near the mouth of a river. The facility depended on the tidal flow for its raw water source which was pumped through the many tanks holding a variety of saltwater species. During the rainy period the river causes the salinity to drop and then the system is closed to the ocean and the water recirculated.

The lobsters I had provided were placed in various tanks throughout the center after I had returned home. In November, the beginning of the rainy season, it was necessary to go into a recirculation mode. Apparently when the water was recirculated its temperature went up enough to cause all the lobster to shake loose their eggs. Almost overnight, all the screens preventing species from escaping into the sea became clogged with the eggs and an unknown quantity of the eggs flowed into the river.

One of the strict guidelines for this project was to not allow any of these "new" lobster species to be released into Oregon waters until all the necessary studies pertaining to the larval characteristics had been evaluated. Not a good start. I still have a copy of the original report entitled "Introducing Deep Water Homarus Americanus into Oregon Waters" by J.J. Gonor and S.L. Gonor, a husband and wife team of the Department of Oceanography and Marine Science Center of Oregon State University. The study was initiated in December 1969.

To my knowledge, the species was never permitted to be introduced to the west coast although a number of the original shipment and their offspring were shared with other universities extending through California.

As it later turned out, Dr. Thomas Meade, another member

of the URI Fisheries School staff, who was responsible for classes in Industrial Fish Products (fish meal and oil) and Aquaculture became involved. Over the years, Tom had reasonable success in growing salmon and other species at the University facilities.

One of the most important changes in sweep durability for me came about by way of James MacLeod of Killybegs, Ireland. James was speaking at one of the University of Rhode Island sponsored Fishermen's Forums. His subject, as I recall, was the "Design and Use of the Scottish Seine." He was the proprietor of a fishing gear company in Killybegs, Ireland. I was on the staff at the URI Fisheries School at the time of his visit and spent most of the time he was here in the U.S. showing him the boats and meeting the fishermen from Point Judith. James spotted our wrapped sweeps and said he used a small rubber disc about 2" diameter with a 5/8" hole that he had a supplier cut out for him back in Ireland. He said he would send me a sample.

About a month later, I came home to find a dozen burlap bags full of discs—some "sample." We made up a three-piece sweep using the small discs that ended up close to the same as our wrapped sweep. The new sweep was virtually indestructible. The only thing that eventually rusted out was the galvanized wire, so we switched to stainless steel. They also worked good for the bottom legs with a washer and wire clamp every couple of feet to keep the discs from sliding and bunching on the wire. James really made a contribution that continues to this day and not only in Point Judith.

Beginning in 1970, funds became available from the State of Rhode Island Technical Services, as I recall. The funds were administered by Walter Gray of the Graduate School of Oceanography. I was assigned as kind of a marine extension agent, working for Walter part time, to identify projects and any equipment that would be paid for by the fund. Back then I was full of ideas.

During trips to Canada, I had seen hydraulic net drums on stern trawlers. The drums were always mounted halfway up the after deck and the net was either pulled up a steep stern ramp or over a roller mount on the stern.

At the time, Harold Loftes, Sr. had built a new steel 65 ft. trawler named the *Miss Ginny* with a small stern ramp. Harold was towing as a typical stern trawler from frames located on each side of the stern. He was hauling the ground cables and legs on the main winch, then swinging the boat around and fleeting the net aboard as you would on a side trawler.

Harold Jr. was working on the boat with his father and I knew from past experience that they were always looking for new innovations. I proposed building a hydraulic powered net drum that would be mounted over the stern ramp so that the whole net could be wound on the drum and then haul the cod end up the ramp. Since the project would be paid for using money from the "fund", they were all for it. Working with the Loftes and Barry Gallup from Rhode Island Engine, we designed the drum. It was fabricated and installed by RI Engine including the hydraulics using a gear motor and chain to power the drum.

I made the right choice picking Harold for this project,. He tried everything possible with the drum and it worked without a hitch. The ramp was not large enough to take most of Harold's catches up the stern, but it was a quick move to swing the boat to take the bag over the side. The big thing was the deck was clear to dump the fish for sorting unlike drums mounted middeck.

While I was working with Harold, I started talking to him about where to go to build a steel boat. He had also been thinking of building a larger steel boat that could carry more than the *Miss Ginny*. He had more or less settled on Atlantic Marine located near Jacksonville, FL. It was a good tip and offered me a place to start.

Based on the performance of the stern mounted net drum, I made sure to incorporate a similar design for the boat that I intended to build. As it turned out, nearly every stern trawler in the northeast now has one or more net drums mounted over a stern ramp. That investment by the "fund" administered by Walter changed fishing gear operations.

The beginning of the spring semester in 1970 brought me back to my full time teaching responsibilities. Having Dick Wing aboard to take over the diesel engine lab requirement gave me some relief, but I still had the time-consuming 2 days "at sea" as part of the fishing operations course.

One of my family responsibilities beginning in the fall of 1969 was to take my oldest daughter, Lynn, to the train station in Kingston, R.I. She took the train every week day at 7:30 a.m. to

Providence. Usually my wife was able to pick her up in the afternoon. Lynn attended Classical High School, going every day for four years as required to graduate. As it turned out, hers was one of the last graduating classes to be able to attend Classical from out of town. Both my brother and I were Classical graduates. The high school was rated as the second highest educational school in New England and still holds that distinction to this day.

Picture of a stern-mounted net drum with rubber discs
on lower legs and ground cables

Chapter 14

The Planning and Construction of the *Alliance*

During the spring and summer of 1970, I was working on the specifications for a new steel stern trawler capable of hauling lobster pots. There were a number of new southern built steel trawlers in the Point by then. Dick Goodwin had built the *Huntress* and Charlie Follett had built the *CindyBet*. No question, steel boats built down south were the way to go primarily because of the price and from what I could determine, the workmanship was satisfactory.

Between trips lobstering on the *Jerry & Jimmy*, I began working with Morris Wilmot, the sales manager for Atlantic Marine, Fort George Island, Florida. This was the company that Harold Loftes had suggested. The yard was located at the fork of the inland waterway and the St. Johns River, not far from the aircraft carrier base at the Mayport Naval Station.

I was faxing my ideas based on an Atlantic Marine standard 79 ft. shrimp trawler. In the end, the vessel did not resemble anything they had built to date. There was a strong interest on their part to do this deal since they could envision selling a number of this design in the northeast. All this preparation was just to establish a base price. My first inclination was to power the vessel with a Caterpillar D379, 520 HP at 1200RPM. This was a powerful engine with a good track record in New Bedford. I knew the sales manager for Caterpillar in New England and when he heard I was building a boat, he asked me to consider installing a new series of engines, and recommended a D346 rated at 480HP at 1800RPM with a 5.17 reduction gear. He convinced me partially because of the lower price and the higher speed engine he said was where Caterpillar was "going" in the future. In hindsight, that was my first mistake especially related to the final selling price many years later.

Going into this venture, I decided to ask Nelson Bourret, the current captain of the *Jerry & Jimmy* to be a 1/3 owner in the vessel. I could not be sure at that time that I would ever be able to go back to fishing full time. Having Nelson committed to continuing on running the new boat made sense. I planned to operate the vessel as a "C" corporation and being totally responsible myself for the financing.

In addition to working aboard the *Jerry & Jimmy* and continuing with the trawling/potting operation that summer, I managed to visit with my dad between trips. He had done quite well with the chemo treatments and it appeared that he was in remission. At the beginning of summer the diagnosis was that the cancer had come back more aggressive before spreading into his lungs. The outlook was not good. Regardless of his condition, he was very interested in the new boat project. By the way, this time I didn't need the financial help that he provided with the *Jerry & Jimmy*.

Working with Morris at Atlantic Marine, we finally came up with a "beginning" price. I knew there would be "addendums" to the contract right from the start but we had done a great deal of work to nail down the price. The proposed contract was for $167,973. In 1970 this was a big price. The price included a $20,000 contract with Marco of Seattle, WA for two hydraulic winches rated at 100 horse power each with drums large enough to hold 600 fathoms of 3/4 inch trawl wire.

The initial temporary financing necessary to sign a contract and begin construction on some auxiliary equipment was accomplished by signing a personal note with only my signature, for $100,000 through the Wakefield branch of Industrial National Bank. I knew the manager of the bank, Hudson Scattergood, for many years. This was also the Fishermen's Cooperative's bank and had a long history of supporting the fishermen of Point Judith.

I wanted to get the contract signed and construction underway before I started the fall classes. Unfortunately dad had taken a turn for the worse, and by the end of August, he was in Memorial Hospital in Pawtucket. I visited him every day and there was little change. I decided to fly to Florida to sign the contract on August 31st. Just as I got to the gate to fly to Jacksonville that morning, my name was called over the loud speaker. It was my mom. Dad had died that very morning. Even though I knew he was very sick, it was still a shock that he was gone. I had visited the hospital the night before, and I guess I convinced myself that he was going to be with us for another month or so.

That next week was hard on all of us. I think it was accepted by my mother because she had been with him every day through-out the year or more of this illness. We managed to get through the funeral and celebrated his life with a party for relatives and friends in the back yard of their home in Lincoln that I am sure he would have enjoyed.

A week later, I did fly to Jacksonville. Nelson and I signed the contract with Atlantic Marine for the new boat on September 11, 1970. We had a $48,000 down payment. I paid $36,000 and Nelson contributed $500 with a "loan" from me of $11,500 to make up the

Plating the hull upside down

$12,000 of the 1/3. As I had ex-plained earlier, it was never my intention to ask Nelson to pay cash into the formation of our corporation.

I suggested that we name the boat *Alliance* since the name suggested an agreement for Nelson and I to operate the boat as a joint venture. When Bob Merriam heard the name we decided on, he said "did you know that was the name of the second vessel to be part of the Continental Navy?" No I did

not, but it was a good name. I definitely did not want any family names since I had seen many boats sold that eventually became run-down wrecks that still had the original family name.

In mid-October two of our students and I traveled to Tam-pa, Florida to run a booth at a fisheries exposition or "fish expo" as they were later called. The purpose of the booth was to generate in-terest in the URI Fisheries School in a different region of the country. After the "expo", Morris from Atlantic Marine and I drove to Jacksonville so I could see the start of construction. Two of the sales reps from Marco in Seattle that had been at the "expo" met us at the shipyard. This was significant because when we were looking at the keel, they suggested that we should weld a 12 inch wide x 1 inch thick plate on each side of the keel. The vessels built by Marco in Seattle were then being built with what they called a "T Bar

Keel", that had the effect of stabilizing the vessel similar to rolling chocks. I thought it was a great idea and would certainly make a very strong keel. This was the first of many "addendums" to the contract that Morris would make.

Throughout the fall there were a steady flow of faxes from my house to Atlantic Marine concerning minor changes, such as pipe fittings through the engine room bulkhead to the forward fish hold, one of two, for use in circulating refrigerated sea water from the refrigeration unit similar to the one on the *Jerry & Jimmy*, which I planned to have installed in the engine room ahead of the main engine. In November, Nelson and I drove to Florida with a prefabricated 44 HP lister with 4" pump provided by Rhode Island Engine.

As late as March 16, 1971 there was a final "addendum" for $12,420. This included two interesting items that indicate how the value of the dollar has gone to hell. 18,000 gallons of fuel oil at a cost of $12,240 or .68 cents/gal, two 55 gallon drums of 30 wt. lube oil for $180 or $1.63/gal. The final total price by the time we were ready for sea trials came to $194,744. I was able to finance $142,000 with C.I.T. Corporation of Jacksonville, FL on March 3, 1971. The contract called for 84 equal payments of $2,554.17/month. Seven years was no big deal but the total with interest came to $214,550.27.

This sounded reasonable at the time, but the costs involved in rigging the boat was not a part of this number. I had already ordered two spools of pre-marked 3/4" tow wire at 575 fathoms a

Back upright   Ready to launch

spool from Wilcox Marine and a pair of 10 ft. wood/steel doors from Westerbeake in New Bedford. As I recall we had assembled at least three nets with different sweep configurations and mesh sizes, plus three cod ends. Coming up in the spring would be the cost of at least 500-600 "bear trap" sized lobster traps plus ground gear. I split the cost of the lobster gear with the *Jerry & Jimmy* since we planned on alternately hauling the gear, but it was still "my" cost. This was all with 1970 money. All it took was a lot of nerve or "whatever".

The last two weeks of the construction, Harlan Stanley, Sr., my engineer on the *Jerry & Jimmy*, and I flew to Jacksonville to see that everything was complete. I wanted Stan to become familiar with the entire engine room including the deck equipment since he would be taking over as engineer on the *Alliance*.

When the *Alliance* was near completion, Bob Merriam with one man flew to Jacksonville to install all the electronics. Back then the flights were either with Eastern or National Airlines. Bob brought a number of antennas and many boxes of equipment with him. The initial installation had a $5,950 allowance in the contract. On the way home to Point Judith every piece of electronics worked perfectly as I knew it would.

With a new boat, there is absolutely nothing that comes with it especially tools. Back then, Arthur Grasso was the NAPA dealer in Wakefield. I sat down with him and figured out the list of tools. Art ordered them all and had them delivered to the NAPA dealer in Jacksonville where we picked them up.

Atlantic Marine's main business was doing work for the Navy. Quite often their welders, etc. would fly to a Mediterranean port to meet one of the carriers based in Mayport and do steel work on the way back across the Atlantic. As a result, all of their welders were certified for Navy contracts. Over the years, I never once came across a bad weld that cracked for example.

During the fabrication of the hull, once the framing was complete and sandblasted, the hull was rolled upside down so that the hull plating could be more easily welded. After each section was welded it would be sandblasted and painted. All the sheets of plating were sandblasted beforehand. During the roughly five months that the steel work was being done on the *Alliance* there was virtually no rain, allowing for a superior paint job inside and outside of the entire hull. For example, the "A" frame mast fabricated out of square tubing never required painting during the twenty year I owned the boat.

I was not present when the *Alliance* was launched. The first time I saw it in the water, I thought there must be some mistake. It looked so big, how could this be the boat I ordered? Compared to the *Jerry & Jimmy* this was a "big" boat. At the time, of course, it had no fuel aboard or cement in the fish holds. Nevertheless, it was impressive as you can see by the pictures included with this narrative.

During the winter school vacation, I flew to Jacksonville with my wife and three daughters. We stayed at the Thunderbird, which was a large facility with a pool, etc. My girls had visited Florida a number of times during the winters either to visit with my parents or as a family. So the first thing to do was to jump in the pool. But this was Jacksonville. The man cleaning the pool was wearing a long overcoat. It didn't matter, cold or not, in they went. We visited St. Augustine and Daytona, and a good time was had by all.

In early December Harold Loftes, Sr. had signed a contract with Atlantic Marine to build a new 79 ft. trawler, he named the "Ocean State". The vessel looked more like the traditional southern shrimper with the wheelhouse forward. The big difference was the size of the forward fish hold which was designed to carry upwards of 200,000 lbs. of trash fish or pogies. The boat had the next Atlantic Marine hull number after the *Alliance.*

In each case Atlantic Marine had the responsibility to have the vessel "measured" for its federal registration number which was 530910 for the *Alliance*. The number was welded on a main deck frame at the opening of the forward hatch. On wooden boats the number was chiseled into a main deck frame. For ease in identification, I had the number painted on each side and the roof of the pilothouse.

This was the full involvement by federal officials in 1971. There was no state or federal fishing license. The only requirements to catch and land fish for sale, at that time, was the hull had to be built in the US, hence the Federal number. At the time, I still owned and operated the *Jerry & Jimmy* as an individual proprietor. The *Alliance* was incorporated in the State of Rhode Island as "Trawler Alliance, Inc." on February 2, 1971.

My primary lawyer for the corporation was Archibald B. Kenyon, Jr. of Wakefield, the registered agent. The successor registered agent was Richard C. Sisco, my accountant at the time, who was also a lawyer. Mr. Kenyon was busy with a major problem right away. Under my contract with Atlantic Marine in the state of Florida, there was a due 3% Florida sales tax based on the total delivery price. The State of Rhode Island also had a sales tax on new boats at the same percentage as a new car would be. First we had to get a waiver from the State of Florida since we were subject to an additional much higher tax in Rhode Island. Archie managed to the get the Florida waiver, then after serious negotiation, he was able to obtain a more acceptable rate in Rhode Island, as I recall of about 5% or $10,000, which was not included in the mortgage.

For many years now there has been no sales tax on fishing boats with a state commercial license, which I still have in 2015 and there is no sales tax on fishing gear and equipment. There is one exception, if you only buy a new outboard motor for your existing boat, you have to pay the sales tax on the motor. Always "one more thing". My last 150 HP Yamaha cost $12,000 plus tax.

During the sea trials in the river around the shipyard, the "driver" from Atlantic Marine who delivered boats to the customers as far away as South America, put the *Alliance* through a strenuous test. At one point while steaming at full speed, around 10 knots, he put the engine in neutral then full reverse until the boat stopped. That was above and beyond any reasonable test as far as I was concerned. This guy was going to be watched carefully since he was going back to Point Judith with us.

With about five days left, Nelson, Dick Winters, one of our four crewmembers, and a college friend of mine, Alan Easterbrooks arrived to bring the boat home. During the last few days the crew worked cutting out and "gluing" down the asphalt deck "tiles" that had been delivered from New Bedford. With the cold weather at home this job would have been impossible, but the warm weather in Jacksonville made it simple and the job looked great. One less thing we had to do when we got home. We also cut and fitted the "checker" boards for the deck and across the opening of the stern ramp. Rather than leave the deck checkerboards in place, we stored them in the stern compartment, along with my fishing poles, since the only thing in that large compartment was the rudder post and steering quadrant.

The morning we took leave of the shipyard, we steamed out of the St. John's River then ran north following the coast about ten miles off to Cape Hatteras. Everything ran like a clock. Put the boat on autopilot and that was it. My plan was to make Hatteras then sail directly to Block Island. By the time we got to Hatteras, the wind was blowing northwest at 25 mph with gusts to 30. This put the wind on the port side with the high bow and the pilothouse up on the second level it looked like we could stay with "the plan" rather than the longer route of following the coast up toward Long Island.

The first sign of trouble was when the boat rolled back to port, fuel was coming out of the vent pipe of the 2,200 gallon after tank, which was about 30 inches high. We switched tanks and started burning the fuel off of the stern tank. This was a long term solution, but in the meantime the fuel oil on deck was softening the asphalt tiles and although most of them stayed in place, the whole deck was now spongy and sticky to walk on. We decided to drive a plug into the unthreaded elbow of the vent pipe and ran the engine off the forward tanks.

The following morning somewhere off Norfolk, VA, I was sitting at the table in the galley having breakfast. I sensed that the table was not as level as it had been and was slanting aft enough to be noticeable. I mentioned it to Dick Winters, who was cooking for us on the trip home. He wasn't sure either. It was still rough and I went up in the pilothouse to look at the deck. It was very wet with water running steadily out the leeside scuppers. I went down to the engine room and switched the bilge pump over from the engine room to the aft compartment. I watched over the side discharge and nothing but the prime water continued to come out. Apparently it was dry back there. I tried switching to the after fish hold and it pumped some water then stopped with only the prime. I decided to slow down and head down wind to visibly check the compartments. When we went out on deck, it was obvious that the stern was down.

We checked both fish holds; they were dry. We needed a hammer to loosen the clamp on the large round flush hatch to the stern compartment and found it was full of water right up to the deck. To make matters worse, all the deck boards we had stored

Easier Handling–Bigger Profits the F/V Alliance by ATLANTIC MARINE

Fishing vessel owners are Businessmen — they know profits are often made just "narrowly."..

The F/V ALLIANCE
..... W-I-D-E-N-S *the profit potential,* through an innovative combination of design and technical craftsmanship.

Atlantic Marine would like to share with you their experience in building one vessel or a fleet that .....

- Cuts Manpower Requirements
- Reduces Elapsed Time To Set And Retrieve Nets
- Control Can Be Directed From The Pilot House
- Safer Handling
- Provides Faster Handling
- Offers Easier Handling For The Crew
- Dual Rigging For Fishing Or Shrimping

These are the specifications for a newly designed lobster traveler with the net reel located in the open stern ramp, designed by *Jim McCauley,* Mechanical Engineer and new owner of the **F/V ALLIANCE** with his partner, *Nelson Bourret.*

ATLANTIC MARINE builds traditional vessels, and now the closest thing to a computer operated fishing vessel.

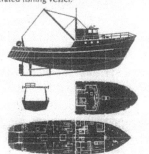

Let ATLANTIC MARINE ... W-I-D-E-N *your profit margin* ...

ATLANTIC MARINE INC.

8503 McKENNA ROAD / P.O. BOX 138 / FT. GEORGE ISLAND, FLORIDA 32226 / (904) 251-3111

back there were rushing from one side to the other. It must have taken an hour to fish them all out and store them under the winches.

It's a wonder they didn't damage the steering mechanism. We still couldn't pump it out. It was obvious the pump intake was plugged. When we pulled up the deck cover we noticed that there was no rubber gasket or "o" ring where there should have been one, and without the seal, the flush hatch had been leaking the whole trip. This was an oversight of the shipyard, but nevertheless we should have realized the problem. Since we didn't have a portable pump, there was nothing we could do. We buttoned it up and again headed for home.

The more I watched the stern settle, especially going over a big wave, I decided we had to do something. Stan and I went down to the engine room and disconnected the fuel line to the 2,200 gallon after fuel tank. We put the bilge pump on in the engine room and pumped out fuel the rest of the way home. In time the whole living quarters smelled like diesel fuel. Ten miles south of Block Island we reconnected the fuel line stopping the flow. We spent the next hour flushing out the engine room bilge.

By now our Atlantic Marine guy was a nervous wreck. I think he had visions of the boat going down sinking by the stern and losing the *Alliance* on its maiden voyage. It was true that 14 ft. of the stern was full of water and fuel right up to deck level. That represented considerable weight, but I never thought of the condition being a serious threat, more of an aggravation. I never considered notifying the Coast Guard or any other vessels.

We made it to the dock around 4:30 pm. We had called home and the Co-op about our time of arrival. We had covered the work deck with every piece of cardboard and plastic we had on board when we tied up on the south side of the state pier at the Point. We had barely tied up when Ted Foley and the crew of the *Jerry & Jimmy* came on board followed by what seemed like everyone in Point Judith. I had installed dark green indoor/outdoor carpeting throughout the living quarters and pilothouse. Within a half hour there were black footprints everywhere.

I never got a chance to enjoy what was turning out to be a celebration. Our Atlantic Marine "guy" insisted that I get him to the airport right away so he could get back to Jacksonville. I didn't get the urgency, but I got him on his way. By the time I got back to the boat it was dark and all the deck lights on the *Alliance* were on with at least thirty people still aboard. Joan and the girls had come down to the Point and took pictures as the *Alliance* came through the breachway. I finally made it home about 10:30 pm. It had been quite a day and quite a trip traveling about 900 miles in four and a half days. Considering how rough it was and our problem, I was pleased with the *Alliance's* overall performance.

The next morning, a Friday as I recall, the crew and I pumped out the water in the stern with a portable pump we borrowed from RI Engine. It was only seawater, so there was no problem pumping into the harbor. When we got all the water out, all we found was some small pieces of the broken fishing poles, reels, some grit and unrecognizable muck that had plugged the pump intake screen. From that day forward we never had a screen on a pump intake. That way we could always back flush the lines.

I had been away from my teaching duties going on three weeks. At least one week was spring break. Dick Wing had covered my engine classes and Chic Krawiec had covered my at sea days of my fishing operations class. At least building the *Alliance* would bring some recent first-hand knowledge to that class.

Over the next weekend we wound all the tow wire on the drums of the two winches. Next we loaded the trawl doors that we had already rigged. The ground cables and legs were wound on the net drum, then one of the complete nets. By Monday morning, we were ready for a test tow. Since I had limited knowledge of towing grounds south of the Point, I was happy to have Charlie Follett on board. Charlie wanted to see how or if all this gear would work.

We set out the gear from the drum without a hitch. When it came to unhooking the idler chain from the connection to the drum, we found that it was way too heavy. It took two men to disconnect it and toss it over the back end of the door. Obviously the idler had to be wire which we changed before going fishing.

Setting the doors and towing was very impressive for a crew that had only worked an eastern rig side trawler. What a spread. I had no idea that there would be so much difference. The big surprise however, came when I tried to turn. Even with the rudder hard over, the boat was turning but it was slow coming around.

Increasing the speed made turning slower as the boat surged ahead. It had never occurred to me that a standard rudder for a shrimp trawler would be worthless on a stern trawler like the *Alliance*.

Hauling back with the new Marco hydraulic winches was a dream. Even with the full drums, the *Alliance* was still going ahead as planned by the engineers at Marco. The winches, by the way, were built for the *Alliance* with serial numbers 1 and 2. The net drum hauled in the 50 fathom ground cables and 15 fathom legs. The bottom legs were rubber discs without a problem and the same with the net. The cod end slid up the ramp under the drum. No problem.

I can't remember whether Nelson took the boat on a trip with the rudder situation, but within two weeks we were hauled out at Norlantic Shipyard in Fairhaven to address the rudder problem. The shipyard fabricated the new rudder with the same wedge shape that they had made for the *Jerry & Jimmy*. The rudder also followed the curve of the hull at the top edge. The steering mechanism worked fine without change.

The *Alliance* was now able to turn around almost in its own length and towing it could turn right around and run back on the wires if necessary. I had to pay the bill, which ran about $5K. My fault, the rudder was right on the plan. However, the rudder was installed in Jacksonville, and the boat launched without me ever seeing it. I'm sure I would have realized it was not enough. Oh well.

Chapter 15

1971-1973 Lobster Trap Seasons

Although I was still employed by the University in 1971, I had my contract revised again with the Dean to nine months at 3/4 of the time. Of course with each reduction in my teaching time, there was a proportionate reduction in pay. Now if I was not teaching or involved in special projects, I was free to work on *Alliance* or *Jerry & Jimmy* problems when they were in port.

By April, I put together as much cash as I could come up with in between the two boats and ordered 500 "bear trap" lobster traps from an outfit in Maine. I paid about 10 grand up front at the time of the order with the understanding that I would pay for the traps as they were delivered. By the time we got to mid-June when I was ready to start fishing traps, only about 175 had been delivered. I found out that the orders were being filled for boats in Gloucester, etc. while we were committed with the advance. It took constant calls and many unfulfilled promises by the trap company to complete the order. It was mid-August, half way through the trap season, before the 500 were delivered. To send a "message", it was almost a year before I paid for the last hundred.

I realized right away that the investment I had in the *Alliance* and in the typical "broken 40" lay or share formula would not be enough for the boat. This was especially true when it came to adding another $50,000 for the lobster traps and associated gear. I explained my position to the crews of both vessels pointing out not only the lobster gear issue, but that I would have an ongoing extra unknown expense to cover the cost of replacing lost gear and my goal of fishing 800 to 1,000 pots in the near future.

My "gang" understood and supported my proposal of the boats taking a "clear 45" or 45% of the gross stock before the boat expenses. That summer the crew made more money than any of them thought possible. The change in the "lay" that I was taking did not go over well with the rest of the Point Judith crews. Most notable was Paul Gorman's inscription on the menus at George's Restaurant that read "Jim McCauley "Friend" of the Fishermen". I guess the guys got over the change since years later they elected me President of the Point Judith Fishermen's Cooperative Association for ten consecutive years.

My focus for the summer of 1971 was setting up both boats, a stern trawler and a side trawler, to alternate fishing the same gear. My major concern with offshore pot fishing was the endless parade of foreign trawlers towing the length of the banks. My solution to best protect the gear was to always have one of the boats on the grounds at all times.

That first summer, we rigged the pots using 1/2 inch "surplus" galvanized wire for ground lines with 5/8 polypropylene endlines that were each 100 fathom in length. My plan was to set the pots along the 80 fathom curve in the area north of Atlantis Canyon which is located about 75 miles due south of Nantucket. We rigged the ground wire with a pot every 30 feet (5 fathom), with 30 pots per trawl line with the result that each trawl line was 150 fathom (900 ft. long), roughly three lengths of a football field. We started with 16 trawls plus 10 replacement pots on deck. In order to haul the trawls on a winch drum, the traps with a 5 ft. poly snood had to be attached to the wire when setting and removed when hauled. To do this, we bolted a 1/2 inch wire clamp to the ground wire every 30 ft. The first set we made we used a snap swivel spliced to the snood and after a clamp went out, we would snap on a pot. When the next clamp came by it would catch the snap swivel and pull the pot overboard.

Ted on the *Jerry & Jimmy* was the first one to haul a trawl and found that the snap swivels were breaking, losing the trap. He lost about five of the thirty traps in the first trawl. He called me at the dock and from then on we used an anchor shackle with the pin only finger tight. I remember Dick Winters attaching the shackles with the wire running between his feet on the deck of the *Alliance* before going out the ramp with a trap. It was safe in that the wire running out was controlled by the winch brake unlike rope trawls that run free. What do you do with 500 snap swivels you can't use?

It took three trips for each boat to bring all 16 trawls to the grounds. The *Alliance* could take 4 trawls at a time with 120 "bear traps" on deck and the *Jerry & Jimmy* half that many. We set the trawls in two parallel lines about ½ mile apart, leaving approximately the length of a trawl between the end of one trawl and the beginning of the next one. The other parallel line was set to fill in the space between the trawls.

For bait, we used mostly frozen herring and occasionally filled in with mackerel. The frozen bait was supplied by Tom Daley for all the years I was trap fishing. We put seven herring in each bait bag with two bags a trap. Once we got rolling we used about 1,000 lbs. a day. We found out the herring fished fast and the bags were picked clean in two days. Throughout the summer, we hauled half of the pots the first day and half the second day, then headed home. The other boat would be on the grounds the next two days. During the trips in or out, we relayed the Loran bearings of the numbered trawls.

I had decided to work the deck that summer as "Deck Boss". All summer I stacked pots with John Tarasevich, who was much taller and a strong young guy in his first season of fishing. It's a wonder my back didn't give out, but I survived. Nelson ran the boat hauling and setting the gear, but my being on deck gave me the advantage of seeing how each trawl was catching, and I was able to direct Nelson to change the locations of trawls to maximize the results.

In two days hauling, the 500 pots allowed each pot to be on bottom two nights, and to our surprise we would land between 8-10,000 lbs. of lobsters for 500 pots, or an average of 16 to 20 lbs. per pot of mostly select 1 ½ to 3 lb. lobsters with an occasional 4 or 5 pounder in the mix. As I recall, the price back then was 80¢ to $1.00 per lb.

The Co-op opened a lobster operation in 1970 in a new building located west of the dehy plant. For several years before that, Gerry Adams with the *Ocean Clipper* and I with the *Jerry & Jimmy* paid a percentage of our lobster landings to the Co-op since we were not supporting the Co-op with fish landings, which made sense and was an agreeable condition. I had been selling lobsters to Wickford Shellfish, but now with the Co-op lobster division in place, the Co-op managers wanted me to land with them. My concern was that my lobsters would be landed from refrigerated seawater on both boats and the volume of our landings. I knew that Wickford Shell was selling most of our landings to Hook Lobster in

Boston the same day of unloading, thereby minimizing holding the lobsters prior to sale. Nobody buys weaks or soft shell bugs, and I was very concerned that the new Co-op facility might realize costly losses. I cannot recall exactly when I started selling our trips to the Co-op, but the sales went without the problems I had anticipated.

Both boats experienced problems with foreign trawlers that summer, especially with the Spanish. If they were towing toward out gear at night we would turn our deck lights on and off, and aim our spotlight at the end buoy radar reflectors and flags when they came within 2 miles of our trap field. We also made contact with our ship to ship radios. If there were a number of foreign trawlers in the area, our boat would remain on station until the other boat arrived. As it turned out, we did not suffer any gear losses throughout the season until we lost two trawls at the end because the boats were back towing for fish and picking up the last of the trawls at the end of their trips. During that short period, the traps were left unguarded.

We had some memorable lobster trips. One day, Ted on the *Jerry & Jimmy* called to ask if I could come out the next day because in one day hauling about 300 pots his tanks were full with about 8,000 lbs. I remember the Rondeiro brothers, Joe and Gino from Stonington, CT, happened to hear that call while they were lobstering inshore. The "word" on what we were doing was getting out. In early September, on my last trip before returning to teaching at the school, we landed a trip of 16,000 lbs. on the *Alliance*. You might know it was a few days after the Labor Day weekend and demand for lobsters was falling fast. We had hauled about a hundred or so pots that had been in the water just one day, but even those pots had significant catches. Since I was still working on the deck, I actually saw many catches of a level takeout basket full of lobsters, about 35 lbs., from just one "bear" trap.

The summer of 1971 was the only time the boats used wire ground lines with the traps that close together. It was also the best fishing, pounds per pot, that we ever had over a five month period. In subsequent years, we used polypropylene ground lines with the pots spaced at 50 feet. Looking back, I believe the heavier wire ground line really anchored all the pots in a trawl with no possibility of movement. The pots being closer together also concentrated the bait as a greater attraction. Overall, the field of trawls were more concentrated than in later years. The main reason for the high catch rate was we were the only boats with traps in the water at the time. The nearest "Prelude" traps were fifty or more miles to the east and no pots along the bank to the west.

I honestly believe the lobsters were really hungry. Once all that bait hit the bottom, with the slick that herring creates, lobsters from the deep water of Atlantis Canyon moved in and stayed there until caught. Over the summer we made only minor adjustments to the field. On one occasion we had a bad set with the whole trawl bunched up in a short distance, about a quarter mile. We set another new trawl, then within one hour, we went back and hauled the messed up trawl and had about 40 lbs. That is fast fishing — unbelievable.

I have not mentioned the level of income the boats were bringing in back in 1971. Generally the *Jerry & Jimmy* stocked around $120—130,000, but in 1971, the *Jerry & Jimmy* stocked $187,000. The difference from the average was four month of offshore potting lobsters. Since the *Alliance* did not have any income that year until late April, it was more difficult to fully analyze its performance. Based on the *Jerry & Jimmy* stock, the 500 pots contributed $60,000. Since the two boats shared the production from the same pots, the *Alliance* showed about $75,000 because of its greater holding capacity. Catching $135,000 or roughly 160,000 lbs. at an average price, as I recall of 80¢ per lb.

We did have a cost for gear of about $25,000, but other costs such as fuel were much less than we experienced in later years. The *Jerry & Jimmy* fuel cost for the whole of 1971 was $10,600. The cost of ice for 8 months was $258. My estimate of crew share was roughly $10,000 each for the 5 man crew for the four months of lobstering. For the whole year, the 4 man crew made just under $20,000, with the captain at $29,000. Today that sounds like they were on welfare, but back then $100 a week or $5-6,000 a year was good money for a shore job.

Our catch in 1971 did not go unnoticed. As the new fishing year of 1972 began, a system of registering the proposed area with the Coast Guard for each lobster enterprise came into play. I believe Prelude from Westport, MA was responsible for initiating the proposal because they filed right away for an area, as I recall, about 120 miles long by 40 miles wide. It was totally unclear what that meant. The purpose of providing the pot field location was that it be specific in order for the Coast Guard to provide the Loran coordinates of at least the four corners plus depth of the field to foreign trawlers. Not surprising, Prelude's nonspecific claim included the area where I had fished the pots during the previous summer in 1971. By June, 54 boats had registered with the Coast Guard to set pots between Cape Hatteras to Corsair Canyon. The Coast Guard estimated that the number of entrants would increase to 85 by July.

In Point Judith, there was an increase from 2 to an expected 26. Of that number 6 were new to the Point specifically for offshore lobstering, while the remainder were conversions from other fisheries. As a result of this influx of new boats, I registered my location from the east side of Hudson Canyon extending 30 miles east from 70-120 fathoms. Not what I really wanted to do, but I calculated that it was so far from the Point and other potential "lobster ports", that we would have the area to ourselves. Meanwhile, we increased the number of traps we fished to 750 as well as replacing lost gear at a cost of $10,000.

Although we had followed a sound policy of marking our gear in 1971, the fishermen got together and established recommendations for setting the pot fields to avoid necessary conflicts among ourselves, especially with draggers both foreign and domestic. The guidelines were to set pot lines along depth contours and as we did, to have a boat in the area at all times, my suggestion, and notify the Coast Guard of the pot location on a weekly basis. Gear markings were to have a red buoy with a mast and radar reflector on both ends of a pot line with a flag on the west end. These markings are still considered the acceptable markings to this day.

One problem we became aware of that first summer, was that big trans-Atlantic ships would slow down as they approached the pot field. Once they became aware that this conglomeration of targets were only radar reflectors being used as gear markers, they would resume their normal speed. We noticed after a couple of months that the word must have spread because most of the ships no longer slowed down. This was their first year encountering lobster trawls in the region of the traffic lanes as well.

At night, when it was foggy, so as not to get run down, we

made it a policy not to lay to and drift in or close to the pot field and we always ran a watch.

Shortly after returning to classes in the fall of 1971, I was contacted by Atlantic Marine to take possession of one of their 79 ft. standard trawlers that had been re-acquired by them through a default on a loan that they had guaranteed. Working with Morris Wilmot, their same sales manager, we laid out a work schedule for the F/V *Dorothy E* to convert her to a lobster trawler. The boat required work by RI Engine. We converted the after fuel tanks to a lobster tank with an insulated floor and walls covered with cement finish as I had on the *Alliance*.

The work was completed by mid-October at a cost of $15,000. All charged to me. In discussions with Atlantic Marine, I was convinced that I could work out a deal to take over the payments for the *Dorothy E*. I went so far as to form a new "C" corporation with Ted Foley and I, the same arrangement I had with Nelson. My original $100,000 note with our local bank was to pay it off with a combination of the *Alliance* financing and the proceeds from the planned sale of the *Jerry & Jimmy*. The deal on the *Dorothy E* fell through when the original lender required that Atlantic Marine would be responsible by cosigning the loan. As they said, they were not in the long-term boat financing business.

As I recall, the *Dorothy E* was sold to a fisherman in Long Island, then after a few years the boat was purchased by my friend Rodney Avila from New Bedford, and it became the *Trident*. Over the years, we fished together with many memorable trips. More about that later.

I was disappointed that I was never able to put together an arrangement with Ted. He certainly bailed me out during the time I was building the *Alliance* and fishing alongside the *Alliance* during the following winter.

In March of 1971 my brother Jerry had gone to work on the *Jerry & Jimmy* with Ted. Jerry had graduated from URI as a chemical engineer and went to work for Pratt & Whitney after graduation, but he really wanted to try fishing. Here is a quote about his experience. "I know it was damned rough and I was seasick from the time the boat passed through the gap until we returned home. Not fun. I think I only lasted about three months". As it turned out, Jerry had a successful career working as an engineer. I have often though about my choice of being a fisherman for all those years. I certainly never recommended it as a way of life if there was a choice. In Jerry's situation, if he had fished with me on the *Alliance* that summer for lobsters, instead of starting out dragging in the winter, the outcome may have been different.

During the summer of 1971, we were using wire for the groundline. By the end of the season, I realized that using the same wire for another season would be a risk. As each trawl came ashore, we filled a few dumpsters with the wire. I ordered a big 50 HP pot hauler from Marco for the *Alliance* and had RI Engine install a hydraulic system on the *Jerry & Jimmy* including a locally made pot hauler. Because we were fishing in deep water up to 100 fathom, I decided to space the pots 5 fathom apart meaning that up to 20 pots would be suspended off the bottom while hauling. Based on talks with the Marco people, I decided to use 5/8 polypropylene line throughout the system. As a result in early 1972, I ordered about 35 miles of rope. Because we were working with draggers with the gallows frames in place, we had to disconnect each pot as it came aboard. The connection to the pot was a "G" link made from a chain link.

Fortunately for me, during the latter part of 1971, Tom Dykstra started building bear traps for me in his father Bill's barn in Wakefield. Tom's pots were the same dimensions as the earlier pots I had purchased in Maine. By spring, I had 750 pots ready to fish with a reliable source of supply when needed.

I neglected to tell the story about bringing the pots from the summer of 1971 up to my yard in Wakefield. Using our two 3/4 ton Chevy "Longhorn" trucks, we stacked the pots four high from the back of the yard almost to the street, about 175 feet, in four rows with a space wide enough in between the rows so we had access to every pot. The month was November, so the neighbor's windows were closed because there was a distinctive "smell of the sea" from the pots. I told my girls to spread the word to the neighbors if they were missing a cat. Sure enough, within two days we caught two. Naturally they were in the bottom pots and we had to move the three on top to get them. I think we got one more a few days later and I can't remember if it was ours.

As soon as the spring semester ended at the school, I was back on the *Alliance*. We loaded both boats with as many trawls as we could carry and headed for our "new" location down by Hudson Canyon, a distance of about 100 miles. At an average speed of 9 knots, it was going to take us at least 11 hours each way. For me it seemed like it was much farther away than Atlantis Canyon where we were the last year. In fact, it was only an hour longer trip.

This time we had fifteen trawls consisting of 50 pots each spaced at 60 ft (ten fathom). This made each trawl 3,000 feet in length, a little over 1/2 mile each. Each time one of the boats took out a load of pots, we would haul the trawls that were on the grounds.

I worked the deck, as I had the year before, in order to observe the catch. Using the new Marco pot hauler on the *Alliance* allowed us to haul the 100 fathom end lines in just minutes. It was located about 8 ft. off the deck and in the forward center of the deck. The line came aboard over a single block at the end of a hydraulic boom. With the power block turning near top speed, the water would fly and the end line ended up in a neat pile. Each pot came up, stopped and was disconnected from the ground line. We always had extra baited pots ready to be reconnected to the ground line while the pot that just came up was unloaded at the rail and rebaited. If a pot was damaged, we set it aside and substituted a standby. The pot hauler had no trouble lifting the roughly eight pots from the 80 fathom depth. This was a much faster operation than when we used wire ground lines.

We were catching reasonably well but we found out right away, that the strong consistent southwest tide caused the trawls to move. The east end of each trawl usually ended up with three or more pots bunched together as near as we could tell and we started using a heavy steel anchor on that end which helped. Trawls that were set around 90 fathom where the Canyon opened into the northwest always caught the best, but quite often slid down the bank into deeper water and the western end of the trawl would come up with each pot filled to the cover with small red crabs. The red crabs also "destroyed" the bait bags.

Each boat was using a 30 gallon garbage bag full of nylon bait bags every trip. I started a bait bag production line at home.

Down cellar, I would cut out the square from a large panel of nylon netting using an electrical tool that burned rapidly through the netting. The whole house smelled of burnt nylon. I would also cut the appropriate length of nylon twine to string the bait bags. My three girls, my wife and even my mother would sit and string the bags. I usually did over a couple of hundred at a time since Ted Foley, running the *Jerry & Jimmy*, was using them up at the same rate.

We didn't have as much foreign trawler problems as we used to back east. In early June of 1972, however, the first major incidents occurred when three pot vessels lost about 75 percent of their gear, about 800 pots, in the area around Hydrographer Canyon as a result of foreign trawling operations. The other "good thing" for us was that we were working well south of the Ambrose to Nantucket trans-Atlantic shipping lanes and encountered very few large ships.

I recall one bad week around midsummer when both the *Jerry & Jimmy* and the *Alliance* experienced trouble with our refrigerated sea water systems. The lobsters you could see in the below deck tanks looked fine but when we pumped out the water, we found that the bottom third of the lobsters were either "weak" or dead. After doing the "sniff" test on some of the lobsters to see if they could be cooked for the meat, I gave up and went out about a mile south of the center wall of the harbor and dumped about 3,500 lbs. of lobsters overboard. Two days later, Ted on the *Jerry & Jimmy*, had the same problem and dumped another 2,500 lbs. overboard. Oh well!

The increase in the number of boats setting traps in the deep water had a negative impact on the price and I don't know how the relatively new lobster operation was able to handle, sell, and pay for all those lobsters. I was not involved in the Co-op management at all back then. I did know that the restaurants and other lobster buyers were notorious for not paying their bills and might not pay for sixty days even though the lobsters they bought live were consumed in three or four days. I can't imagine what the Co-op receivables must have been.

It was not what you could call a good year. With the especially rough winter, the *Jerry & Jimmy* for example made about 30% less than the previous year and the *Alliance* didn't do that well either.

The summer of 1973, both boats started back setting pots for lobsters. We had lost very little gear the previous year and my records show that each boat had only $1,500 worth of lobster gear cost for 1973. I decided to try working the same general area where we had such a successful summer in 1971. Although "Prelude" and others had laid claim to half the "edge" in early 1972, there were still open areas where we could fit in our 750 pot field. There were other boats trapping around us but seldom setting any closer than two miles of our gear. There was a much lower catch rate than we had in 1971. For two boats working the same gear, it was only a "living" compared to the previous years. I was never sure if the gear we were fishing with all rope bottom lines, was able to catch the way the wire ground lines did. Other boats with similar number of pots seemed to be having comparable landings, making me come to the conclusion that it was more likely that the population of lobsters offshore was already being thinned out. The other possibility was that unlike 1971 when we were alone and our pot field was the only food/bait around, that we attracted lobsters from a very large area. Now there were all kinds of bait to attract them to the many pot fields.

I began to feel uncomfortable tying the *Alliance* to the dock so much while we alternated trips. The obvious answer was for the *Alliance* to fish the gear alone which made sense if the catch remained similar to what the two boats were catching. As I recall in late summer, the *Jerry & Jimmy* started ground fishing around the "corner buoy" south of Nantucket. The catch of lobsters was better as expected with the one boat, but was not nearly the numbers we had in that area especially in September of '71. The other problem that I had anticipated with all these boats trapping lobsters was a noticeable drop in price with a nose dive after Labor Day.

That fall, with only one boat, it seemed we would never get all the gear back to the dock even with pots stacked all over the boat. Fortunately there were no lost trawls mostly because there were no substantial hurricanes affecting our area.

The *Alliance* at the dock in Point Judith

Chapter 16

"The *Alliance*"
Decision Time

The most important issue that I faced going back fishing fulltime was to refinance the *Alliance*. The initial financing by CIT in Jacksonville allowed me to complete the *Alliance* according to the contract. The interest rate on that note was high compared to the fishery loan I had on the *Jerry & Jimmy*. At that time, the best financing for commercial fishing boats was with The Southern New England Production Credit Association, a subsidiary of the Farm Credit Service established by the Federal Government to provide financing for farmers.

On July 13, 1973, Nelson and I, as Trawler Alliance, Inc., signed a seven and a half year loan agreement for $225,000 with payments of $2,500/month with interest at 6%. I still have the card showing the monthly payments. Right at the beginning, I made an extra payment and remained one payment ahead until the loan was paid off on February 5, 1981. The loan consolidated all the loose ends including all unpaid bills. A clean slate.

In the fall of 1973, as Captain of the *Alliance*, we fished with Ted Foley, captain of the *Jerry & Jimmy* for yellowtail, black backs, and gray sole south of Nantucket in the area of the former Nantucket Lightship. I can't recall how we found out about a big "pile" of yellowtails being caught way to the east by some of the New Bedford boats. We took about 40 ton of ice on the *Alliance* and with the *Jerry & Jimmy* headed east on the next trip. It was early in October.

As it turned out, the fish were found 50 miles NE of what was later, in 1984, the "Hague" or Canadian Boundary Line. The fish were in 50 fathoms at 66 degrees W and 42 degrees N. It was a long trek of about 300 miles to get there and took us 32 hours averaging 9 ½ knots. We all hoped this was not a "Wild Goose Chase," especially not knowing what kind of bottom we were going to be fishing on. We set out and towed about an hour and caught about 2,000 lbs. of clear yellowtails, 2/3rds of which were large. I doubt

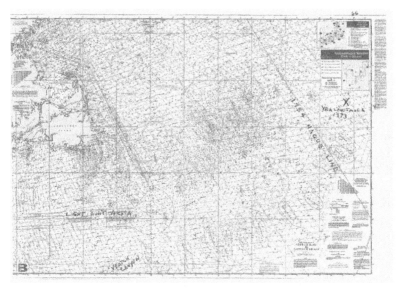

Fishing grounds NE of the Hague Line

there was 50 lbs. of trash—mostly skates.

That first trip, we caught 58,000 lbs. in 33 hours of fishing time. We did sort the fish. The large were iced down in the after hold and regulars iced down in the forward hold. We stopped because we were generous with the ice and had run out. Meanwhile, the *Jerry & Jimmy* had caught over 40,000 lbs. and was ready to make the return trip to Point Judith. As it turned out, the New Bedford Fleet went on strike about the time of our first trip. During subsequent trips, there were no New Bedford boats on the ground.

We talked about the strike situation which I understood was called for a number of issues other than the price paid for yellowtails. Our fish, landed at The Point, were mostly sold to fillet houses in New Bedford, and I did talk to Jake Dykstra about continuing to fish on yellowtails. I got the impression from him that we would not get any medals, so to speak, if we stopped fishing in support of the strike. Our near water boats fishing around Block Island and Nantucket would still be fishing yellowtail, so we returned to the grounds on a second trip. As I recall, we averaged about 35 cents/lb. for the trip for $20,000. Remember, fuel was cheap.

We loaded up with books from the library and, with more ice, headed back on another 32+ hour trip. At the time, Dave Sterling was running the *Suzanne* while the captain/owner, Jack Westcott, took some time off. Dave decided to make the trip to the grounds with us. I always assumed Jack gave him the "green light" to make the trip. The fishing on the next trip was even better. With only a few boats working in the area, the shoals of fish did not "break up" as they would with a fleet of boats towing the area. The *Alliance* trip was completed with a total of 75,000 lbs. We took out 50,000 lbs. of large, all in the after hold, full except for the space under the hatch. The 25,000 regulars were in the forward hold. In all the years I owned and ran the *Alliance*, this was the most yellowtails I ever caught in a trip. The *Jerry & Jimmy* did well that trip and Dave Sterling filled the *Suzanne*. Thank God!

The *Alliance*

I believe we made one more trip that October. We were doing so well, that I decided to continue into November. The *Jerry & Jimmy* and the *Alliance* headed for the "spot." As we got near the grounds, the seas were getting worse all the time with northwest winds blowing 30-40 M.P.H. We drifted for a day waiting for the seas to calm, jogging back into the wind every couple of hours. The weather reports call for diminishing northwest winds so we waited. This went on for three days. I was so frustrated that I almost set the net a number of times. Common sense prevailed. If I had a screw up of some kind trying to tow, we would be in big trouble being this far from home.

Finally, in the morning of the fourth day, I talked with Ted, and we decided to head in together. It took us almost two days to get to the "corner buoy" south of Nantucket. The wind didn't let up one bit. At times, I wouldn't be surprised if it didn't reach 50 MPH. The rest of the trip to the Point was not so painful. We were gone on that trip for six and a half days and never set the net on either boat. In my "hang book," I wrote "Never go to George's in November" so hard with a pencil that it tore through the paper.

Based on that unforgettable trip, I decided to haul out the boat every November, and we fixed everything we could, including nets and gear, so that we wouldn't have to put up with dealing with all kinds of maintenance issues during the winter months.

Since that time, I have often thought about those yellowtail trips and if they are still available in large quantities in that region. It is unlikely that the Canadians are even looking, never mind trying to fish that far from their ports with the current cost of fuel.

1974 was an especially important year in my fishing career. The first "decision" I made was to sell the *Jerry & Jimmy*. At the end of 1973, the balance sheet of the boat's financial statement showed a "basis" of $99,131 with "accumulated depreciation" of $79,425, leaving a "book value" of roughly $20,000. If you have any knowledge of accounting, you will recognize that any sale of the *Jerry & Jimmy* was going to result in a taxable capital gain, State and Federal.

The decision to form a "Corporation" when I contracted for the *Alliance* was because I had asked Nelson to become a participant in the venture. At the time, I was still employed at the Fisheries School and thought it necessary to have a committed partner that I could count on to run the vessel during the times I could not go to sea. The "Corporation" solved any liability problems which might occur with a partner. It was similar to many of the arrangements that

New Bedford absentee owners had with the Captains of their vessels. In most cases, similar to my own, the Captain, in this case Nelson, did not provide much or any capital to the corporation.

Selling the *Jerry & Jimmy* meant that as an individual, I was liable for a sizable capital gain tax while at the same time, I had all kinds of capital losses in the "Trawler Alliance, Inc."

In the spring of 1974, I sold the *Jerry & Jimmy* to Frank Lamy, an experienced Captain that had fished out of the Point for years. I sold the boat to Frank for $90,000 as I recall, and I did pay a considerable tax on the $70,000 capital gain. I have often reflected on that decision. The boat, although built in 1945, was in good condition with a relatively new engine and a total renovation of the hull. The most important consideration was that I would lose Ted Foley, who had been a productive and reliable Captain for me. There was no position on the *Alliance* for Ted as Captain or mate now that I was back fishing fulltime. Now, looking back, it was a serious mistake for what cash I ended up with. "Uncle S." did well as always.

My second decision that spring was to put out the word that all my lobster gear was for sale. Based on the increasing number of new participants including new offshore lobster boats to the deep water fishery, I concluded, at the time, to get out of the business. Compared to the new entrants, the *Alliance* was in a much better position to continue in the fishery. Again, looking back, I should have stayed in and tried to outlast the newcomers.

I was approached by the owner of one company that owned a couple of offshore lobster boats to sell him the gear with no money down and payable over the next two years. What a great offer, top dollar too. I thought he was kidding, but no, it was really his proposal. If you, as a reader, missed the point of the proposal, here it is. The collateral for the "loan" would be my lobster gear at sea in some unknown location subject to a high rate of losses. "Goodbye."

I did sell all the gear to "Butch" Winters, who was fishing out of Atlantic City for cash. I had known "Butch" for years, and I made sure he got all the gear including the two pot haulers from both boats. All the gear was in my yard, and it took three flat-bed trailer trucks to carry it all. I was out of the offshore lobster fishery after being the first out of the Point to give it a shot. All I can tell you, I was in it at the beginning when the catches were beyond belief.

Even fishing the gear with only one boat during the previous fall, it was obvious that the bonanza was over.

As it has turned out since the year 2000 on, there is room for a limited number of boats dispersed along the offshore banks to make a respectable living. At times, in the last decade prior to the 2007 & 2008 recession, lobster prices have been, in my opinion, quite impressive, especially compared to my early lobster dragging days when culls and large were 40 cents and selects were 60 cents.

Although I was now out of the lobster trap business, more fishermen were still entering the trap fishery along with a number of new boats—many called "investor" boats owned by speculators new to the industry. At the time, there were no license requirements and "limited entry" programs were years away. Now, as a year-round dragger fisherman, I was concerned with gear conflict issues with so much of the offshore grounds continuing to be proliferated with pots, especially during the six months of the "summer" or calm season.

There was another decision to make in the early spring of "74" that was really a "no brainer." The Caterpillar Company Headquarters had decided to ask me if I would be interested in overhauling the main engine in the *Alliance* at no cost for parts and labor. The engine was a new model, and they wanted to see how much wear had occurred since the boat begin operation in March of 1971. My only contribution would be the loss of roughly three weeks of fishing time. As a direct result of the overhaul, Caterpillar installed an improved piston and rings modification that did result in a noticeable reduction in lube oil consumption. Not a bad deal.

The fishing activity in 1974 focused primarily on fluke. Beginning in the winter, if the weather pattern showed a period of five days or more of fishable weather, we would start the trip using a 5 1/2 inch cod end for fluke. By fishable weather, I mean running offshore with the clearing northwest wind of 25 plus knots after a storm, then hopefully get westerly winds under 25 knots for a few days with diminishing winds at the end of three days. By that time, fishing 24 hours/day, which we always did, we could count on having 8-10,000 lbs. of large and jumbo fluke and a mix of angler and tile fish.

By the third night, we would change the back end of the net

using a 2 1/2—3" tailpiece and cod end. Usually we were near areas like Veatch Canyon, where we could pick up some butterfish at night and squid during both night and day. We would still catch the large mesh species, but these continued to be large fish and not undersized by any means because of the small mesh. No harm done.

When there were stretches of bad weather, we would make two or three day trips for butterfish. If we got on the fish, we could catch 40,000 lbs. or more during one night. In these situations, I would stay up and have all hands on deck so we could get the fish iced down before hauling back the next tow. If we were really on the fish, the tows could be as short as twenty minutes or as long as an hour depending on how the fish showed on the fish scope. I liked to catch no more than 10,000 lbs. a tow so that we could take the bag up the ramp in one shot. Towing too long would mean splitting the bag over the side like a sidetrawler which wasted a lot of time in my opinion. It really was possible to judge the size of a catch if you watched the scope throughout the whole tow.

The offshore fluke fishing started to wind down in April. The last trips, strangely enough, were always in deeper water. Usually all winter, the fluke were in 60 to 70 fathom, but in April, they were found out to 80 and even 90 fathom. The weather was usually good so we could fish five or more days each trip. We still had a box on deck so we usually had three or more thousand pounds of "drag" lobsters. Up until the end of April, this was a typical winter pattern of fishing not unlike the years with the *Jerry & Jimmy*. From then on, in order to continue to chase fluke for a living was a learning experience.

In 1974, I bought fishing licenses for the *Alliance* in the states of New York and Massachusetts. In May, we started towing for fluke exclusively with large mesh right up on the beach in as little as 30 feet of water mostly along the "Hamptons" at the eastern end of Long Island and east of Shinnecock Inlet. At times, we would go as far as Moriches Inlet. During the day, it was like being a tourist as we towed along with a clear view of all the beachfront mansions. They were very modern in design compared to the Newport mansions in Rhode Island.

We were not popular with the locals fishing out of Shinnecock. It was bad enough that they had to put up with the

Montauk Fleet, but at least they were New York boats. Our worst offense was that we fished around the clock when the locals were exclusively day boats. Also, with our heavy gear when towing in shallow water, we left a mud plume that was visible on the surface behind the net.

The fluke off Long Island were more mediums (under 2 lbs.) than anything we caught offshore. But, using a 5 1/2 cod end, we avoided catching fish under 14 to 15 inches. Not like the catches I had seen being landed in Virginia when I was fishing with Silas "Dub" Barrows. Most of the trips landed down there were less than 14 inches at the time.

By the end of May, we moved to Nantucket Sound. Thanks to Jack Westcott taking his case allowing out of state boats to fish Massachusetts waters all the way to the Supreme Court back in the mid-60's, we were able, with a license, to fish anywhere in Massachusetts waters. Jack, fishing with the *Suzanne*, fished the Sound in the summer months. He worked the west end of the sound, but I never fished with him. Working the west end of the sound, you really had to know the ground. I never gave that a thought and steamed right through that area and fished the east end of the sound where the bottom was mostly clear or at least more forgiving.

I remember setting out in the channel one night back when I had the *Jerry & Jimmy*. There were two other boats fishing there so I gave it a shot. I towed about 15 minutes and hung up. With a fair tide, I thought I was going to lose the works. Enough of that.

We set up a pattern for working Nantucket Sound that was very productive over the years. Come dark, we would tow east and west and south of Tuckernuck Shoal, in an area called the "Quahaug Grounds" that was outside of Nantucket Harbor on the north side of the Island. We always caught at least two or three times more fluke there at night than we ever did in the daytime. The dayboats working out of the harbor would come out and have a good daylight tow, then the catch would drop off for the rest of the day; and if they fished the sunset tow in to the dark, they would have another good tow. Very few of the boats lasted that long and normally returned to harbor by late afternoon. The bycatch in that area was conchs, a spiral shaped shell mollusk. At the end of a three day trip, we often caught up to 6,000 lbs. of conch, which we sold at the Co-op.

Night fishing on the Quahaug Grounds was relatively easy, even in the fog because there was little traffic running to or from the Island at night. The only exception was the 11:00 p.m. ferry to Hyannisport. I usually called the ferry if I was in the area to let him know that I was towing and the direction of the tow.

During the day in the summer, there was continuous traffic and on foggy days, I made it a point to tow up in the northeast corner of the sound. On calm fog bound days, it was very difficult to determine the direction of a becalmed sailboat or if it was small, it could be a conch pot buoy which became numerous in the 1970's.

Over the years, I had many encounters with sailboats. Most were very surprised to hear the horn indicating a boat towing and almost without exception, they would attempt to cross in front of us. When they did see the *Alliance*, it must have been a scary sight with a twelve foot bow coming at you at 3 or 4 knots. I often wondered if in sailboat classes, they were warned never to go in back of a trawler because of the tow wires or fishing gear extending over the stern when we were hauling back. On those few occasions when I thought they were too close, I would slow down and take the engine out of gear. The boat would actually settle back about twenty feet with the weight of the gear. Nice to know.

I was washing up in the head one early afternoon, when the boat slowed almost to a stop. Nelson had the afternoon watch from 1:00 to 7:00 p.m. He sounded the towing signal, and I looked out the open porthole, and there was an 18 foot sailboat passing down our port side no more than 30 feet away. There was a man and a woman sailing the boat, and I have seldom seen anyone with such a shocked look on their faces at their close call. Close ones don't count.

During the early daylight hours through the day including the sunset tow, we fished around the shoals such as Horseshoe Shoal, Southwest Ground, Broken Ground, and many unnamed structures. Each time when we hauled back the net, the twine was plastered with dead vegetation that had accumulated alongside the shoals. When the bag of fish and junk including mud was dumped on deck, it was a near solid mass. We learned that the only way to work through the mess was using long-handled potato rakes and the deck hose. Although a lot of work, we had significant catches of large, black sea bass, large scup, and fluke. Every time we hauled back, we had to set the net with the cod end open and tow it around to clear the meshes, especially in the lower wings and belly.

Since we worked around the clock with a crew of five, this left two men on deck, so I hired a senior in high school to go on deck most every day to help wade through the catch. It worked out so well that he fished with us every summer for four years until he graduated from college.

I don't remember the exact year, but we had a Fisheries School crewmember, going transit as we call a temporary crew member, with us. As the trip reached the third day, we still needed more fish to make it worthwhile. The problem was that he was graduating the next day. About four o'clock that afternoon, we made a tow just outside Nantucket Harbor primarily because the wind was blowing hard from the southwest. During the tow, the fish scope was really "lit up." When we hauled back, there were scup stuck through the meshes all over the wings and face of the net. By the time we cleared the net, we had caught 17,000 lbs. of large scup and made our trip. We sailed for port in time for graduation. I honestly can't confirm that he attended the ceremony.

I neglected to tell about the important squid fishery that took place each May when we first started fishing the Sound. The concentration of squid was in the northeast corner of the Sound up toward Hyannis Harbor where there were a number of fish traps. The traps were and probably still are "fixed" in place with twine hung from poles driven into the soft bottom.

We fished for squid with the net rigged very light on the sweep with the headrope loaded with floats and the backend or tailpiece constructed of 1 1/2" twine including the liner inside the cod end. The Point boats fishing the early squid in the Sound were often put on a trip limit by the Co-op, as I recall, of 25,000 lbs. because there was so much squid being landed by our boats and the "floating" fish traps around Point Judith. The price wasn't great, but we could catch a trip in less than 24 hours fishing with the nights being equally productive.

A "Sound" story. Nelson always listened to Channel 16—the emergency channel monitored by the Coast Guard. One day, he told me about a panic call he heard. A power boat called *The Hy-*

annisport Station requesting a compass course to the port. Picture this. It was thick fog, and the Coast Guard after a few minutes asked the powerboat for his position. The response: "If I knew where I was, I wouldn't have called you!" Oh well.

By mid-July, we usually moved out of the Sound and fished for fluke towing north and south along the west side of Wasque Shoal which is located on the west side of Muskeget Channel. During that period, we would also tow east and west along the south shore of Martha's Vineyard at various depths. As I recall, we were usually alone towing that area. That area was also "dirty" at times.

From there we moved to the south side of Nantucket Island, sometimes towing in as close as 25 feet of water. We towed around Miacomet Rip then through a 45-55 foot hole, then east past the Nantucket Airport going toward Sankaty Head Light until the water shoaled to about 30 feet where a Loran tower was located. This area could be productive for at least two weeks or more each summer.

I recall one day that one of the small "day boats" towing by the airport caught a small, high winged, single engine plane in his net. When he got the plane up high enough, towing it off his stern, he came on the radio that it looked like there was someone still in the cockpit. The last we saw the boat, it was towing the plane toward Sankaty Head Light with a plan to meet up with the Coast Guard. We never heard that there were actually bodies aboard. The activity did break up the day and gave us something to talk about. Over the years, I caught quite a few pieces of aircraft.

While I'm still telling stories about that general area, I got into a pile of scup on my birthday, early in September one year, and in five short tows about a mile south of Muskeget Channel Buoy, we caught over 50,000 lbs. of scup. For a number of years, I tried to catch scup in that area around my birthday and struck out.

During the month of September, we continued catching fluke along the twenty fathom edge west of the "fingers" of Nantucket Shoals. We did pull a trip or two between the two "fingers" north of Davis South Shoal. The tide in there ran like a river. Towing into the tide at maximum RPM's, making about 2 1/2 knots. Towing fair tide, we could only catch if we almost idled the engine and still were towing over the ground at nearly four knots. Otherwise, towing fair tide at normal towing RPM's, you were lucky to catch a couple of fish. The fish found between the "fingers" back then were almost all jumbo-size ranging from 4-8 lbs. or more.

I remember one trip along the twenty fathom edge west of Davis South Shoal, when we caught 25,000 lbs. of mostly jumbo and some large in 24 hours of fishing. All the fish had extended bellies full of squid. There was always a bushel or two of beautiful hard lobsters with each tow in that area.

I had one day fishing in that area that I will never forget. We got to the grounds just after daylight and set the net. No other boat was in sight which was good. After towing about a half hour, fresh coffee in hand, I looked at the fish finder, and it was lit up like a "Christmas tree." We hauled right back. The first of the king-sized dogfish began in the end of the wings and with all hands on deck, we cut heads off the dogs and yanked the bodies out of the twine. We finished bringing the full cod end aboard just before dark. I couldn't begin to estimate how many were in the net. The cod end alone probably had 8,000 lbs. in it. Over the years, I caught a lot of dogfish, but that time was, without doubt, the most. Now that I think of it, we never sold a single pound of dogfish in all my years of fishing. Always were cents/lb. in my day.

It was sometime in the "eighties," as I recall, that lobster-men started setting trawls in this area along the twenty fathom edge. It was such a dangerous area for gear conflict with the draggers that we called them "suicide" pots, and I do think they set only their old-est pots in that area. After a period of time with both sides in the conflict having had "enough," we all came to an unwritten agree-ment that the draggers would stay west of Loran line 14125 or maybe it was 14150, anyway it worked reasonably well for many years.

I remember one night in that area, the *Alliance* towed up a trawl. There was a pot hanging on the portside door with a trawl line running back with pots visible in our wake. We cut that pot free and of course, the net had the rest of the trawl. As we started to bring the legs aboard on the net drum, I felt and heard a pot tangle in the propeller. By giving the engine a quick burst of speed in reverse, I was able to clear the prop. This same thing happened at least five times during the haulback and the prop came clear each time. After cutting out the pots caught in the face of the net, I steamed around for fifteen minutes or so to make sure the propeller was clear and set in again. That was the worst mess I ever had by way of gear conflict, although I caught my share of discarded and active trawls over the years. Had that string of pots been constructed of vinyl coated steel, like they are now, I would never have been able to break clear. Lucky sometimes.

In October of '74, we were back fishing south of the "banana shoal" in the "light ship area". The fluke were moving off and now mixed with the combination of blackback flounder, yellowtail flounder, grey sole, and lobsters. This completed the cycle before starting offshore in December. It would turn out to be kind of my own niche that I would follow through the rest of the 1970's right through the mid-80's with variations as necessary.

Over the next ten years, the fishing was lucrative enough to pay for my three daughter's college educations using my paycheck only. Nelson also put his two daughters through nursing schools. Nelson's son, Edward, joined the crew around 1975 after serving in the Navy. His last assignment was aboard the carrier *Intrepid* which was decommissioned at Quonset Point, Rhode Island in 1974. Ed stayed with the *Alliance* until it was sold.

In November, I stayed with my pledge to take the *Alliance* to the shipyard which was exclusively Norlantic Shipyard in Fairhaven, Massachusetts. I had been talking to Bob Merriam, my electronic expert, about a state of the art fish finder. We settled on a Koden Dual Frequency Color Machine that sold for $12,000. The transducer was installed at the shipyard under Bob's supervision. The viewing unit was installed on the portside of the wheelhouse facing inward so I could easily see the screen from my comfortable leather captain's chair. The fish finder ran almost continuous for the next fifteen years without a service call. The bottom and fish showed clearly even at full speed of 10 knots over the bottom. It caught a pile of fish for me over the years and was well worth the initial cost.

The other major project accomplished at the shipyard was to weld on rolling chocks. They extended out 10" from the v of the hull roughly half way between the hard chine and the keel and ran for about 15 feet along the middle of the hull (10" x 1" thick x 15'). In my opinion, it added additional stability without a noticeable change in hull speed. This was my preference to installing booms with heavy "birds" for stability. Back then, the booms in service were held in place by wire cable bracing and supports. After all the weather I experienced on the *Jerry & Jimmy*, I couldn't see how the booms would survive with the seas that were generated by 100+ mph winds. I had heard stories of booms collapsing, using cutting torches to clear the wreckage, etc. Not for me. On the *Alliance*, we cleared everything off the deck, sealed up the ramp with heavy beams pinned in place, opened all the scuppers to allow the water to clear the deck. Once buttoned up, we could sail along without considering the need to go on the deck.

As it happened, all the years I fished the *Alliance*, we only ran into winds of 75 mph a couple of times without incident. I attributed that to better weather reports plus the ability of the *Alliance* to steam into the wind with relative ease, instead of a slow jog which often let the bad weather catch up with us.

Alliance entering the harbor

Chapter 17

The Point Judith Fishermen's Cooperative Association, Inc.
"The Co-op"

This chapter on the Co-op includes only a brief history. The main purpose for writing it is to tell the reader what it was like from my experience as a member and a boat captain/owner.

The Co-op was established in 1947. According to what I have read about the early years, George Gross, a former Naval Officer, had the vision and the resolve to make the Co-op a reality. He became its first general manager. George Thompson was the first president of the Association. The office manager was Americo "Reek" DiSista, who was with the Co-op forever and was one of the staff. We all had a great deal of respect for what he contributed to the daily operation. Jacob "Jake" Dykstra started as the dock foreman, prior to becoming President of the Co-op in 1952. The President is technically the Chairman of the Board of Directors, one of seven directors in the Co-op structure.

The main dock was in operation in 1948 with the second floor housing the offices and marine store added a year later. The Co-op added to the main building and leased other nearby buildings located to the south along the bulkhead, as their scope of operation expanded under the supervision of Joe Lewis, who became General Manager sometime around 1949. I believe the Co-op hired

Jacob "Jake" Dykstra

Joe from New Bedford. When Joe had the job, he also sold the fish to outside buyers in New York and other major east coast cities.

In addition to sales, Joe established a sizeable fillet operation for blackback and yellowtail flounder. A freezing operation was also operating in adjacent buildings. As I recall, the finished product was sold under the First National and A&P store labels as well as the Co-op label.

Throughout my early years fishing on the *Dorothy & Betty*, the *Whitestone*, and the *Jerry & Jimmy*, Joe was the general manager until about 1969, I believe. A few years later, Joe bought the fish market located at the head of the state pier from Milton Pariseau, the original owner. The Lewis family ran the market for many years.

The Ryan DeHy started operation about 1951. My first experience fishing/seining on the *Mary Ann* was in 1953, and we unloaded our pogies at the plant. It was a major complex with multiple steel holding tanks in addition to the main building. I remember the first time I went into the plant. It was at night and processing was taking place. The smell was noticeable outside, but inside, it was just like the pogie smell on the *Mary Ann* only ten times worse. Add the noise and the heat, and it was a forbidding place at best.

I became a member of the Co-op around 1958 when I was fishing with Sam Cottle. At that time, Paul Champlin and Norman Gilbert were the two other crew members. Along with Sam, they were all Co-op members. Other than William B. Rose, my former neighbor who guided me through my masonic degrees, I don't believe the members of the Board of Directors knew who I was. Paul's brother, Leon "Bud" Champlin, was also on the Board at the time, which probably helped my cause. I do know it was a very important event in my career as a fisherman.

I don't know what the Board thought of me bringing the

The Pump Deck at the Plant   Inside the Plant

Jerry & Jimmy into the Co-op fleet in 1962. It certainly looked like a big old sled with the rusty steel scallop sheathing on both sides. By the way, at that time, the members were Jake Dykstra, Melville "Mel" Strout, James White, Forrest Hoxie, Jack Westcott, Paul Champlin, and Ken Winter. This was the year before the Ryan De-Hy closed, and if Ken Winter had not been involved at the time, the Co-op probably would not have bought the plant in 1963. Ted Harvey managed the plant from the beginning until the changeover to a fish meal facility. It ran for the next ten years as a meal plant.

The new addition   Installing the new Fish Meal Dryer

The storage building in Peacedale

The fish meal generated by the meal plant was stored in a holding building owned by the Co-op alongside the railroad tracks at the east end of Church Street in Peacedale. The meal was shipped by rail to the buyer and used for animal feed as a supplement. It has been many years since there was rail service to this area of Rhode Island.

I remember the days when all the Co-op boats took ice in 300 lb. blocks. The blocks came from the Co-op ice house on the north end of Kingstown Road down the Pier. Moe Tucker, usually the only night man on duty, would show us how to slide the blocks to the ice crusher then tip them one by one into the crusher. The crushed ice was then moved down the dock by a screw conveyor, then down a chute into the fish hold of the boat. Back then, I usually took fifteen tons of ice, or roughly seven blocks to a ton, which would be 100 blocks. Considering we usually took ice at 10:00 p.m., it was a workout for the crew before we left the dock to go fishing.

Ice-making plant once owned by the Co-Op

Not long after I started fishing the *Jerry & Jimmy*, the Co-op built an addition on the north side of the main building between the Coast Guard Station as an ice plant. Initially, it only made about 30 tons/day. After a few years, more ice machines were added, and the ice was delivered on the next dock north of the main unloading dock. The new system used a blower that delivered the ice though a 10 inch hose to the boat. Either flake ice, preferable for butterfish, scup, or any other short trips, was available, or a more course ice, similar to the old crushed ice, could be used. If you were going to take thirty ton or so, it was safer to order the ice in advance.

In order to pay for the new ice plant, the Co-op assessed the boats a small percentage from each trip. The assessment was continued for a number of years until the debt was paid off.

The Co-op facility ice plant in the left background

The Point Judith Fishermen's Cooperative Association, Inc. was established in 1948 as a cooperative similar in structure to the many farming cooperatives. The growers of cranberries came together as a cooperative, for example, and is now Ocean Spray. The structure allows smaller units, such as each of our fishing boats that are either owned as an individual or a corporation, to join together to market their fish.

In the Co-op's operation, there were many additional benefits. Blue Cross was available to members and crews as a group plan. The Co-op also had a welfare fund which paid so much a week if a crew member, including the captain, could not work for whatever reason. This program was looked after by the welfare committee of three members, and payments were limited to one year.

The Co-op also made available boat insurance both hull and personal injury. The Co-op had an exclusive agreement with the Sam Snow Agency in Providence that insured the boats with the Home Insurance Company in New York. A story: each year, the boat owners would make an appointment through the Co-op office to meet with Sam at the Co-op office on a weekend when the office was closed. I remember one year I had my meeting at 11:30 on a Saturday. Sam had a little ritual of offering a shot of whisky with each of us when we renewed our policy. By 11:30, Sam had met with five captains and was beginning to show signs. He asked me how I was feeling, and I told him that I was dealing with a back problem. Sam said he had a back problem and exercised every morning. All of a sudden, he said, "Let me show you," and he got up, laid down on his back on the office floor, and proceeded to do knee pullups—suit, tie, and all. All I could think of was if someone comes in, especially another captain, they will think I decked him. My boats were always insured with Sam, and the "Home" until the late 80's. Sam was a good guy. I still do those exercises every day.

In addition to the ice, diesel fuel was available at several locations on the dock, and the boats were fueled by Co-op employees to ensure that there would be no spillage. The marine store on the second floor of the main building carried about everything a boat might need including wire or wire rope cut to your specifications. Same with chain and netting of various mesh sizes. Kind of a mini-West Marine.

In later years, there was another deduction for the Defense Fund. I don't know how Jake came up with the name, but it was appropriate. The Co-op needed funds available to use for things related to the politics of the industry and government outside of the Co-op.

Of course, the main reason for the Cooperative in the first place was to sell the fish delivered to the Co-op by the member boats. By the late 70's, there were about 70 boats, and members were building new steel draggers that were both larger with more power, thereby increasing their catch. Quite often, the boat they sold to step up to the larger vessel remained in the fleet.

In order to sell the fish, the fish salesman, of which we had a number of excellent people over the years, had to move the fish as soon as possible after they were unloaded. It was almost Co-op policy to make sure to spread the fish to all the fish "houses" or buyers each day. When fish were scarce, usually because of bad weather, an effort was made to keep them satisfied. In the New York City Fulton Market, there were a dozen prominent houses the Co-op supplied daily. Then there were additional houses in Philadelphia and

Baltimore in that direction, then strong buyers in Boston who resold to Chicago and the West Coast.

The reason for the concern of keeping those houses on line was as the Co-op grew and landings continued to increase, the salesman had to have a home for the fish even to the point of asking dealers to take more fish than they normally handled. The system did work because we provided a very fresh product in quantity.

The salesman tried to obtain a near common price by getting a starting number from the lead houses for each specie sent to market each day.

It's important to understand that the Co-op trucked fish to New York and other ports every day. The Co-op unloading dock took in fish seven days a week, starting at 7:00 a.m. and finishing as late as 9:00 p.m. as long as the fish could be in Fulton by 2:00 to 3:00 a.m. when they were unloaded and the fish were displayed for purchase by local New York restaurants and fish markets. Since a number of our boats fished days, it was common for a restaurant in New York, for example, to have a fish on the plate that was 24 hours or even less out of water. The same scenario could be true even in Chicago where a Boston buyer had trucks waiting at the Co-op doors loading fish that was coming off the boats. Then they would air freight the fish to its destination the same day.

Because our trucks unloaded their boxes of fish to the New York houses early in the morning, the buyers were able to look at the condition of the fish prior to selling to their customers. By 9:00 a.m., most of the fish had been sold. The buyers could then settle on a price with our salesman. Once he had confirmation from each house, he would come up with the average price paid for each specie. Either he or the office could deduct the costs of unloading, boxes, ice, dock help, trucking, and profit margin and arrive at a payment price to the boat. That's when the boat captain and crew found out what their trip was worth. Once in a while, they would get a pleasant surprise, but generally they had visions of high prices before they even docked the boat. Of course, it was always the fish salesman's fault when the price was lower than expected. One of the requirements of a fish salesman was to be able to handle the flak.

It was imperative that the houses pay the Co-op within five days, for example. Back in those days, the checks came in the mail.

No wired funds. I think someone from the office checked the post office box twice a day. Unlike the houses in New Bedford that pay the boats within hours after the trip was unloaded, the Co-op paid once a week. For example, fish unloaded between Sunday and Saturday August 16th, would be paid on Monday, August 25th. A vessel making trips of four to six days, like I usually did, would be paid nine days after they unload.

Again, in my case, we would leave for the next trip two or three days after unloading so we wouldn't get paid until we came in from the next trip. For a crew member who was making every trip, it didn't really matter because we had a check from the previous trip waiting. All of this explanation about selling the fish is oversimplified. In practice, it was a complex business.

For most of the larger boats, there were trips of butterfish, for example, of 40-50,000 lbs. These fish would usually be unloaded by fish pump or by hand in baskets and shipped in 1,000 lb. fiberglass tubs (about 800 lbs. of fish plus ice). These fish were sold to processors who would sort and freeze the fish in boxes for shipment for Japan. A similar procedure was carried out when we caught large trips of squid. For the most part, the price to the processor was negotiated beforehand going out a month or more. Most of the squid went to Spain.

The good thing about fishing with a fixed price was not only did you know what each tow was worth, but it didn't matter if there were other boats working together to catch their trips. The price would be the same, and since the species were caught during a relatively short season, the processors wanted as much as you could land unless they could not process the volume. The payment to the boats was the same time frame as fresh fish.

There was a significant change in the operation of the Port of Point Judith when the Fishermen's Co-op's Board decided to cease operations of the fish meal processing plant in the fall of 1973. Over the years, under private ownership, then under Co-op ownership, the plant played a major role in the success of the port. The plant apparently was no longer considered profitable. In addition, there had always been odor problems with the plant, and trying to solve the problem to the satisfaction of our neighbors in and around the port was actually impossible, especially after the construction of

FRESH-FISH PRODUCTS:
The table below indicates the broad range of fresh-fish landed by the Point Judith CO-OP fleet.

Generally Used North American Names:	Scientific Name:	Additional Names:	Principal Harvesting Season:
	Examples of North American Fresh-Fish Landed by the Point Judith Fishermen's Cooperative		
American angler	Lophius americanus	Goosefish, monkfish	JAN thru DEC
Bass, striped	Morone saxatilis	Striper, rock, rockfish	MAY thru JUL
Butterfish	Peprilus (Poronotus) triacanthus	Dollarfish, shiner	APR thru JAN
Cod, Atlantic	Gadus morhua		DEC thru MAY
Dogfish	Squalus acanthias Mustelus canis	Spiny dogfish Smooth dogfish	APR thru NOV APR thru NOV
Summer Flounder	Paralichthys dentatus	Flounder, fluke	JAN thru DEC
Windowpane	Scophthalmus aquosus	Brill, spotted flounder sand dab, sand flounder, "turbot"	JAN thru DEC
Witch flounder	Glyptocephalus cynoglossus	Gray sole, Craig fluke	JAN thru DEC
American plaice	Hippoglossoides platessoides	American dab, sole, Canadian plaice, plaice, blackback, flounder, plie	JAN thru DEC
Yellowtail flounder	Limanada ferruginea	Yellowtail, rusty dab	JAN thru DEC
Winter Flounder	Pseudopleuronectes americanus	Blackback, sole, dab, lemon sole, flounder	JAN thru DEC
Herring, Atlantic	Clupea harengus harengus	Sea herring	JAN thru DEC
Lobster	Homarus americanus	American lobster, North American lobster, Canadian lobster, Maine lobster	MAR thru DEC
Mackerel, Atlantic	Scomber scombrus	Mackerel	MAY thru NOV
Menhaden, Atlantic	Brevoortia tyrannus	Pogy	MAY thru NOV
Ocean pout	Macrozoarces americanus	Eelpout, mutton fish, "conger eel"	FEB and MAR
Pollock	Pollachius virens	American pollock, Boston bluefish	APR thru AUG
Red hake	Urophycis chuss	Ling, squirrel hake, white hake, mud hake	JAN thru DEC
Scup	Stenotomus chrysops	Porgy	APR thru DEC
Silver hake	Merluccius bilinearis	Whiting	JAN thru DEC
Skate	Raja spp		JAN thru DEC
Squid, long-finned	Loligo pealei		JAN thru DEC
Squid, short-finned	Illex illecebrosus		JAN thru DEC
Swordfish	Xiphias gladius	Billfish	JUN thru SEP
Tautog	Tautoga onitis	Black-fish	JUL thru AUG
Tilefish	Lopholatilus chamaeleonticeps		FEB thru JUN

A list of fish landed by the fleet can be found above

the Dutch Inn, a large hotel complex located about two hundred yards from the plant.

I remember after the plant closed, that under the State of Rhode Island Land Lease Agreement, the Co-op was responsible to clean up the site. The entire plant, a truly massive facility, was torn down, and the site cleared at considerable cost to the Co-op. The only Co-op building remaining in that north end of the inner harbor was the lobster operation. Rhode Island Engine Company was the next building to the east along the bulkhead that ran approximately east and west.

In later years, a large fish pump was installed beside the bulkhead that had the ability to pump fish such as butterfish, herring, squid, etc. into Co-op owned tank trailer trucks for delivery to Co-op leased processing facilities or for sale in bulk to outside customers. An inground truck scale already on the site weighed the truck before and after pumping to provide the weight of each catch.

One trip, after pumping out our butterfish, I moved the *Alliance* farther east along the bulkhead and tied up so we could pull some gear off into our truck. The boat was there for about three hours and the tide had gone out. When I put the boat in forward to "spring" the stern out away from the bulkhead, there was a loud thump that shook the whole boat. When the tide had dropped, the propeller must have been laying against a large rock. We broke off one of the four blades of the propeller. The rock was there for years I guess, and we were "lucky" to find it.

Over the twenty eight years, mostly as a boat owner, I found the Co-op members similar to a brotherhood. There was a positive relationship that existed with regard for looking after each other at sea including putting member boats on fish. There was also an undercurrent of competitiveness. I know I hated to put the boat name on the "board" when I had a broken trip that only took a half hour to unload. At our Co-op annual meetings, we had a big dinner at George's or the Dutch Inn after the meeting, and it was a late night.

During the years prior to 1976, Jake Dyksta was fishing with his brother, John, as a crewmember. After that, he was employed by the Co-op fulltime. The main reason for the change was the passage in Congress of the Magnuson Fishery Conservation and Management Act of 1976. The Fisheries Management Councils were a direct result of the act. Jake became the first chairman of the New England Fisheries Management Council. Leonard J. Stasiukiewicz was the general manager of the Co-op for all the time I was a captain/owner of a Co-op boat. The job description included everything. Bob Smith was a member of the Board of Directors almost as long as Len was the manager and was the vice president under Jake for most of those years. Bob was a fulltime fisherman and captain owner of the *David D*.

Leonard J.
Stasiukiewicz

Around 1979, the Co-op Board decided to close taking new members. By that time, there were about 75 member boats and over 150 members. The Co-op facilities were at capacity. Fish were being unloaded onto a long conveyor on the north fuel/ice dock, and the next dock south of the main dock was also turned into an unloading dock, and at one point was rigged out with a pump.

I recall days when there were one thousand pound tubs full of butterfish or squid in every space in the first floor of the building and outside, with covers, between the space between the ice plant and the main building. Even unloading at five stations, it was more and more necessary to wait until the next day to unload. Day boats were always given the opportunity to unload each day.

Closing the membership opened an opportunity for other fish buying operations and in 1980, Town Dock opened for business.

Robert D. Smith
and the F/V *David D*

Then in 1985, Handrigan's Seafood also began buying fish. In most instances, the Co-op boats continued taking out, but there were new entrants coming to the port every year.

It was not my intention to attempt to write a history of the Co-op. This is only a brief introduction to the operation and the people involved during those middle years.

The pictures of the meal plant were a few of 50 or more given to me twenty years ago by Ellis Norman. Another face of the Co-op.

Ellis Norman

Chapter 18

Unloading Fish at the Co-op

The best way to describe how the Co-op worked is to take you through a typical landing day of the *Alliance*. Depending on where we were fishing, we would leave the fishing grounds in time to dock at the Point around 5 a.m. The first stop was at the end of the Co-op dock to check the Board. The Board showed the boats that had arrived before us, and we would put our name down. Knowing who the boats were helped in guessing when we would likely get to a door to unload. For mixed trips, there were three unloading stations, one on each side of the 100 ft. long main dock and one across the end. We would also drop in our hail slip at the dock foreman's office in an enclosed box to insure the privacy of the hail or estimated quantity of fish by specie. Depending on the species landed, the rate of unloading might be 8,000 lbs./hr for a whiting trip that did not require sorting, to a mixed trip of fluke, sea bass, scup, etc. that had to be graded by size, which might take out 4,000- 5,000 / hr.

Once we got back to the dock, which for years was one dock south of the State Pier, we might go home for a while if there were ten boats ahead of us. I always called the dock foreman at 7:00 or 8:00 a.m. to get his estimate on when he wanted us.

The dock foreman at the Co-op for at least most of my fishing years was Fred Messa. I considered Fred to be the "Face of the Co-op" since we had more contact with him than anyone else.

It was Fred's job to run the dock including hiring the dock workers, training, and supervising them. His day, as I recall, started around 5:00 a.m. and lasted until he was satisfied that the late crews were organized to finish up and complete the loading of the trucks, and that

Fred Messa,
Dock Foreman

could be 9:00 p.m.

Over the years, I would meet people all the time that said they once worked at the Co-op dock after school or during the summer. I think half the male population of South County worked there at one time or another, and they all knew Fred.

At times as more and larger boats joined the Co-op fleet, it might not be until the next day to unload, if that was the decision, I would call the crew and tell them they had the day off. For this example, we were the fourth boat to unload with a 9:00 o'clock estimated time-frame. We could tie the boat up on either side with the *Alliance* since the Co-op had booms at each door.

We usually had a steady lumper who worked the boats every day. His job was to fill the baskets with fish down in the fish hold, then guide the basket up through the hatch. One of our crew usually ran the winch, wrapping the line around the winch head and hoisting the baskets, about 80 lbs., one at a time until the trip was finished. A typical trip for us was 30,000 lbs. of mixed fish.

Ed Bourrett swinging a basket down the hatch

Once the basket was dumped on the cull board, the ice used to cool the fish on the boat had to be removed. The Co-op wanted a true weight of fish, not ice. Then, if the trip was fluke, for example, they had to be graded by weight. Under 2 lbs. down to the legal size of 14", although at the time, there were no legal sizes and still is called a "medium," from 2-4 lbs. would be considered large, and over 4 lbs. a jumbo. This was not as difficult as it sounds. When you have handled large quantities of fish as the lead Co-op cull board man, it only requires a glance to know what size the fish is with only a confirmation with a separate scale to confirm that a jumbo is 4 lbs. Whatever size is prevalent, the cull board man sets up a scale at the end of the cull board and just has to push the large, for most of our trips, into the basket. The other sizes were placed in their basket in the case of the jumbo size fluke that is often sold as sushi these days.

Once the basket reaches 100 lbs. plus, a fish or two extra, no extras on jumbo fish, it was dumped in a wooden box that had a shovel full of ice already in the bottom. Often, when half the basket is dumped, another shovel full of ice is added. When all the fish are in the box, a healthy shovel full of ice is thrown on top, the cover goes on and is nailed. The boxes, three or four high, were then wheeled down to the truck dock after being clearly identified by a black marker as to the specie and size.

The dock foreman or someone from sales usually stapled a tag indicating where in New York the box of fish was sold. There was always what looked like a chaotic scene when three doors were unloading fish of different species. Fred as foreman never seemed rattled, but calmly supervised the workers which numbered at least 15 for the three doors plus the boat crews working on the cull boards.

Quite often, I would hire extra people to work with the unloading so that Nelson could do upkeep in the engine room, and usually Bill Conley and I could work on the nets.

Most fishermen would think we were insane not to

Bill Conley

The author

stay at the cull board all through the unloading of the trip. In most places, you had to see that the weights were right, the cull by size, and the correct number of boxes, etc. At the Co-op, the opposite was true. The Co-op crews favored the boats' owners or crew and made sure everything was right.

I have already mentioned that there was one price for each specie and size each day. This was the only way the Co-op could keep track of the fish. That meant that a day boat landing fluke which was hours old would be priced the same as my trip of fluke where my first day of my trip's fish might be five days old. It was imperative that we do the utmost to care for the fish such as icing fluke in the pens white side up so that side would have a minimum of bloodlines. This did not necessarily happen during a trip. Shelving the fish was also critical to keep the weight off the fish at the bottom of the pens. On the *Alliance*, we had two shelves for each pen. Figuring a total of six feet of fish, there were two feet of depth of fish times three in each pen.

I realized the problem I must have caused back when I first started landing large trips of yellowtails with the *Jerry & Jimmy*. I could now understand why the Co-op directed me to take out the fish in New Bedford where each trip was judged and paid for on its own merit. The fact that I had seconds or poor quality of the fish on the bottom of the pens did not fit the definition of Co-op fish under the one price/day concept.

Back to unloading the trip. When the last of the fish was unloaded, the captain was given a tally card with the weight of each specie. At the bottom of the card would be the name of the head cull boardman responsible for unloading the trip.

As soon as the fish were out, we would move the boat for the next boat in order. It was always my policy to wash down and scrub the fish hold and the lumberyard full of pen/shelf boards which were interchangeable. Unless there was a large amount of ice left in the hold, the lumper would remove the old ice and we would dump it overboard. We would next go to the ice dock, now that there was a new ice plant, located on the next dock north of the main unloading dock. We would then take the ice for the next trip, usually 15-20 tons. At the same time, the Co-op fuel man would replace the fuel used on the trip. Each fuel tank had sight gauges marked to the preferred level in the engine room which would be monitored by a crew member/engineer.

The cook meanwhile cleaned out the fridge, and I would tell him how many days to shop for and when to get the food and other perishables. By then, we were back tied to our dock or a dock. Most important, we were ready to make the next trip, weather permitting. We lived our lives with weather reports, so it was possible to plan ahead. With the *Alliance*, unless it was calling for gale force winds, I would plan to go.

During the unloading of the boat, I would pick up the settlement for the last trip from the Co-op office, check with the fish salesmen on their guess for the prices for today's trip, and comment on the prices on the settlement.

Sometime during that day, when I got home, I always made out the crew settlement and their checks for the next morning. The following page has an example of what a 1975 late winter trip crew settlement would look like without any deductions from the marine store. Since the annual gross stock for the *Alliance* in 1975 was $329,082.30, this example is realistic.

Most interesting is the fuel cost of only $1,070 for a trip in this example. The actual annual cost of fuel for 1975 was $32,840. We made at least 35 trips/year, so again, this example is valid.

Taking out the fish at the Co-op simplified the job of making out the crew settlement because all the deductions for a particular trip would be the costs associated with that trip.

Anyone looking at the sizeable boat share might think that I as the owner was making a killing. If you have ever owned a boat, you have experienced the endless cost to maintain it. In 1975, there was only $9,600 for repairs because the boat was relatively new. $11,000 in gear, $8,000 in nets, rope and twine, $9,000 for insurance, and much more. The costs to run an 85 foot trawler have only

SETTLEMENT EXAMPLE FROM THE CO-OP

#5				
BOAT: ALLIANCE			**DATE: 3/27/75**	
8500	Joe Fluke	@	1.25	$10,625
2500	Large Fluke	@	1.10	2,750
800	Med. Fluke	@	0.90	720
	Small Fluke			
6000	Butterfish	@	0.60	3,600
	Scup			
9000	Squid	@	0.60	5,400
3000	Whiting	@	0.20	600
550	King Whiting	@	0.30	165
	Stk. Cod			
	Mkt. Cod			
	Haddock			
550	Lg. Tile	@	0.80	440
700	Med Tile	@	0.70	490
300	Kitten Tile	@	0.35	105
250	Mackeral	@	0.20	50
150	C. Bass Lg	@	1.10	165
800	Angler	@	0.70	560
140	Stk Hake	@	0.45	63
33240		TOTAL:		$ 25,733
Deductions:				
	Fuel 3/27			$ 1,070
	Ice 3/27			250
	Welfare			22
	Galilee Groc. Food			186
	Total			1,528
	Net			**$ 24,205**
				(Ck. No. 1047)

increased over the years since 1975.

When paying the crew, they would have no deduction for federal or state income taxes. Fishermen are treated the same as farmers in that they are required to pay an estimated tax based on their actual average income of the previous three years. As the owner of the boat, I was required to send them a 1099 statement at the end of the year. They had to sign a W9 form to insure that the social security number was legitimate.

All the years owning boats, I always made out the crew settlement sheets with a copy to each crew member. As an employer, I was sent a tax guidebook that had tax deduction calculations. I would include a suggested tax withholding figure which, hopefully, they would set aside until they had to pay their taxes.

As you can imagine, getting a check for $2,500 for a five day trip in 1975, generated thoughts of buying upscale things. In actual fact, the annual crew share that year was about $33,000. You had better set aside something for taxes before the day of reckoning.

Throughout my years with the Co-op, we were fortunate to have a Co-op lawyer Richard "Dick" Billings from the then law firm

CREW SETTLEMENT

4/5/75		
Copy of Trip Fish Prices Attached		
Settlement for Trip 3/27/75		
Gross		$25,733.00
Boat Share – 45%		(11,579.85)
Balance		14,153.15
Less:		
Fuel		1,100.00
Ice		200.00
Galilee Grocery		186.00
Welfare Fund		50.00
Total Crew Deductions		1,536.00
Crew Share Total		$12,617.15
5 Crewman – each		2,523.43
Capt. 5% Boat Share 578.99		
Mate 5% Boat Share 578.99		
(Deducted from the boat share)		
Capt.	$	3,102.42
Mate		3,102.42
Crew		2,523.43
Crew		2,523.43
Crew		2,523.43
Suggested Set Aside for Taxes		

of Hinckley Allen in Providence, Rhode Island. Although I was not involved in the Co-op business until years later, I was aware that there was legal representation familiar with the limitations of a cooperative. Dick was always present at our annual Co-op meetings.

I have no idea how many trips that were unloaded at the Co-op dock counting both boats. There was one trip that stands out. We were unloading the *Alliance* at the north side of the dock. We had come in from the trip just at the beginning of a major snowstorm. When we started unloading, the wind had increased and standing in the open door, the same size used in a one car garage, catching and dumping the fish on the cull board was worse than brutal. I think Bill Conley was hoisting the baskets on the opposite side from me. I had my rain gear, oilers buttoned up as tight as I could, but the snow was continuously blowing directly into our faces and would work its way down your neck. In no time, our faces were red until someone brought us ski masks from the marine store upstairs.

This went on for about four hours. Even alternating with the other crew members every half hour only gave each of us a short break. We had lowered the door down as far as we could and still had room to bring the basket of fish through the opening. I don't remember anything about the catch. The man on deck swinging the baskets up out of the fish hold actually had the best job since he was facing with the wind at his back.

I am sure that the fact that I was a Co-op boat owner was one of the reasons I was able to obtain a National Marine Fisheries loan when I rebuilt the *Jerry & Jimmy*. The Co-op boat owners over the years had built a reputation for being reliable financial partners with the local banks as well. Again, this held true when I was able to get a $100,000 loan with just my signature to start building the *Alliance*, from who was then the Co-op's banker. The fact that I was a Co-op boat when I refinanced the *Alliance* with the Production Credit Association, that was accustomed to loaning money to farm cooperatives, was probably the reason I was able to obtain that substantial loan at favorable rates. I assume the other Co-op members benefited the same as I did.

Chapter 19

Incidents in the 1970's

Jake Dykstra, Co-op President, called me one day in the fall of 1974 asking for some help. TimeLife had called him about having two of their people go out on a fishing boat. TimeLife was in the process of publishing a book on navigation and wanted to include a chapter on the electronics fishermen used. Jake thought the *Alliance* would be a good modern boat for the project. What could I say but all right. The TimeLife people had a great deal of experience reporting for the magazine all over the world Jake was told.

We made the arrangements and planned to leave for an offshore trip about 10:00 p.m.. The two TimeLife people, one a reporter/writer and the other a photographer. Nice guys, in their late 30's. We left Point Judith about 10:00 pm heading east of Block Island. Before we even got to the Island, they were both seasick. They hit the bunks, alternating using 5 gallon buckets. As I recall, they really didn't surface at all even when we got to the fishing grounds 75 miles south of the Point.

I can't recall what exactly broke back on the stern where the towing blocks were mounted, but it was serious enough, that we could not fix the problem that required an experienced welder. We headed back to the dock. Only two people on the boat were happy that we had to go in. Back at the dock, the reporter went all through the fishing procedures with me for the written part of the article. The photographer worked with Paul Bennett, one of my crew, and showed him how to use his elaborate camera.

The next trip out, I didn't go for some reason. Paul took all the pictures that appear in Chapter 5 entitled "Rich Haul for an Automated Trawler," Pages 142-149 in the TimeLife 1975 edition of "Navigation." The funny part of the story, I thought at the time, was that Paul was directed to give the camera to a bus driver of a particular bus line that would deliver the camera to the photographer in New York City. As it turned out, Nelson Bourret, my partner, had his picture in some really good shots in the wheelhouse. They also caught a good tow of butterfish. Our one claim to fame.

Another incident, we had made a fairly long trip on the *Alliance* during the fall of 1976. We came in and unloaded at the Co-op and took on fuel and ice as usual. I headed into my assigned dock at the north side of the first one south of the State Pier. My practice was to cross the end of the dock, back down, then go straight in to the dock. This time when I slowed down and put the clutch in reverse, I heard a slight thump and the engine revved up and there was nothing— no backing down at all. The *Alliance* continued forward at 3-4 knots. I looked up ahead, and there was the stern of the *Charles H* with Clarke Chappell, the Captain, coming up from the engine room. He heard my crew member up on the bow hollering, glanced back, and took off running forward. I had just enough speed to steer the bow away from the *Charles H* and glance off the side then continued ahead about a boat length and hit the steel bulkhead with the bow. By then, we had slowed down enough that there wasn't even a dent in the bow. Fortunately, the *Charles H* was not damaged either. We sure gave my old engineer "Chappie" a scare. The bow on the *Alliance* was about 12 feet high above the waterline.

We quickly determined that the propeller shaft had broken right ahead of the prop, because the shaft was turning evenly indicating that the cutlass bearing at the end of the shaft was intact. I managed to get hold of a diver on short notice, and we pointed out where we were in relation to the docks. Within an hour, he found the propeller, then had a day boat hoist it up out of the mud.

The propeller on the *Alliance* was a 70 inch diameter by 54 inch pitch, not a cheap item. I was more than lucky that this incident occurred right there in the harbor after the distance we had travelled during that trip. The propeller shaft was another matter. The shaft installed initially was a 6" steel shaft, and I was not surprised that it failed, and I was not about to replace it with another steel one. I think it was Holgate's Shipyard that located an Aramco stainless steel 6" shaft 17 feet long. I know it came from somewhere down south, and it cost far more than it should have normally to get it trucked to Rhode Island. Then it had to be machined to fit the propeller, and we changed the inside coupling. No small matter, and we lost three weeks of fishing time. Insurance doesn't cover wear and tear.

As a follow up on the propeller shaft incident, in March of 1977, I flew down to visit Atlantic Marine to go over with them in detail the problems we had over the years with the *Alliance*. They were in the process of building more boats for the Northern Fishery, principally for New Bedford. One of the items was welding on rolling chocks which we had done in November of 1974.

I also advised them to narrow the fuel tanks in the engine room. Boats up north did not need 17,000 gallons of fuel capacity where boats of that size, even with big power, would probably burn less than 30 gallons of diesel an hour. The *Alliance* burned 18-20 gallons an hour.

My partner Nelson Bourret

The rudder size and configuration was another major and necessary change. Altogether, there were about twenty items from hydraulics to windows that would make a better boat, and I think the engineers at the yard took it as advice, not criticism.

Another incident: I had made arrangements with Pete Laurie of Point Judith Welding to deliver our set of trawl doors to the *Alliance* at the State Pier. I had made plans for Nelson to take the boat that trip after the trawl doors were delivered. Pete had to finish up some of the welding and brought the doors to the boat. I was there that morning to see the job on the doors and make sure the boat sailed. It was in the fall of 1977, and it was a good day weather-wise. The boat left to go about 10:30 a.m. We often sailed on trips in the morning. Since we fished twenty-four hours per day, it didn't matter except we usually left the dock by 8:30 a.m.

Nelson and Bill Conley, my long-time crewman, told me the story. They were heading out for the Nantucket Lightship area south of the Corner Buoy—more or less a southwest heading. Bill said he saw a dragger fishing off to the south of their heading. I think he recognized it as the *Two Brothers*. He and Nelson were sitting in the matching captain's chairs in the wheelhouse. Bill always sat in the starboard side chair visiting with me for hours.

Next time Bill looked in the direction of the *Two Brothers*, it was gone. He told Nelson that he was sure something strange happened. With the other three crewmen on deck, they went over to the area where Bill had last seen the boat. Apparently, they didn't see anything at first, then they saw the heads of people in the water. I don't recall how they got everyone on board, but they managed to save Bill Dykstra and his crew along with a couple of visitors that were aboard that day. The first time I heard about what happened was when Nelson called to tell me they were back at the dock.

Sometimes at sea, sinkings and other occurrences can be fatal, then there are days when things work out like the *Alliance* sailing late in the day then being in the immediate area when the *Two Brothers* sank. Almost every fatality that I know about happened so fast that there was little or no time to react.

Everyone in Point Judith was in disbelief on September 23, 1978, when the 75 ft. *Lobsta I*, similar to the *Alliance*, an offshore lobster boat, disappeared with five young crewmen aboard. There was never a clear explanation to my knowledge as to what occurred even after the hull was located. Surely whatever caused the loss happened so fast that there was no time to respond.

Another incident: I believe it was in the spring of 1978. When I came in from a trip, I heard that the *Jerry & Jimmy* had run aground in the rocks around Cuttyhunk Island. There was no possibility of getting the boat out of the rocks as I once managed to do on Block Island years before. I believe the Coast Guard was able to take the crew off without incident. Apparently, it took quite some time before the boat was flooded. The *Jerry & Jimmy* was one rugged dragger.

Ronnie Falulli, from Newport, acquired the "wreck" and was able to raise the vessel and managed to put the *Jerry & Jimmy* back in service. I heard that Dale Chappell, who had worked on the renovation of the *Jerry & Jimmy* for me years before over at Holgate's Shipyard in Snug Harbor, did quite a lot of work on the boat after it was salvaged.

For many years, the *Jerry & Jimmy* worked as the fish trap boat towing the big open work boat and skiffs to the fish trap sites off Newport and Narragansett. The fish were brailed out of the traps on to the *Jerry & Jimmy* similar to the way we brailed pogies aboard the *Menco*. I used to see the *J & J* off the traps in Narragansett all the time. A far cry from the two 100 mph storms I rode out on the vessel years before.

Another incident: In October of 1979, we were fishing in an area south of Hudson Canyon for some reason I can't recall. It was about 1:00 a.m., and I had just gone off watch when Nelson came down the stairway from the wheelhouse. He said someone was trying to call us on the single sideband radio from a boat back at the Point. We were able to hear the weak signal, and it was Bob Conley, my crewmember Bill Conley's brother.

The message was that Bill's son, we couldn't make out the name, was killed in an automobile accident about an hour or so ago. Well, that was the worst news that anyone had to pass on. Bill was, of course, destroyed by the news. He had two sons in their early twenties, Bill Jr., who usually worked on the *Alliance*, but had taken the trip off, and Bobby, who had also made trips with us. Bill's comment to me was that it was either one, and he just shook his head.

We hauled back right away and headed for the Point. The problem was, it was twelve hours to the dock. Bill alternatively sat on the couch we had in the living quarters or in his captain's chair in the wheelhouse all night until we reached the dock. By daylight, we were close enough to connect with a landline to call his house. It was either his daughter or his wife that confirmed that it was Bill Jr. that had been killed with no other casualties involved. To me, that call was one that every fisherman dreads. Being away from home so much of the time leaves all the responsibilities primarily on your wife. I can honestly say that was the worst trip of my career. What could you say or do?

We all attended Bill Jr.'s funeral and the burial in the Jamestown Island Cemetery. Bill fished with me on the *Alliance* for fifteen years and was like family.

Another incident: We were fishing for scup in early November of 1979 northeast of Hudson Canyon in 50-60 fathoms as I recall. We were in our third day of fishing and had about 28-30,000 lbs. of scup and a couple of thousand sea bass aboard. Off and on during the trip, I could see the *Jan-Bet*, Dub Barrows' boat at the time. Sometime in the afternoon, he called me on the VHF and said that he was unable to move. I think he had the net or bull rope tangled in the propeller. He needed a tow.

We were alongside within a half hour and figured out how we could rig the tow. Dub had a heavy tow line aboard, and I shackled our tow wires together so we could tow evenly from both sides of my stern to make it easy for us to steer. As I recall, the *Jan-Bet* was an eastern rig side trawler of about 90 feet.

We got under way, and it was an uneventful tow. Since we were about ninety miles to the Point, it took about ten hours, although we slowed toward the end to arrive off the Harbor around daylight. I didn't try to take him into the dock. It was most likely, now that I think about it, that he had a diver come out to solve the problem. Towing each other was not unusual in the Point. I never heard that the insurance company ever objected, in fact, they were probably in favor of the idea. I mention this incident only because I had an opportunity to help Dub out after having been fortunate to have been part of his crew on the *Whitestone* during my early training years.

Another incident: We were fishing for butterfish in December of 1979 in our usual spot by the 71 Fathom Shoal. I could tell by the "color machine" that we should have a decent tow. I liked to guess that we could have around 10,000 lbs., so that we could haul the tow up the ramp in one big cod end load. That always saved time and did not hurt the quality of the fish since it would slide up the stern ramp rather than lifting a bag.

On this occasion, we had a few more than 10,000, but I decided we could take it. The crew strapped the cod end with room to spare, and I started hauling the bag up the ramp with the falls or three part block and tackle. When the bag was about one-third of the way in, it jammed under the net drum. There was enough slack so one of the crew could slowly turn the net drum to push the bag through, a common practice for us. I took another turn on the winch head and the bag started to come, when bang! The strap on the bag broke. The single block hooked into the strap came back toward me in an instant and came within a foot of my head and hit the back end of the wheelhouse. That came close to being my last incident. As I have stated before, "close ones don't count."

Chapter 20

Foreign Fishing Effort

Throughout the 1960's, there were usually foreign fishing vessels in sight during our offshore trips with the *Jerry & Jimmy*. At times, we would be fishing less than a mile from Soviet side trawlers estimated to be about 180 ft. long. In addition, there were stern trawlers of 300 ft. If there was a fleet of eight or ten side trawlers working on a body of fish, they would be accompanied by a processing vessel of about 600 ft.

At first, fishing in close proximity to the Russians and often being the only U.S. boat, I was concerned about how things would work. The Cold War with the Soviet Union, 1947-1990, was a major U.S. concern back then, and here I was 60 miles from the Point right in the middle of their fleet. I have to say that they were just fishermen like us, and there was never a problem.

The Soviet vessels did not seem to be too selective as far as targeting a particular specie. It appeared that the target was a reasonably large body of fish that they could exploit with multiple vessels. Once processed and frozen at sea, there was a worldwide market for their catch.

There were always single vessels looking for fish. I assume their top fishermen were designated for that job. Based on my own observations, they would fish on cod, yellowtail flounder, whiting, and squid for example. Herring was always a top priority.

The big advantage their fleet had over local boats was that they never left the fishing grounds since they refueled at sea and offloaded their catch to refrigerated cargo vessels. Once on a body of fish, they could stay on the fish until they wiped them out, or as often happens, the shoal of fish breaks up and scatters into small pods that are not worth chasing. Within days however, the shoals of fish often reform. As long as a vessel is assigned to look for that to occur, the fleet could target them again. This is the same way menhaden up in the bay behaved.

A story. One night in the fall of the year, I was heading for the Nantucket Lightship Area on the *Jerry & Jimmy*. We saw a cluster of lights off to the south of our heading. I decided to check it out. There was a small fleet of a dozen mixed sized Soviet vessels and a mothership working in 40-45 fathoms south of the area designated on the charts as the dump or dumping grounds as we call it (south of Martha's Vineyard.)

I was very curious to find out what they were fishing for so I made a tow of about 45 minutes. I could see fish off bottom on the fish scope, but not something I could catch with my bottom net. When we hauled back, we had about 2,000 lbs. of scup heads. I assume the finished product was to H & G (head and gut) the scup like we do whiting, then freeze them. I could only speculate how much scup they caught that night, but in all probability, they pretty well wiped out that body of fish since the fish were clearly visible on the fishscope.

In addition to the Soviet fleets, there were significant numbers of Japanese and Spanish trawlers. In my own experience, I encountered the Japanese trawlers in the winter months. The trawlers were all the same and were about 300 ft. long. They seemed to operate in groups of 4 to 6 vessels. The Japanese trawlers belonged to fishing companies rather than the government sponsored fleets of the Soviets.

During the winter when the Point boats like mine were fishing for butterfish at night in the 65 to 80 fathom edge, the Japanese trawlers would show up and fish all night with us. I could never figure out what they were fishing on during the day because they almost always came up to us from the south, yet they were never visible to us off in that direction. In that they had mid-water trawling capabilities, they could have been fishing anywhere. Since most of the butterfish we caught was packed whole and frozen then sold to Japanese customers, There was no question what at least one of their prime targets was.

The Spanish trawlers we came upon were always working on loligo squid which had always been common to Southern New England waters in large quantities. Again, our Point boats caught significant quantities of squid with most of it graded by size, packed and frozen whole, then sold to Spanish customers. The Spanish trawlers were not quite as large as the Japanese, but were still capable of fishing worldwide. Again, they were company-owned vessels. The Falkland Islands was one of their favorite fishing grounds as well as the U.S. waters.

Probably the greatest advantage the foreign fleets had, especially the Soviets, was that they accumulated decades of catch records that was made available to their fleets of vessels on a worldwide basis. Year after year, the same species will appear in almost the same location and usually within a week of when they did the previous years unless the water temperature is noticeably different.

In my experience, having worked with foreign joint ventures when I was President of the Co-op, the Japanese and Spanish company vessels maintained their catch information for their own use. These operations were highly successful and caught an enormous amount of fish. The Japanese and Spanish employed far fewer crewmen on a similar sized vessel compared to the Soviets. I also got the impression that the individual captains worked with other company vessels, but were competitive at the same time just to keep their jobs.

Around 1962, when I became aware that the foreign fleets were fully exploiting the East Coast fish populations, there had not been any effective effort by the U.S. to establish a basis for our fish population. On the other hand, the foreign fleets were operating at what could be best described as "the beginning." To this day, to the best of my knowledge, this vast amount of information of what fish were present on the grounds back then, has never been obtained from the foreign fleets by our research scientists.

During the virtual free-for-all that took place for all those years until the passage of the Magnuson Fishery Conservation and Management Act by Congress in 1976, the foreign fleets fished with no guidance or limitations. The Act created an exclusive Fisheries Conservation Zone that extended out to 200 miles from our shoreline, effectively ending the foreign fleet activities.

In all that time, the foreign fleets were operating with increasingly accurate catch information. By comparison, none of our domestic vessels had the size, horsepower, or the technology of advanced high opening and mid-water nets to compete. Over all those years, we still have no idea of the quantity of fish that was removed from the original or base population.

Those of us fishing at the time in 1976 truly believed that when this foreign effort finally ended, and the Hague line was put in place in 1984, establishing what was U.S. and what was Canadian waters, that there would be more than enough fish for the domestic fleet for eternity. One reaction to the passage of the Act was that it encouraged the banks and other lending institutions to loan the money for fishermen to build new and larger vessels. There was also limited participation by investors building boats giving young fishermen an opportunity to captain a boat. There was also a corresponding increase in the number of crewmen, many of them who had never considered going to sea before, totally unlike the years I put in trying to get a decent "site."

Common sense should tell us that the devastation of our fisheries through the 1960's and 70's, once stopped, should have allowed an opportunity for our fish stocks to recover. Even in the closure of facilities like the Trash Plant in Point Judith, that consumed millions of pounds of fish over those years, once stopped, should have allowed those fish stocks to recover over the last forty years.

With the addition of new vessels coming into the Point Judith fleet, there was a steady increase in the pounds of all species being landed. The Co-op was already selling to buyers that packed and froze fish for export. In the early 1980's, the Co-op leased a packing plant and started exporting frozen product under the Co-op Lighthouse label that soon became recognized overseas as a quality brand.

During that period starting in 1986, the Co-op began operating with joint ventures. I was President of the Co-op at the time and was directly involved in the process. With the increasing landing at the Co-op, we made the decision to give our boats an opportunity to land as much fish as they could catch for as many days and nights they chose to fish by offloading their fish at sea to foreign processing vessels. The joint ventures were contracted with foreign fishing companies with the necessary approval of our Federal Government.

The Co-op vessels and other domestic non-Co-op boats participated. There were two Italian venture vessels, two Spanish, and one Japanese all working on loligo squid. The boats were paid 28 cents per pound for regular size and 30 cents for large. The Co-op was paid 2 cents per pound for all the squid landed. For example, the Spanish took aboard 163,983 lbs. of squid at 30 cents per pound worth $49,194.90 in the month of August, 1986.

To give the reader an example of the efficiency of the Japanese company that I worked with through their representative, the vessel was fishing off the coast of South Africa, then fished off the Falkland Island, South America, then moved on to the Cape Verde Islands for haul out and maintenance. The vessel arrived in Boston on the date we had contracted for nine

The Bridge of the Japanese Trawler

months prior. In addition, the individual I had worked with in Japan was on the boat in Boston when I arrived to plan for the summer. He assured me that he would be aboard during the term of the venture.

On the Co-op side of the venture, I was able to hire Blaire "Moe" McDonough, who had worked with me on the *Alliance* over the years. It would be his job aboard the Japanese vessel to coordinate the transfer of squid from ten Co-op boats and others. I remember hiring Bob Zeittel from the Point to work with six to eight of the Point boats while he was aboard one of the Italian vessels.

Moe took many photographs while aboard the Japanese

Japanese Crew Sorting Squid Below
on Processing Deck.

A Cod End of Squid Hauled on Deck

vessel. The way the transfer worked was for Japanese vessel to move ahead slowly and drop a large red float astern with a heavy hauling line. The Co-op boat would detach his cod end with the squid and attach the cod end to the Japanese hauling line. The cod end of squid was then pulled up the stern ramp of the Japanese vessel, the squid dumped on deck, then the empty cod end was floated back in the ships wake for pickup by one of our boats. Once dumped on deck, the squid was dropped below to the processing deck where they were graded to size, packed in boxes, then frozen.

The main deck with trawl winches

These foreign Joint Venture vessels worked with our boats all summer. Periodically, as necessary, they were resupplied by small freighters. Their frozen product was off-loaded to these vessels. The Japanese trawler worked with us off Nantucket for loligo squid until about the end of July then moved down off New Jersey to work on ilex or summer squid. Some of our boats went with them, and as I recall, some Cape May boats took part in the venture.

A the conclusion of the joint venture with the Japanese in early September, the ship went to New York and made a crew change. As I recall, their next assignment was fishing off New Foundland.

A Russian joint venture was tried early on in that summer of 1986, fishing for red hake and whiting. The larger Co-op boats participated working with a 600 ft. mothership processor. The cod ends were pulled up a tunnel-like ramp in the stern which proved to be a more difficult maneuver than the traditional stern ramps of the squid venture boats. The price paid to the boats

Freighter alongside the Japanese Trawler

was 6 cents for whiting and 4 cents for red hake. The Co-op share was .05%, which was fair had the production been something like we had selling to the trash plant years before.

Rhode Islanders may have seen one of these 600 foot processing ships, the *Professor Baranov*, that was anchored a mile or so south of the Old Jamestown Bridge for a number of winters beginning in 1990. The ship was buying and processing herring from Point Judith boats through a joint venture between Russia and the Co-op through their agency "Scan Ocean," based in Gloucester, MA.

Even with the increase in the number and size of the U.S. domestic fleet, we never came close to landing more than a handful of fish in the late 1970's and 80's compared to the foreign catch. Our pristine waters, no doubt the cleanest in the world since stopping the practice of ocean dumping in the early 1990's, have the capability of feeding the nation. As I pointed out in this chapter, fish from our waters once supplied the world.

One thing we learned from the Japanese venture was that at no time during the summer working with as many as ten of our boats, did they ever exceed their processing capability. With whole fleets of trawlers from different countries operating 24 hours/day year after year, the volume of fish removed from our waters is beyond calculation.

Some of Moe's Fleet

Deborah Lee   *Karen Sue*

Darana R.
Newport, RI & North Carolina

Miss Shannon

Linda Ann
Newport, RI and North Carolina

Capt. A.T.
Newport, RI and North Carolina

Luke & Sarah

Ian Keyes

Chapter 21

Fishing in the 1980's

The 80's, in my opinion, was a time of expansion in the Point Judith Fleet. There were a number of significant steel stern trawlers built in southern yards beginning in 1980 which replaced wooden boats that the owners had fished for years. These new boats contributed substantial increases in landings at the Co-op. It was not surprising that Jake Dykstra and the Board of Directors began to plan the construction of a new Co-op facility. It sounded like a good idea to me. The old Co-op buildings were maxed out years earlier with the amount of fish being landed. Now, in the 80's, there was no question of the need.

About that time, we experienced a major failure with the engine on the *Alliance*. If it had not been such an unexpected event, I might have taken the time from fishing to install a new engine. As it turned out, we had the Caterpillar dealership in Massachusetts rebuild the engine at about half the cost of a new engine. Most of the crew was on hand to help when they could, which was the way we always did things in those days. There was another reason I didn't replace the engine and that was my last payment on the boat was coming up in February of 1981, and I had it in my head that we would be debt-free rather than re-financing a new installation. Not a good reason because it would have been easy to do with my track record of payments.

Butterfishing with all these new boats could be an experience. When we jumped on a body of fish at night with every boat in close proximity to one another, you really had to pay attention. The result was some really substantial landings, much of which was sold in 800 lb. tubs to Multifoods in New Bedford and Freshwater Fish Company in Boston, who packed and froze the fish for export to Japan.

Sometime in the late 70's or early 80's, I started fishing for fluke alongside of Rodney Avila, the Captain/owner of the *Trident* out of New Bedford. Rodney's uncle was John Bothello, Captain/owner of the eastern rig, *Catherine and Mary* out of New

Bedford. John was one of the first fishermen I came to know when I joined the Seafood Producers Association back when I first started fishing the *Jerry & Jimmy*.

Rodney and I caught a pile of fluke over the years, going farther east past Hydrographer Canyon in search of jumbo fluke. I believe that we would hit bodies of fish that may never had been fished before. For whatever reason, we began to address each other on the air as "Admiral." The name stuck and continued for years.

In the 1990's, Rodney and I were on the New England Fishery Management Council. One day, we asked Council Chairman, Joe Brancaleone, if we could address the Council. Our purpose was to point out to the Council and especially the Woods Hole scientists Council Members, that the Woods Hole survey ship that determined the stock levels of all species, did not make any tows over the years anywhere near where fluke were prevalent. The ship was primarily conducting ground-fish surveys, and the nearest survey sight was in fifty fathom where we knew there was no fluke, whereas we were catching fluke in 72 fathom and deeper. The groundfish survey was also considered as adequate as a fluke survey. The strangest part about our presentation was the absence of the Woods Hole members. It was obvious that they did not want to hear any criticism of the survey program. The established survey sights were set and that was the program.

I might add that in my twenty-eight years of fishing, I never once came across one of the survey ships. Then again, my total landings of codfish was less than 50,000 lbs. No doubt that was true with many of the Point Judith boats, yet we have been governed by the surveys in that they were the determining factor in arriving at the estimate of the stock population of all the species in the Northeast.

Back to catching fish. During the winter months in the eighties, Forrest Hoxie was a member of our crew. He was a very personable guy. About 10:00 a.m. many mornings, he would call up to me from the kitchen on the deck below the wheelhouse and ask if I'd like a Western (omelet)? I can remember that call as if it were yesterday. Another one of his specialties was quahog chowder. He would bring the quahaugs aboard nearly every trip. He was aboard for many memorable fluke and butterfish trips over the years.

During the summer months, Forrest was a swordfish spotter

flying a single engine Piper Cub out to the grounds on Georges Bank. Usually the planes flew in pairs, perhaps for safety purposes. During the summer, I would be towing along in Nantucket Sound, and Forrest would fly by at my level in the wheelhouse, a plane on each side heading in for the day. As an aside, Forrest and Bill Conley, my longtime crewmember, teamed up in retirement repairing lawnmowers in a shed out back of Forrest's house. They resurrected an old push mower of mine that Bill said was in the worst shape of any they had seen. All they would save was the engine. Forrest told me that he advertised his business once in the local paper and from then on, they could barely keep up with all the work.

I came across only one tally card from the Co-op that was for the *Alliance* dated 4/13/81.

I remember the trip because we put in some bad weather, and when we took out the fish, there hadn't been a trip landed at the Co-op in about five or more days. I saved the card because of the "high prices."

This trip, like most, was fishing the bad weather with large mesh at first, then finishing the last couple of days with a liner. That change contributed the butterfish, squid, whiting, and mackeral.

If you strain your eyes, you can see on the card the Loran bearings where the fluke was caught, then toward the end of the trip, we moved east from 14413 to 13944 to find the butterfish and squid. Both locations in 65-77 fathoms. Good numbers. Probably more fish there now than there was back then. The trip, 36,810 lbs. valued at $34,681, was less than a dollar/lb. average.

On July 10, 1982, my middle daughter, Pam, married Tim Scott. They spent their honeymoon on Martha's Vineyard. The story was that I was towing for scup and black sea bass in Nantucket Sound only a mile east of the ferry route to Nantucket. This was a few days after the wedding when I got a call on the VHF from Pam in the wheelhouse of the ferry. She came out on the bridge deck and gave Dad a wave. Was I surprised? Not really!

In 1982, Bill Palumbo, a deep water lobsterman from Newport, started the Atlantic Offshore Lobsterman's Association. The main purpose was to bring the lobster pot fishermen and the dragger fishermen together to find a common solution to the worsening gear conflict situation. Bill asked me to be Vice President representing the draggers. I was Vice President for two years while we evaluated every conceivable proposal to solve the problem. The membership of the association included most of the leading offshore pot fishermen working the Southern New England grounds. There were enough concerned dragger fisherman as members to provide a balanced discussion of the gear conflict issue.

The nearest we came to a possible solution was to set aside alternating 100 microsecond sections for pots then draggers. We approached some members of the Seafood Producers Association with that proposal just to get a reaction—not good. It was possible to get acceptance of a good proposal on a voluntary basis, but that was not a solution.

Many years later, as chairman of the Gear Conflict Committee of the New England Fishery Management Council, we came close, then I resigned from the Council, but my successor as chairman finished the work and a solution was reached which became the current gear conflict regulations.

The regulations were implemented in the 1998-99 time frame. In all the interim years since the lobster pot gear became a fact off-shore, there was always the possibility of gear damage or loss. In my own case, if there were pots in the area I was towing, I would mark my then paper plotter with the bearings of the end markers and was able to avoid problems for the most part. The tile fish long lines were far more difficult to avoid even though they had end markers. Winding a long line full of hooks caught in the net on a net drum was about the most dangerous situation my crew had to deal with.

Over all the years I went to sea and especially on the *Alliance*, I would read constantly throughout a trip. I had an arrangement with the head librarian at the Beverly Hale Library in Matunuck where I would take out a box of a dozen books to read during our long trips. Two of my daughters had worked summers at the library. In the later years of fishing the *Alliance*, my crews tended to be older, experienced fishermen, and they were usually readers. Making two hour tows for fluke gave them the off-time to read. There was always someone's bunk light on at all hours night and day.

We had a TV with a roto-antenna that required constant attention to keep the picture. Strangely the ads would always appear constant and bright compared to the regular programming. Apparently, the stations would power-up the signal when the ads were on. Movies on tapes were more reliable but aggravating when a crewman had to go on deck to haulback while an off-duty crewman continued watching the movie.

In 1983, I was asked to become a member of the Co-op Board of Directors. Charlie Follett was the President of the Co-op at the time. Jake Dykstra had resigned and was fishing with his wife, Kathy, on their own boat. Bob Smith was now the member of the New England Fishery Management Council. I decided to go on the Board primarily because Charlie had started construction of the new

Co-op building in the same location as the old trash plant. I had been in favor of a new building and was certainly interested in the project. Forrest Hoxie was also working on the planning of the building. As I recall, most of the meetings of the Board had to do with the new building. An architect had been hired for the new building and the new docks. Engineers were involved in both projects, and Harbor Marine Corp. was contracted to build the docks. As a board member, I had no active part in any of the early planning and construction phases.

Back to fishing. With a regular crew, we would haul and set the gear without a word being said except when I said "okay" on the loud-speaker, meaning to set the doors. My new son-in-law, Tim Scott, came aboard as the cook. For the first time, we had a photographer aboard.

The following is a set of photos showing the hauling and setting of the gear.

Hauling in the wire on the Marco winches

Unhooking the idler chain from the steel trawl doors

Winding in the ground cables followed by the legs on the net drum

Ed Bourret running the net drum with Bob Conley opposite side in this sequence

Winding on the net

Hauling the cod end up the ramp

Hoisting the cod end
and dumping the
catch on deck

The crew tying the knot
of the cod end. Captain
and author looking over
the tow.

Foreground:
Spare net on extra net
drum located in center of
work deck. Deck box for
lobsters.

Re-setting the net and
legs. Rubber discs on
ground cables and
bottom legs.

Bob Conley
looking at the catch

Ready to set the doors

"Being the Captain"
The author in the wheelhouse

During the mid-80's, everything was going good for us on the *Alliance*. There were minor issues that would come up, but that is normal in any fishing operation. Most mornings, Bill Conley would come up and visit in the wheelhouse, and we would listen to other boats on the radios. Over time, you could recognize the voices. In the afternoon, on his watch, Nelson would be in the left hand chair (portside).

In the wheelhouse—Jim and Bill

The crew did not just sit around or lay in their bunks reading:

Winter: A tow of butterfish. Running the fish below through an open deck plate. 8,000 to 10,000 lb. tow.

A two hour tow of fluke
350-400 lbs.

Bill Conley with a "Slamma"
south of Nantucket

By the fall of 1984, the new Co-op building was beginning to take shape. The perimeter foundation was finished, so now there was a clear picture of the total floor area. There had been more work setting the pilings as I recall. The ground was originally marsh land and the steel pilings ended up being much longer to hit solid ground. The new docks were also completed. The project was well underway.

In mid-January of 1985, Charlie Follett resigned as Chairman and also as a member of the Board. At the time, I was very surprised at this development. He had worked hard to bring the building to this stage, and I expected he would manage the project to completion.

There were members of the Board that I thought could take over as President and Chairman who had been on the Board for a number of years. I was unaware that the Board members had decided to ask me to take over the position. I realized that if I accepted the position, I would no longer be able to continue going to sea because of the demands on whoever held the job of President.

It took me several days of talking to my family and Nelson

as well as the other Board members to come to a decision. I was 53 years old and maybe it was time to go ashore. As I recall, I asked Nelson if he would take over as Captain of the *Alliance*. In the end, Nelson decided to take a shore job as well. I asked Harlan Stanley, Jr. to take over the *Alliance* and the crew would be his choice. Since my son-in-law, Tim Scott, was new to the industry, I advised him to find employment on the beach. I believe that was a good move for him and having him at home would be in the best interest of my daughter in the long run.

I made the choice to accept the position and became the Co-op President on January 23, 1985. Nelson and I made a decision at the time, not to sell the *Alliance*. In the event this life-changing decision did not work out, we could resume fishing.

The Freshest of Fresh Fish

Point Judith Fisherman's Cooperative
Association, Inc. logo

Chapter 22

My Years as Co-Op President

When it came to writing about my ten-plus years as the Co-op President, I decided that the subject was much too complex to be of interest to most readers. There was so much going on that I filled ten large spiral notebooks with comments on the daily activities. Reading through all those notes made me realize that my decision to take on the job was way beyond my expectations.

When I first started, I took over the President's office, which was located on the second floor of the Co-op building adjacent to the administrative office. Even through the office had worked for the previous two presidents, it turned out to be very disruptive for the staff with all the visitors that came to see me.

As a result, we rehabbed an area on the first floor that had been a fresh fish market. The room was large enough for my desk and a long table that was adequate for Board of Directors meetings. My new office had a glass door that opened right on to the main street that runs through Galilee and was also right across from what was the Galilee Grocery.

As soon as I moved in, I had an endless flow of fishermen members dropping by, each with his particular problem or suggestion. From then on, for all my years at the Co-op, I did all my serious document reading and writing at home at the dining room table. I remember the staff had a computer installed by my desk when they converted the office over to computers. I don't think I ever turned it on – too busy!

There were significant landings of fish at the Co-op my first year and at times, fish that were being sold to outside processors in New Bedford, for example, were unloaded into large, gray tubs that could hold 800 lbs. of fish in slush ice. These tubs were even placed outside the buildings because all the storage coolers, loading dock, and corridors throughout the building were full of boxes or tubs. Landings at this level were the reason for the new building construction.

For example, that fall, I remember Jim Thayer came in one morning with a request. His boat, The *Luke & Sarah*, was scheduled to be next at the dock, and he had around 100,000 lbs. of fish. He wanted to take out at both doors on the south side of the main dock. We went out and talked to Fred Messa, the Dock Foreman, and set it up with an unloading crew at each door. Jim had two hatches and the unloading went without a problem, and he finished in half the time. As far as I know, that was a first.

During my second year at the Co-op, there was a problem with the boat insurance when The Home Insurance notified Sam Snow, our agent that had provided boat insurance for the Co-op for many years, that they were no longer going to insure fishing boats. After a difficult interim period with another insurer, the Board of the Co-op decided to look into an alternative.

Several members of the Co-op Board and I had a breakfast meeting at the Larchwood Inn with Frank Ostrow and Bill Scola of Ocean Marine Insurance Agency (OMU) based in Warwick, Rhode Island, and Barry Gristwood, Managing Director of Sunderland Marine Mutual Insurance Co., Ltd. in Sunderland, England. Also in attendance was Guido Zamperini from the Bank of New England, who had financed many of the Co-op boats. From that initial meeting, The Point Club, Inc. was organized.

There was considerable work done in a short time. The coverage on the boats began when I notified the new company that, by a vote of the Co-op Board, we would not renew our Fleet Insurance on June 23, 1986. By July 6, The Point Club had signed up 50 boats. My first policy on the Alliance issued by The Point Club, Inc. had a term from June 23, 1986 to June 23, 1987. In a short time, nearly all the boats originally signed up with the Sam Snow Agency became members of the "Club" and additional fishing boats from Massachusetts were insured by the Club.

The original Point Club Board of Directors were myself as Chairman/President; Jacob Dykstra, Vice President; Frederick J. Mattera, 2nd Vice President and later President (1998); Professor Dennis Nixon, Secretary, a marine lawyer from the University of Rhode Island; David Roebuck, Treasurer and Co-op boat Captain/owner; Barry Gristwood, Sunderland Marine, retired from the Board in 1988 and replaced by Barry Gallup, Rhode Island Engine

Co. Point Judith; Frank Ostrow, Ocean Marine Underwriters (OMU); Bill Scola, OMU; Dan Arnold, Captain/owner from Marshfield, Massachusetts; Bruce MacLeod, Captain/owner Point Judith; Robert McVey, Co-op Captain/owner and OMU; Frank Mirarchi, Captain/owner from North Scituate, Massachusetts; and Brian Turnbaugh, Co-op Captain/owner.

The first Board meeting took place on July 3, 1986. As Chairman, I directed the meeting where we discussed the Articles of Association, By-Laws, and Election of Officers. On the agenda was approval of the Lightship Management Agreement, a subsidiary of OMU, that would manage all claims. How to form underwriting an claim committees recommended by Barry Gristwood. How deductibles would work for machinery—based on age. Inclusion of small boats in the Club—lobster boats, etc. Expansion of the Club to other ports, for example Dan Arnold and Frank Mirarchi. This brief description of a meeting of the Point Club tells how involved we as fishermen and boat owners would continue to be in the management of our insurance. I was privileged to be President from 1986 to 1997. It was necessary for me to now have a second briefcase.

Later that year, I was appointed to the Board of Directors of Sunderland Marine Mutual Insurance Company, Ltd. as their U.S. Representative. Now I had a third briefcase. I served as a Board Member until my retirement in 1998. Sunderland insured fishing boats in all the English speaking countries worldwide. Our Board meetings were primarily in England and Scotland. Over the years, I attended meetings in Holland, Ireland, Canada, New Zealand, and Australia. Fortunately, on occasion, the wives were invited.

I usually made no more than two meetings in one year that took five days because of the travel time. Bob Kraines, the Co-op VP, covered for me during any absence. Fred Mattera replaced me on the Board as the member from the U.S.

It is time in this narrative to tell what was happening with the *Alliance*. When I took the job as President of the Co-op in January of 1985 and Nelson took a job in the stock room at Rhode Island Engine Co. that he referred to as his "Little Job," the *Alliance* was paid for, along with all bills and significant cash in the boat account.

In 1983, the value of our landings was $407,482, in 1984 it was $342,358. We both were taking home a decent annual pay. In

1985, my annual pay at the Co-op was a third of what I was used to, although the membership probably thought I was being paid too much.

For the year 1985, the landings dropped to $254,291 and stayed in that range. In the summer of 1986, the *Alliance* fished in the Squid Fishery unloading to the Japanese vessel. Harlan Stanley, Jr. fished the boat through a year or so and maintained it just as we had done over the years. Then there were a number of other Captains. Not an easy job pushing a boat that size. The picture shows the booms used to increase the stability that were installed by R.I. Engine Co. in 1985.

The *Alliance* coming up to the Japanese processor.
Picture by Moe McDonough

As the first few years went by, I was so busy I more or less ignored the boat business although I still made out the trip settlements. In order to stay current with the bills, I borrowed from my bank with personal notes until the fall of 1986 when Hospital Trust Bank required that we take out a mortgage on "Trawler Alliance, Inc." for $120,000. In 1988, I had to increase the mortgage to $160,000.

Right then, I should have resigned my position at the Co-op and gone back fishing to save my business that I had worked so hard to make a success. I didn't do that; I decided to sell the *Alliance* instead.

Once the word got out that the boat was for sale, it became more difficult to hire a Captain and crew. There was one opportunity to turn the situation around. Peter Reposa asked me if he could run the boat. At the time, he had a good job as mate with Harold Loftes, Jr., and I told him I didn't think he should give up a good job since he would be out of a job when the *Alliance* was sold. What a mistake that was. The *Alliance* didn't sell at my price, and like all the Reposa's, when he did get a boat, he never shut the engine off and pushed a boat to its limit. Peter turned out to be a prominent Captain and owner. He would have done the same with the *Alliance*, all because I thought I was being a good guy worrying about his job.

In March of 1989, Neil Stoddard of Hull & Cargo Surveyors, Inc. came up with a valuation between $320—$350,000 and a replacement cost of $950,000. There was only one offer after a year asking $300,000 and in 1990, I agreed to sell the boat for $240,000 to Ed Todd, a Point Judith Fisherman. That's not the end of the story.

On the last trip, the boat Captain got into a known hang, marked on the chart with Loran co-ordinates. They ended up losing everything but one trawl door. Since the sale included the lost gear, it cost over $5,000 to replace everything which included one door that Fred Mattera from the *Travis & Natalie* happened to have.

Before the sale could take place, the boat had to have an out of the water survey. I paid the last Captain to go with me to Norlantic Shipyard in New Bedford. One of the survey requirements was to test the thickness of the hull plating. The tests determined that the hull plating at the stern above the propeller was unacceptably thin and had to be replaced. An area about 5-6 square feet. This included part of the two stern fuel tanks and the steering compartment or lazarette. After cleaning the tanks, cutting out and welding in the new plating, the bill from Norlantic came to $11,210. Take note, if you own a steel boat that is twenty years or more old, the same situation may exist.

Now comes the bad part. In order to keep going, I had taken out a home equity loan of $5,500 on my house. Another 90-day note with a personal guarantee for $58,000. We still had $144,000 principal remaining on the boat mortgage. By the time I paid all the invoices from Merriam Instruments, Trawlworks, Norlantic, boat insurance balance, and accounting fees, I had spent the $240,000 and still had an unpaid bill with Rhode Island Engine Co. for $24,000. I knew that there was not enough from the sale to break even so I left the last one to pay myself since R.I. Engine Co. required a personal guarantee for all their work which was a wise and practical practice. Believe it or not, I was satisfied with the end result because Fleet Bank held the $5,500 home equity loan and the $58,000 note and wanted to take out a 1st Preferred Mortgage on my house. No way was that going to happen with the kind of money I was making. I was not going to touch my personal investments either.

The Trawler Alliance Inc. was dissolved as a corporation in December of 1990. The last full year of operating the *Alliance*, the gross landings were down to $236,692. Obviously, those kind of landings do not support an 85' stern trawler. More on the *Alliance* later. Since taking the position as President of the Co-op, I had worked harder through an endless list of problems with some success than I ever did fishing. Shore jobs? Losing roughly $50,000 in the value of your main business each of the last five years would not seem possible, but it happened.

Nelson was in the process of moving to Florida that year, and the way the business with the *Alliance* concluded ended our long relationship. Not surprising because we both assumed that the *Alliance* could at least operate without incurring new debt. We both were required to sign the 1st Preferred Mortgage on the boat which was a wake-up call that things were going downhill, but to not get a dime out of the final sale was too much.

The sale of the *Alliance* had a lasting effect on me. The Gillnet Swordfish Fishery, for example, had I been running the boat at the time that fishery started, I certainly would have been in on it. Over the years, I observed landings of a number of species that were truly impressive, that I could have caught.

The construction of the new Co-op building was an issue in my early years as President. The foundation and the docks were complete and in time, we were able to organize the financing to continue the project. During 1988 and early 89, I spent part of each day watching how the work was progressing.

The whole steel structure was completed by the early fall of 1988. The preparation of the floor area before the cement was poured was impressive. The whole floor area was interconnected with heavy steel rods. In some areas, there were two levels or rods tied together.

Point Judith Fisherman's Cooperative Association, Inc.
New facility in Galilee, Rhode Island

When the cement was pumped in, there was a continuous line of cement trucks supplying the cement. The floor was a complex project in that there were floor drains throughout the floor area with the floor pitched to direct any water into the drains.

I should comment on one incident that was not actual Co-op business but had a direct effect on the price of fish in our first year of the new plant's operation.

In the spring of 1988, under the guidance and persistence of George Whidden, a Point Judith Offshore Lobsterman, the Coalition to Cease Ocean Dumping was formed. George had observed an increase in a shell disease apparent in the lobsters he was catching. George was so convincing that on July 11, 1988, I believe he was aboard, the *R/V George W. Powell* using the sub *Delta*, checked out the dumping area where the barges carrying all manner of waste from the New York City area had been dumping for years. Bottom samples were taken and were apparently toxic. Throughout all this, George was even on National TV spreading the word of ocean pollution. In time, legislation was passed stopping the practice of ocean dumping.

From 1987 to 1991, I was a Regional Director of the National Fisheries Institute, NFI. Most everyone in the seafood industry was a member and one of their primary focus was the promotion of seafood. I called Dick Gutting at NFI Headquarters in Washington, DC, to give him a heads up on the expected run of bad publicity the industry could expect. There was no way ocean dumping could be stopped without convincing the public, through the press, that the "ocean" was being or was already polluted and that was what happened. Even my mother told me she wouldn't eat fish anymore.

The long-term result of stopping ocean dumping gave us the cleanest ocean water anywhere in the world. We have no way of knowing the extent of ocean dumping off the less developed nations. There is no doubt that George Whidden deserved all the credit for stopping the ocean dumping practice.

The day finally came to officially open the new plant. On Friday, March 31, 1989, we had a dedication ceremony.

In preparation for the program, we covered the floor with a large rental carpet in the southeast corner of the building near the garage-sized door adjacent to the day boat conveyor. Tables and chairs were set up for a buffet luncheon. We were unsure how many to expect, but it turned out to be around two hundred as I recall.

This would be the first time that most of the guests would have been inside the plant. As part of the program, we planned a tour and a demonstration of the unloading systems.

U.S. Senator Claiborne Pell was among the first wave of guests, so after I made a few opening remarks, I stayed with the Senator. I knew him reasonably well having had meetings on fisheries issues several times in his Washington, D.C. office, and he had visited the old Co-op facilities once since I had become President.

As I recall, it was approaching noon, when, without any warning, we lost our electricity. Since the plant had an extensive lighting system with no windows to speak of for light, we were in the dark. The nearest large door was opened and one of the truck loading doors which helped, but it was the end of March and hardly a summer's day. The guests did stay for the luncheon, but the planned tour was out.

The police were contacted, and there was a reported auto accident that had cut the power to our area. There was no information on when the power would be restored. After an hour or so, we called it a day.

The docks in use by the new Co-op building were designated by letters. Starting at the east end, Dock "D" was the pump dock. The left or west side was where the boat would be positioned. The east side belonged to Rhode Island Engine. This dock was leased from the state. Dock "E" had a conveyor running along the left side and was primarily used by the smaller day boats. There was enough room on the right side for a forklift to go out on the dock to unload tuna or swordfish. Docks "F" and "G" had two long tubes, one for each side, that acted as flumes delivering the fish to a de-waterer and an angled conveyor that delivered the fish on to hydraulic powered culling boards where they were sorted by specie and size, weighted, then iced down in heavy cardboard boxes with the Co-op logo. This was the end of using wooden boxes.

Docks F and G were for trip boats and allowed four boats to unload at the same time at a rate of 15-20,000 lbs. an hour for each boat if the trip was a straight run of whiting for example. The east side of the long Dock "H" was also leased by the Co-op from the state. Initially, Dock H was not part of the unloading program. Several years later, a second day boat conveyor was installed on the shore side section of the dock. After that, a second fish pump was purchased by 13 member boat owners and installed on the middle of the dock.

The movement of fish from the unloading area was usually into the cooler until it was time to load the trucks going to market in New York, etc. There was now an extensive loading dock that could accommodate five trailer trucks and two delivery-size trucks.

In the Spring of 1989, we had a test run with the new facility. The '95 foot *Trinity*, owned by Ed Page, was at one of the flume docks with over 100,000 lbs. of fish that was caught in one day. As

Ed explained the fishing: after only a short tow, they had so much mixed fish the crew could only sort part of the tow when Ed thought he should haul back again. The same mix of scup, squid, seabass, whiting, and fluke. The fish were all good size and marketable, so Ed ran the tows down the fish hold without any sorting and just iced them down.

We started unloading his trip and could only pick out the fluke, and I think it was the squid. The rest was run into our 800 lb. tubs. We set up long culling tables all over the unloading area dumping 500-1,000 lbs. at a time with four or five people working each table. Dave Roebuck and Jack Westcott, from the Board of Directors, were there that day, and we brought workers over from processing. The salesmen were out there, and I found a set of "oilers" and joined in for what turned into an all-day workout. It was a good trip, and we charged Ed extra for the work. We also told Ed and the other boat owners that was the only time we would handle an unsorted trip like that.

In July of 1989, I had a call from Rodney Avila, owner of the *F/V Trident*, the Admiral, that I used to fish with catching fluke. He asked me if the Co-op would be interested in buying trips of swordfish. After talking to a major buyer in Boston and our salesman, we started buying the trips. This was a new fishery with the boats catching the fish with very large mesh gillnets. The *Trident's* very first trip selling to us was a total of 185 fish. Swordfish were categorized as "Pups" - 100 lbs. or less, "Markers" - 100 to 200 lbs.; double markers or XX—200-300 lbs., XXX—300-400 lbs., etc. Most of the gillnet swordfish trips had an average size of 160-170 lbs. That trip weighed out at 30,000 lbs. The Co-op unloaded, stored, trucked, and sold the fish for 15 cents/lb or $4,500. That summer, there were two additional boats from New Bedford that landed swordfish with the Co-op. The buyer in Boston bought 40% of the landings for that summer. At the time of the landings described, none of the details were available to anyone other than those involved in the sale.

This new Gillnet Fishery was a significant part of the history of the New England Fisheries. Similar to when I started trapping lobsters offshore that first year, the swordfish landings did not go unnoticed. This was the beginning and a number of Point Judith boats joined the fishery in 1990. Quite a sight to see that many pallets mounded up with ice covering swordfish in our cooler.

The most important headlines in the summer of 1989 was the medical waste, needles, etc. washing up on the New Jersey beaches. This confirmed to seafood consumers that the ocean was definitely polluted. Ocean dumping stories were bad enough but did not have as much impact on the fishing industry as this "news." The landings of whiting, one of the big moneymakers for the Co-op, virtually stopped. The price of whiting in the New York and all other markets got so low that by the time the cost of unloading, trucking, and even a 2-cent profit, left the boat price at a nickel or less. As I recall, only one boat continued fishing for whiting hoping for a jump in the market. All the other species, especially scup, were also hit with low prices, making it near impossible for our boats to make money.

In 1988, the Co-op landings were valued at $26 million. There was a profit at that level. By the end of 1989, there was a catastrophic drop in value to $16 million. Not the kind of results that we were in a position to deal with and certainly not what we projected before resuming construction of the new building.

In the late fall of 1989 and early winter of 1990, we were unloading herring using the pump on Dock D. Back then, the Co-op owned four insulated milk-type trailers. The pump was arranged so the fish could be pumped into the building or into the trailer. The truck scale on the east side of the building would weigh the empty truck and trailer, then weight it again when the tank trailer was full, giving us the weight of the fish. Most of the herring were sold to a Canadian processing plant located in Blacks Harbour just over the Maine border.

I believe it was in early January that there was eight hundred thousand (800,000) lbs. of fish unloaded at the plant in one day. Included were the four trucks of herring, about 120,000 lbs., a similar amount of mackerel, the rest was butterfish, whiting, and a mix of everything else. A busy day.

The herring joint venture with the Soviet processing ship, the 600 foot *Professor Baranov* that I had mentioned in the Chapter on Foreign Fishing, began on February 7, 1990 when the ship dropped anchor in the west passage of Narragansett Bay. Dave Ellington, of Scan Ocean based in Gloucester, MA, and I worked for three months to set up the venture in that we had to have approval from the State, the Navy, and the Coast Guard. I was very familiar with the Bay and suggested the anchorage should be just north of Dutch Island and South of the old Jamestown Bridge. The location was in relatively protected waters and far enough north not to be subjected to ocean swells since our boats would come alongside the ship to pump the herring. David Borden from the Division of Fish and Wildlife of the Department of Environmental Management, DEM, was the contact with the state.

Flynn Seafoods of Newport was included in the venture to encourage the Newport Fleet to participate. The first day the ship was ready to take fish, two of the Point boats unloaded. The first week, the ship took 195 tons. Scan Ocean had a man on board to communicate between the boats and the crew. There were two hundred in the crew of the ship working in three shifts, allowing the boats to unload 24/7. The boats were paid $87/ton for the fish and the ship wanted fish of about 7 1/2 inches long and in good condition to process. Any rejections were processed into fish meal. In practice, the operation was satisfactory to the boats. The Co-op shared $10/ton with Flynn Seafoods. The venture went on for many years. We still had boats unload herring at our dock.

The new building became a processing facility soon after the start up. Our main focus was to clean squid. Prior to occupying the building, the Co-op had always been primarily an unloading facility and sold bulk fish like squid and butterfish to outside processors on the same sales terms of payment in seven to ten days as the New York and other fish buyers.

The Co-op staff had been working with The Squid Machine Co. in California on an experimental basis using the former Co-op lobster building which had ceased operations. The machine cleaned the squid using a combination of cutting blades and high water pressure. By 1992, the Co-op had set up a number of squid machines on a second floor in the processing area constructed for that purpose.

The cleaned tubes and tentacles came down on to a long, wide belt conveyor where they were examined by a dozen workers on each side of the long belt to insure the squid was perfectly cleaned. At the end of the conveyor was a large packing table where the cleaned tentacles were packed on the bottom of each 2 1/2 lb. water resistant cardboard box. The tubes were carefully aligned on top. The boxes were weighed on electronic scales, the boxes were placed in aluminum pans, then the pans were placed directly into the plate freezers that were used exclusively for the 2 1/2 lb. package.

The aluminum pans cut the freezing time by 30%. When the squid was frozen, the individual boxes were slid into labeled, plastic bags, then packed in master cartons which held 20 of the 2 1/2 lb. boxes. The squid was held in freezer trailers on site or in public storage until sold. Most of the product was pre-sold to a Boston company and were trucked to their destination.

Almost from the beginning, in addition to the Point Judith Brand, we added a second brand under the trade name Calamari U.S.A. The second brand was usually used when we cleaned squid that was previously frozen and not considered quite the same quality. In times of heavy landings by our boats, we had no choice but to freeze the squid whole in large cartons in our blast freezers for future cleaning.

On the days when we had butterfish to pack, we had to bring in another 25 to 30 workers in addition to the 50 working on the squid. For many years, the butterfish, graded by size, were packed in 5 kilogram boxes, 11 lbs., using what was called a "swim" pack. The pack meant the fish all facing left, as I recall and placed on a slight angle in overlapping rows. When the fish were sold in Japan, the buyer could open a box and count the number of fish to insure they were a large size counting 35 fish to the box for example. Very labor-intensive.

The total number of "contract" workers in processing on a busy day would be around 75. To insure that we would have the number of workers to match up with the landings, the sales department had installed a Qualcom communication system in the sales office along with the single sideband and VHF radios. The new system was completely secure, and we would know what time to expect the boat and a detailed tally of what was on board. Most of the trip sized boats had the system installed.

The Co-op's financial problems operating at this level began with the weekly payroll. The contract workers alone based on a five-day week was around $20,000 back then. There was another

$12,000 for the key employees and another $18-20,000 for the 40 permanent employees working on the docks and supervising the contract workers when overtime was factored in.

Then, of course, the boats had to be paid in at least eight days for the fish being processed. If the fish products coming out of processing were paid for in 30 days and often a longer period of time, there was a constant shortage that had to be addressed by using a line of credit or factoring.

When I was working at the old Co-op building, I often took small groups of four or five staff, member fishermen, or visitors over to the Landing Restaurant across the street for coffee or lunch.

When we moved to the new building, I continued the practice and would often walk over to the nearby Portside Restaurant for lunch. There was usually only one waitress on duty no matter how many customers there were. Jeanne Lane had been there for years and knew most of the fishermen and what they usually ordered. The thing was that she couldn't begin to know all our names so she called each of us "Schwartz." She later went into selling real estate as I recall. Twenty years later, I was in line at Iggys Doughboys and Chowder House in Point Judith to buy chowder and clam cakes, and a voice called out, "Is that you Schwartz?" Her son, a fisherman, named his own boat *Schwartz*.

The summer of 1990 was significant with an increase in the number of boats taking part in the Gillnet Swordfish Fishery from Point Judith. My records show the landings from 1991, but in 1990, I believe Mike Monteforte, Fred Mattera, Jim Thayer, and Bob McVey landed swordfish. There were also landings of yellowfin tuna and big eye tuna. The fish dressed weight ran 60-80 lbs.

I believe it was 1991 when Harold Loftes Jr. and John Tarasevich were longlining swordfish and tuna. Longlining is set up with miles of line with hooks spaced the whole length and usually baited with the large ilex or summer squid. Generally, the swordfish were smaller, under 100 lb. dressed weight, than the gillnet fish.

During one summer, we shipped our first giant Bluefin tuna, caught by Rod Sykes using rod and reel, by air freight to Tsukijii Market in Tokyo, Japan. This was the beginning of a service the Co-op would provide by shipping one or two, if they were smaller fish, in large, heavy cardboard "coffins" that were strapped to wooden pallets for ease in handling. Our CFO went to Tokyo to meet with the buyers of our butterfish. He visited the market and while in the city was treated to some exotic food and also made a regular trip to McDonald's to survive.

As soon as we moved into the new building and started processing squid, we had a call from the manager of the Town of Narragansett's sewage treatment plant located just south of Scarborough Beach. He was seeing fish and especially squid pieces in the waste water coming into his plant, and it had to stop. From then on, instead of washing down the plant with our heavy duty fresh water hoses, the floor had to be swept up and nothing but water down the drains. In the old building, the fish dock was always washed clean with a salt water hose and everything went into the harbor.

With the new plant, we had to have a large tank where all the discarded fish from the sorting conveyors and the floor sweeping were dumped. Periodically, during the day, the tank was pumped into a specially designed, water-tight, commercial dumpster located outside on the north side of the building. Every two or three days, this dumpster was delivered to a company in the western part of the state to be mixed with compost material. The end result was bagged and sold to gardeners. I don't recall the name of the product, but our employees called it "black gold."

One thing about the new building. Being about 30 ft. high above the foundation, the view was spectacular. It was also perilous to go out on the roof because there were hundreds of seagull nests spaced over the whole expanse, and they didn't like visitors. They would swoop down, making a lot of noise. It was an ideal location for a nest since the roof was inaccessible to all except flying predators. Half the population of seagulls in the area must be from those nests.

The Co-op leased a large tract of land where the new plant was located. With the approval of the state, we sub-leased a section to a company called ProPark for Block Island parking. Over the years, it has been a benefit to the many travelers using the Block Island Ferry System. It was also helpful in paying our land rent.

Leaving the port of Point Judith

Chapter 23

The New England Fishery Management Council
1991 - 1997

Since my years at the Co-op, I had been directly involved in the operation to some degree. Now, in 1991, with a full-time General Manager in place, I decided it would be better for the business for me to back off. The position of a Member of the New England Fishery Management Council held by Bob Smith was coming up for renewal. There were three other contenders for the Rhode Island position along with Bob. I discussed the situation with Bob, and we came to the conclusion that he might not be reappointed since he had already served several terms since replacing Jake Dykstra on the Council. I suggested that if I applied for the position as President of the Co-op, Bob had been Vice-President under Jake when he was appointed, there was a good chance of keeping the seat for the Co-op. We did directly represent a considerable number of member fishermen. As it turned out, I got the appointment from the Governor and was sworn in as a member of the Council that year of 1991.

I already had started to fill another briefcase for Council matters since I had been attending the monthly as well as selective committee meetings since becoming President. Throughout that time, I would address the Members of the Council from the floor on various issues usually after brief conversations with our Council Advisor, Lucy Sloan, who was paid by us through the Defense Fund. She would also address the Council on our behalf. Lucy had been working in this capacity since the mid-70's or about the time Jake had been Council Chairman back in the beginning.

Now with me being on the Council, I could still speak out on matters of concern to our members and all other issues brought before the Council for consideration. Incidental to this Council business, all the traveling, usually in the Gloucester, Massachusetts region, then sitting all day, was raising hell with my back. During the meetings, I often had to stand with my back against the wall. Many days when I got home at night, I would have to hang on my driver's side door until my back could straighten out enough to walk into the house.

Beginning in 1991, I served for two, three year terms until 1997. During that time, I was a member of a number of committees and was Chairman of the Monkfish and Chairman of the Gear Conflict Committees. We came close to solving the problem between the Draggers and Fixed Lobster Trap Fishery, and my successor completed the plan over the years.

I was the Liaison to the Mid-Atlantic Fishery Management Council when John Bryson was the Director. Although I did not have a vote on that Council, I was a member of the Squid, Mackeral, and Butterfish Committee and Dimersal Finfish Committee. Being in that position was important to our Point Judith fishermen since those species were the primary targets of our fleet. The Mid-Atlantic Council was more of a quota base system of management. The quota or annual catch for each specie was determined using the information on stock status from the Woods Hole scientists. The Council worked with the Atlantic States Marine Fisheries Commission, ASMFC, which included 15 members from all the states on the Atlantic Coast, to allocate a percentage of the annual quota for each state, including Rhode Island, based on their historical catch records. This is a very simplified explanation of how the system worked because there was input from fisherman at Council meetings and public hearings at various ports in the Mid-Atlantic region, New York to North Carolina. I reported back at the New England Council meetings each month.

The Director of the New England Council for most of my years on the Council was Douglas, "Doug," Marshall. He had staff members that prepared all the relevant information on the species such as groundfish for each of the committee meetings, and the assigned staff member was always present to explain or answer questions on their current presentation. The system worked and gave the committee members all the information beforehand that was on the agenda. Again a simplified explanation.

By the time I became a member of the Council, I actually thought that over the next few years, the various fish stocks would be found to have recovered to the Point where the regulations in place would be relaxed and the fishermen would be gradually allowed to direct more fishing effort on the various species. That did not happen at least on my six year watch. Eventually, haddock made a recognized comeback and scup as well.

There were many issues that came up that were of concern to Point Judith fishermen. At more than one meeting, there were serious discussions that a boat could only have one mesh size on board. This was a request by the Coast Guard and NMFS because they could not enforce the use of small mesh if it was aboard the boat when fishing for large mesh species. As I recall, the Gloucester Whiting fisherman were also opposed to that requirement. Tom McVey, the Liaison to the New England Council from the Mid-Atlantic Council, my counterpart, was in opposition to the one mesh concept since it would impact their fluke fishermen.

At that time, I explained that it was common practice to fish for large mesh species first, such as fluke in my case, because they had a longer shelf life when well-iced. Then, depending on the weather or availability, changeover to small mesh, make the change with the adjustable sweep to eliminate bottom tending fish, then catch butterfish, scup, whiting, or squid, for example, which had a short shelf life of two days or so to be acceptable in the market. I explained the concept of the adjustable sweep which about all the Trawlworks built nets had and were used by our Point boats. The response, although polite, was that only one mesh on board was what was favored by NMFS.

I mention the small mesh issue because discussions like that brought me to the realization that fishermen in general were now considered as the "bad guys," meaning that stringent regulations were necessary to bring "them" under control. Up until then, I was always sure we were all working in an honorable profession, catching fresh fish for the U.S. population, risking "life and limb" going to sea.

One of the first significant moves was to require all fishing vessels working in Federal waters to have a fishing license. It was decided the license was for the boat, and the owners were responsible for its operation regarding all fishing regulations. In our State, the landing license was in the operator/owners name. More on that subject in the last chapter of the book.

I recall the day when all the Council members were introduced to the fishing logbook. The logbook originated at NMFS Headquarters outside of Washington, D.C. in Silver Springs, MD. As I recall, we had no input in its preparation. The fishing log was for the boat and required a signature indicating that the information submitted was accurate. The logbook entries became the official landing record of the boat. At that time, not every fisherman realized that the future participation in certain fisheries would depend on whether or not the historical catch record indicated qualification in the groundfish fishery for example. Over time, very few of our Point Judith boats met that requirement for groundfish. In fact, most of our boats deliberately fished on the more underutilized species to lessen the pressure on the depleted species such as cod.

Early in my first three year term on the Council, Lucy Sloan moved to Japan to work for a group of Japanese fishing companies. As a result, I asked Jake Dykstra if he would be interested in representing the Co-op by speaking from the floor at Council meetings, etc. We came to terms on his compensation which came from our Defense Fund, as it had with Lucy. It became our practice that I would pick up Jake at his home in nearby Kingston and drive to the meetings. During the drive, we could talk about and plan what needed to be addressed at the meetings.

Over the years, the Council used to hold public hearings in Point Judith. We would meet with a number of fishermen prior to the hearing so that they were informed enough to speak on the issues from the floor. Not all the fishermen at the hearing itself had been at the pre-meeting, and at times, their comments and their presence was considered to be intimidating to those Council members running the meeting. As a result, the Council decided to move the location of the hearings away from the harbor.

The members of the Council and the Council staff were all what I call "good people" and dedicated to achieving the Council objectives. In time, I became "involved in the process" and the actual fishery problems became secondary. It is a long road to bring a plan amendment to a point where it can be submitted for approval. Other Council members or former members have expressed similar thoughts when I asked them.

The Council system, in my opinion, is set up as a democratic operation. There is always an opportunity for fishermen to address the members at council meetings on agenda subjects and also participate in Committee meetings.

The work of the Fishery Councils is based on the stock assessment for each specie. During my time on the Council, the stock assessments were determined by the scientists at Woods Hole based primarily on trawl surveys carried out by their own vessels. The surveys were for all the fish species. Based on comparing the survey results from the same locations over the years, a determination is made on the estimated population of the fish in the Northeast Atlantic in our case. If the estimated population reaches or goes below established parameters, that species may be considered as overfished requiring the directed fishery for cod, for example, to be reduced by limiting fishing effort until there is a recovery to the level where the population would be sustainable. This is a ridiculously simple explanation of a very complex process that would probably require a thousand pages to have a complete understanding.

The problem for most fishermen was and is their lack of confidence in the survey results. For example, I received a phone call in my Co-op office from one of our boats through the Boston marine operator. He was fishing for whiting well east of Nantucket and had just had a call from the Captain of one of the survey vessels fishing nearby. He said that he just had a tow of 150 lbs. of mixed fish using fine-mesh in the back end of the net and asked what the Co-op boat was catching. I was called for an opinion on how to answer. It was the middle of the afternoon and he told me he was on his last tow to make 100,000 lbs. of whiting since daylight. He was unsure that if he told the survey vessel's Captain, the area might at some point by closed to prevent overfishing. Stories like this were common.

This situation was understandable because the Co-op boat was towing a net that was designed to catch whiting. The same would hold true for scup, squid, butterfish, and even fluke.

I have described the type of gear that was in use built by Captain Bert Hillier in the Chapter on the URI Fisheries School. That gear was basically a hard bottom groundfish trawl. At various times over the years, surveys were carried out by commercial fishing vessels resulting in considerably larger catches. As far as I know, this information was not considered as usable in the final stock assessments.

The scallop fleet did their own supervised surveys since the NMFS vessels were never outfitted with scallop dredges to carry out surveys. The scallop surveys were very complete and as I recall, including photographs of the bottom clearly showing the abundance level of scallops in the survey areas. I believe that over the years, these NMFS recognized surveys were the primary reason for the long, successful history of a sustainable scallop fishery.

The real job of the Councils is to develop regulations to control fishing effort. Deciding how to control effort without causing fishermen's business to fail is a near impossible task. Sitting on the Council, we often heard fishermen from all over New England testify that our decisions to curtail fishing was causing them to go out of business." Every boat has a "number" or financial minimum they have to make for their business to be sustainable. I know this firsthand, based on my experience with the *Alliance*.

Other than the fishermen on the Council, the members seemed to tire of hearing that plea over and over again. The pleas we heard were real. The sad part was the position the Council Members were in. We were obligated to carry out our duty by the oath we swore to when we became Council members.

Over the years, we developed systems like limited the days at sea to control effort. Regardless of the measure employed, it always came down to fairly allocating the days to the boats. In time, the log books with the confirmed catch record of the boat would be the determining factor. I never fished under all these controls. In my fishing days, there was an element of trust that the fishermen would do the right thing by way of conservation. The word "trust" does not appear anywhere in existing regulations.

Chapter 24

The Co-Op Business

Throughout the early 1990's, the Co-op's focus was on cleaning squid. Our Point Judith Fishermen's Cooperative label on the 2 ½ lb. frozen package was a top of the line product and was distributed not only in New England but all over the eastern states as well as the major cities like Chicago. This was a time when calamari was fast becoming a favorite appetizer in most of the top restaurants.

There was no doubt that processing all the mid-size squid, 4-6 inch tube length and selling the large squid into the fresh market or freezing the large for export stabilized the price to the benefit of the boats. Our staff projected that this one product could reach sales of 8-10 million dollars/year.

To achieve that level of sales would require a line of credit well beyond what would have been available to the company in the best of times. We even formed a separate company to raise funds from the members and friends of the Co-op to use as an added line of credit.

In early 1995, we cut back on all processing except the 2 ½ lb. package. By the beginning of June our payments to our long-time vendors were in arrears to the point where they hired a well-known law firm to represent them as counsel to the Co-op's unsecured creditors. Our law firm appointed a very able lawyer to guide us through this crisis. A work-out company was brought in to handle the Co-op financial affairs.

On June 15, 1995 at a special Co-op Board of Director's meeting, our lawyer informed us that on advice of the Co-op financial consultants, the Co-op could not continue to operate based on short-term cash flow predictions. Continued operation would not provide for payment of payroll and failure to make the payroll becomes a liability for the management and the Board of Directors. There was a complex motion that was passed regarding the creditors and a receiver. It was decided that the business would close at noon.

With our lawyer's assistance, the employees were told that they were all on temporary layoff. It was over.

The Co-op filed for a state receivership at 4:15 p.m. on Thursday, June 22, 1995. The same lawyer and law firm that represented the unsecured creditors was appointed as the temporary receiver and later was appointed the permanent receiver.

The following day, the receiver, our lawyer, one of the financial consultants, and I had a meeting at the Co-op to plan the future of the company in receivership. It was determined that the business could continue to operate on a limited basis including the ice plant with oversight by the receiver. They decided that under our then general manager's supervision, a profit could be realized. All supplies, trucking, etc. would be on a COD basis. Initially the period was through September 8th when the auction bids on the main building and the ice plant were due.

A "Petition to Sell the Assets Free and Clear of Liens" was prepared and presented to the Superior Court by the receiver. The petition eliminated the claims on all the equipment in or attached to the building on the day of the bankruptcy. This included blast freezers and fish pumps purchased by fishermen and the unloading equipment, etc. financed by a Federal agency.

It was no more than a few weeks after the bankruptcy that I had "the call" from one of our long-term fish buyers located in the Fulton Market, New York City. He and his family were interested in buying the business. In the discussion, it was clear that the property and equipment, which was just over six years old, was secondary.

In the negotiations with the receiver and the State of Rhode Island, that had guaranteed the bonds for the construction of the building, the "new company" agreed to assume the bond obligation. By 1995, one third of the original debt had been paid off by the Co-op. In mid-October, the Purchase and Sale Agreement for the processing facility and for the ice plant were signed.

The agreements included payment of any and all outstanding debt owed to the State and the Town of Narragansett. The new company also had to agree to desist from dumping any squid processing water from the plant into the Town sewer system.

In the final settlement of the Co-op, the sale of the old lobster building and a piece of the original Co-op building that the Co-op had been leasing to a lobster operation, generated about $500,000. That amount of income was probably not enough to cover the legal costs incurred by the bankruptcy.

The reason I provided this limited amount of information on the Co-op bankruptcy was to inform the readers that the State of Rhode Island did not lose any money because of the failure of the Co-op business, and the same with the Town. At the time of the bankruptcy, the press was speculating on how much money had been lost by the State even to the point as to how much it was going to cost each Rhode Island resident. My and others' response throughout the period was "no comment." We, of course, knew that the original cost of the building and equipment was close to six million dollars plus the unknown value of the business including the boats that continued to unload fish through the bankruptcy and most would continue selling to the new owners. The receiver knew what he had for value from the beginning. In my opinion, the whole process was well planned and executed right down to the final sale.

To me, the one good thing that came out of the sale was that the new owner asked all the permanent employees to stay with the new company including the General Manager. The new owner also wanted me to work for him without specifying what my role would be going forward. The new owner did not know anyone in Rhode Island other than talking to the salesmen, the General Manager, and me. Quite a "leap of faith" to acquire an operation of that size.

There was a significant amount of money lost by all of us fishermen when the Co-op failed. The Board of Directors and the fishermen investors owned boats that would provide future earnings in order to recover. They could continue to sell their catch to the new company or sell anywhere else in Point Judith or in other ports since they no longer had an obligation to sell to the Co-op. For my own situation, at this time in my life I needed the job with the new company.

The unsecured creditors did not realize anything at all from the sale. They had become close friends in many cases over the years and the managers of the new company made certain that they would have an opportunity to continue doing business with the new company.

When the business resumed under the new owners, there

was a focus on how to dispose of the wastewater generated by the squid cleaning operation before processing could begin. This was an order by the Court. We managed to get approval from the EPA and a number of state agencies to dump the water while moving in an area south of the "hooter" Buoy about 5 miles south of the Point Judith Light. We hired the F/V *Ocean State*, owned by Bob and Glenn Westcott, to carry the wastewater. The new company purchased a diesel powered pump for the boat. Our maintenance crew installed a large fiberglass holding tank on the bulkhead to collect the water generated during the day.

Several years later, a 100 ft. barge was rented for the same purpose but with greater capacity. A local Captain, who owned a small tug boat, brought the wastewater to the same location. This time, there was a new EPA requirement to measure how long it took to disperse. The company hired Dr. Joe DeAlteris, the then Director of the Fisheries School, to professionally do the monitoring and provide a report to the EPA. The work was done using his own boat under his privately owned company, not associated with the University.

Chapter 25

The Transition to a Rod and Reel Fisherman

      In 1992, I received the National Fisherman Magazine High-liner Award at the Fish Exposition in Boston on October 16th as President of the Point Judith Fisherman's Cooperative and "in recognition of my contributions to the fishing industry."

      In addition to a dinner for the four recipients that year, I was presented with a Furuno GPS. That GPS sat on my workbench in the cellar all winter until that spring when I decided to buy a boat for the GPS. A good reason. Our banker had three Boston Whalers at the time and wanted to sell the oldest one, a 1975, 20-foot model with a 175 H.P. Johnson Outboard, that his kids called the "wave breaker." Going into a 15 knot breeze at 20 knots, it would really pound. A good, stable boat that I still use through the 2016 season. I was working all the time and was still on the Fishery Council, so the boat sat on its' old trailer in my side yard until 1996 when I began renting a dock in Jerusalem from Bob Smith.

      After the Co-op bankruptcy, I was in what I guess you could call a depressed state of mind, and it was a good thing for me that I was working for the "new company." I decided it was time for me to resign from my various positions. In 1996, I resigned from the University of Rhode Island Graduate School of Oceanography Advisory Council. I had

MAC-1

been appointed to that position by Dr. John Knauss, Dean of the School in 1985 as the only fisheries person on the Council. The Council was chaired by former Rhode Island Governor Phillip Noel. Other members were from the oil and gas companies, Admiral Stanfield Turner, former head of the CIA, Nicholas Brown of the Brown Family of Rhode Island and Head of the Baltimore Aquarium, to mention a few. I sent my letter of resignation to Dean Margaret

Lineham, Dr. Knauss' successor after he left U.R.I. to become the Administrator of NOAA. As I recall, Dick Allen from my Fisheries School days took my place.

In 1997, I did not attempt to renew another three year term, after six years, on the New England Fisheries Management Council. I sent in a letter of recommendation to the State in favor of Frank Blount, owner of the Francis Fleet of head boats out of Galilee. At the time, there were no active former Co-op boat owners interested in the position which is very time consuming for a trawler captain/owner. Also I could not say that I officially represented the fishermen. I did not attend any meetings after leaving the position.

In 1997, I resigned my position as President of the Point Club, renamed the Nor-East Point Group in 1991. I had been in the position since 1986 and Fred Mattera, the VP took my place. In 2016, Fred is still the President with 50-plus boats insured.

In 1997, I also resigned as a Director of Sunderland Marine Mutual Insurance Company Limited in Sunderland, England, a position I had since 1988. Fred also took my place as the Director from the U.S. The Company has since been absorbed by a larger insurer, but Fred is now a Director for that company as of 2016. All of this "In My Wake" so to speak.

I was still working part-time for the "new company" in the year 2002 when the EPA informed the company that after a certain date, dumping the squid waste water at sea would be prohibited. The company hired Joe Federico from Beta Group, Inc., a Lincoln, RI engineering firm that specialized in wastewater treatment. In the end, a Canadian company called Zenon was selected because their specialized filtering system was the only one that could clean the wastewater to an acceptable level to run into the Town sewer system.

The Xenon Plant

The contract with Zenon was signed in June, 2003. The whole project from the extensive foundation, tanks, and prefabricated equipment structure cost almost as much as the main plant. There was no agency assistance, the "new owners" had no choice if the squid processing was to continue. The whole complex system of pumps, etc. was run by computers with a visual monitor located in the sales office. The plant was capable of processing 35-50,000 gallons of waste water each day. There was a monitoring station where we or the Town could sample the discharge. It was as clear as drinking water and without any detectable odor. The resulting sludge was pumped into tank trailers and disposed of at commercial disposal sites. Rob Brule, manager of the Ice Plant, ran the operation from day one. Rob and Carl Webster, now the dock foreman in the main plant, mixed sludge with the sand, etc. and grew all kinds of flowers and vegetables. Some of the local champion pumpkin growers tried the sludge mix, but the pumpkins grew too fast and cracked. I don't know what would have happened if the Co-op still owned the plant facing another major expense. The Xenon company was bought out by General Electric as part of their interest in improving the environment.

Back in 1987, I was appointed to the National Fish and Seafood Promotional Council. My selection as a member was because of my affiliation as a Regional Director of the National Fisheries Institute (NFI). The council was composed of industry men and women from all over the U.S. The Alaskan Representative was involved with a separate Alaska seafood promotional council. We selected a staff and Tom Jones was made Executive Director, based in Washington, D.C.

The Council was formed under the direction of the Department of Commerce and funded with 6.5 million dollars. We were responsible for national television advertising through 1991. Our main theme was "Eat Fish and Seafood Twice a Week." The purpose was to promote the U.S. Seafood Industry.

I bring this information up at this time because like the government's encouragement to expand the U.S. fishing fleet and shoreside support facilities during those years, it shows the contrast with today's government approach of drastic fishery management control measures that are bringing the industry to its' knees. What happened to U.S. supplied seafood and the "Twice a Week" theme?

As I mentioned in my chapter on the Fishery Council, we were now being viewed as the "bad guys" to the extent that we are required to hire "monitors" on board the groundfish boats to insure that we are not cheating in the trip reports. They already know the ones that cheat and have for years. Ninety-nine percent of the fishermen are the finest people you will ever meet.

There is now a group called the National Ocean Council Committee to Combat Illegal, Unreported, and Unregulated Fishing and Seafood Fraud focusing on imported fish. Imported fish is now a common substitute for U.S. caught fish. According to recent NMFS information, the U.S. is now importing 20 billion dollars of seafood compared to total U.S. landings of 5.2 billion dollars in 2015. An NMFS rule is scheduled to appear in the Federal Register on 1/9/2017 for the SIMP or Seafood Import Monitoring Program, with an implementation date of January 2018. The first phase will cover 13 species or 9 billion dollars of the total. The intent is that the importer of record would be required to supply information mirroring the current U.S. fishing vessel logbooks.

I repeat that the U.S. waters are the cleanest on Earth. I have never seen our local waters as clean and clear as they are now. Organizations like our Save the Bay in Rhode Island have worked for many years to insure the conditions we have now would become a reality. Every sewer processing facility now operates at the highest level of efficiency and continues to upgrade facilities as new technology is developed.

Back in 1982 when the Alliance was making serious money, I bought a condominium on the West Coast of Florida. This was the spring before my daughter Pam's marriage. My wife and I were visiting my mother in St. Petersburg for two weeks. My mother needed a dress for the wedding, so we took a ride to Madeira Beach to a dress shop specializing in high-end women's clothes. I decided to sit in the back seat while my mother was driving. When we drove across the causeway over the inland waterway, there was a big sign advertising new condos for sale. While they were looking at dresses, I took a walk over to the 200+ condo complex. They didn't buy a dress, but I bought a condo.

I rented the property to my cousin Bill McCauley and his wife for several winters at a price that would pay the taxes, condo fees, etc. that were very reasonable. I was in on the sales early so I had my choice and ended up with a second floor, "no bugs", two bedroom unit overlooking a waterway and the docks. We rented until 1997 when we started staying there January 1st until the end of March. A few times, I did fly back to R.I. to deal with issues at the Company. I had paid off the small mortgage years before, so the whole arrangement was very affordable.

For the first year or so in Florida, I did my fishing from the Reddington Beach Fish Pier about five miles north. I learned about Florida fishing by watching the "regulars" as to where on the Pier to fish and the best rig to use. I finally caught a 29 lb. kingfish off the end of the pier that nearly "spooled" me, that is I had about five wraps of line on the reel when I stopped the fish's first run.

It was several winters before I was invited to go fishing on one of the Yacht Club member boats. Once I made a trip or two, I became a regular. In addition to "knowing boats," I could also clean fish. Everett "Moose" Orlando was a top notch rod and reel fisherman and owned a 23 ft. Sailfish powered by a 200 H.P. Yamaha. Jim Bince, from Ontario, owned a 25 ft. Sailfish powered with twin 115 H.P. Yahamas. Jim always ran at full power. Quite often, we alternated boats. If either of them bought a new piece of equipment like a color depth/fish finder, the other would have the identical unit the next trip. Every year Moose had a fish fry for all the members of the Condo Association. Our trips were dedicated to catching enough fish for the fry. Most were large, gray snapper fillets. I remember one year that it was coming near the "fry" date and Moose was concerned that he might not have enough fish, so Moose, Jim, and I made another trip. In the Gulf, you had to go 15 to 20 miles offshore to get to a depth of 45 to 60 feet, where we always could catch fish. This particular day, it became rougher with the wind picking up as we went out to the grounds. Finally, all agreed that it was just too rough, and we returned to the dock. This was the only time we had ever called it a day. When we got back to the dock, Moose and Jim went out to breakfast, and I declined. Later, shortly after noontime, Moose's wife Tess had to call the ambulance. Moose was having a heart attack. In the ambulance, the medics lost him once but managed to revive him before they reached the hospital. Talk about close ones don't count.

Moose made it to the fish fry and within a couple of months was back fishing. In later years, Jim Bince became Chairman of the Board of the Yacht Club and did a great job. Tess couldn't keep Moose from going fishing and over time, we had to give him a lot of help to get him aboard Jim's boat. One tough fisherman.

I owned that property for 25 years and sold it in the spring before the "crash". We rented at the Yacht Club for a couple of years, but it was not the same. A number of our friends there had passed, and the remaining spouse had to return back North to be with family. I will say, it was nice never to have to think about winter. I very seldom saw a Rhode Island license plate even during the three years we rented on the East Coast. Most Rhode Islanders apparently become Florida residents when they retire and do their six month stay to be legal.

Back in Rhode Island, I started using my Boston Whaler a couple of times a week. At first, I fished for striped bass sometimes alone, but usually with one other retired friend that was available during the week. My brother Jerry and I were fishing with the heads of fresh menhaden one Saturday just north of Point Judith lighthouse when I caught my 53 lb. striper. Over 50 lbs. is kind of a milestone that all striper fishermen try to achieve. I did sell it at the company, and it was the largest bass sold there that summer until mid-October when a 57 lb. fish turned up.

Jerry and the author: 53 lb. striper

Over the years, I took my grandchildren out on the boat to catch their first striper. James Scott was on board one day when we caught a few; this was his first 28 lb. fish. At the time, James was only about 14 years old. After 5 years in the Coast Guard, he now works for NOAA on a research vessel in the Pacific. He is a big guy at 6'3", and works as a commercial mariner.

James Scott and Grandpa

A more recent picture of my grandson Jake when he was 12 years old. This was his first "keeper" that made the 34" commercial size limit that weighed 16 lbs. Jake is now 6'2" and another big guy. He is a baseball player on his California high school team.

Over the years since I started rod and reel fishing, I found that the fishermen who had a commercial fish license that allowed them to sell their catch were more aggressive than many of the dragger fishermen. Considering the boat size, usually 18 to 23 feet, they go every day the "weather permits" from mid-April to mid-November.

Jake Rifkin and Grandpa

About a dozen of those boats

unloaded their catch for the day at the Company. They would unload at the bulkhead at the east end door by the day boat dock. A number of them fished alone as I did back in the nineties. We all fished for fluke most of the summer with a mix of black sea bass. I was able to keep my fish in two live wells in the boat rather than carrying ice.

Over the years, the fish prices for the fish we caught, which were only hours old, increased significantly. Since 2013, for sushi grade fluke, we have been paid $5-6/lb. for jumbo (4 lbs. and over), $4.50/lb. for large (2-4 lbs.), and $3.50/lb. for medium (14 inches to 2 lbs.). Black sea bass range from $1.50/lb. to $3.90/lb. for jumbo size.

In Rhode Island, the limit for fluke in the early Spring has been 100 lb./day, then it has gone down to 50 lb./day for most of the year. In 2015, we were allowed to catch 50 lbs./day of black sea bass for eight consecutive days in the Spring, then again in early November. The rest of the time, they went back overboard, even though they were everywhere and easy to catch.

The one thing that is an understandable gripe for the recreational fishermen is the size discrepancy compared to the commercial size. On fluke, the minimum size is 14", recreational 18", black sea bass is 11" compared to 14", and scup is 9" compared with 10". The commercial size is determined on a coast wide basis, and the smaller sizes have been in place for many years because of the influence of the states of North Carolina and Virginia whose fishermen have traditionally caught smaller fish.

In practice, since we commercial fishermen can only catch 50 lbs./day, we try to high-grade each day to catch large and jumbo fish. Quite often that requires us to fish 15 to 20 miles away from the harbor such as South of Block Island. In 2013 and 14, the price of fuel was high and most of the recreational fishermen that fished weekends stayed within two or three miles of the harbor. Come Monday morning, the close-in areas were fished out.

This concept was similar for the larger draggers. Since most fish had relatively low catch limits, most boats restricted the distance they ran from port unless they were certain of catching fish on day one. Back when I fished the *Alliance*, I usually fished at least 70 to 100 miles from the harbor. I know the day boats from Point

Judith could never accuse me of catching their fish.

In 2006, my world changed when I re-powered my Whaler, MAC 1, with a 150 H.P. Yamaha 4 stroke outboard. From then on, I could count on trouble-free fishing. When fluke fishing, the one thing that determines the catch was the speed of the drift. I have a newer Furuno GPS that gives me accurate readings in knots over the ground. On some of the "pretty days," with no wind or tide, the drift is 1/10 of a knot. I used to troll with the engine but had to kick it in and out of gear continuously to keep the rig on the bottom even with a 10oz. sinker.

The engine in the up position when the boat is running at full speed

In 2010, I solved that problem by constructing a motor mount in the middle of the boat on the port side. I bought a 4 H.P., 4 stroke Yamaha with a long shaft. Now I can set my speed, usually 7/10th to 1 knot on calm days. I run the main engine at idle, turned hard to starboard and keep the boat going sideways steering by kicking the main engine in forward or reverse. This system has worked well, and we can fish up to five lines, and the rigs never foul up. Does it work? We have had some good days.

My granddaughter Emily Scott, can really catch fish. Regardless of how rough it gets, she stays totally focused. The fluke she caught in this picture was on August 17, 2013 and weighed over 10 lbs. She caught the fish south of Block Island fishing in the middle be-

Emily Scott

tween my brother and I and brought it up with no indication that it was a big fish until we first saw it coming to the net. I idled down the 4 HP until we had the fish in the boat. Our lines were still in the water and when my brother picked up his rod, he had a 9 pound fish.

Every October, we fish for tautog in rocky areas along the coast. We use a half of a green crab for bait that I catch in crab traps right at the dock. Tautog are really fun to catch. There is a very subtle bight. I watch the end of the pole and a bite will show as an up and down movement. It is important not to move the bait which is not easy on a rough day. I fish with 40 lb. braided line with the drag set up tight so that it's hard to pull the line off the reel.

When you strike the fish, it's like a mini explosion on the end of the line, and the fish drive hard to get to the bottom where there usually are caverns or crevices, and they will often hang you up on a snag. I only use one hook to minimize the hangups. The key to tautog fishing is anchoring the boat exactly where you have caught fish before or on obviously rocky bottom. I drop a buoy where I want to end up; otherwise, it is a hit and mostly miss proposition.

Over the last few years, we have sold our tautog live for $4—$5/lb. It is not a problem if the fish are caught in 30 ft. or less. If caught deeper than that, the fish need to be vented using a hollow needle, sold for that purpose, inserted above side fin. Otherwise the fish will float belly up in the live well and will be dead by the time you hit the dock, then you get paid $3/lb.

Years ago, we could sell 20 fish/day during the opening season; now it is limited to 10 fish/day at 16 inches. The live fish are preferred to be less than 6 lbs. No big money but fun.

Over the years, we have had a lot of fun and caught our share of fish. Selling the fish has provided enough money to pay all the expenses and buy all the equipment every fisherman just has to have from fish poles and reels to electronics.

From 2014, I have been reporting my landings to the State on their website. Prior to that, we sent in our landings in an official log book each quarter whether you fished or not.

Chapter 26

My Observations and Opinions
of the Fishing Industry

During my lifetime in commercial fishing, I have witnessed the movement of fish species to cooler waters. Back in 1961, I described catching boatloads of whiting when I was fishing on the *Lucky*. From the 1950's on through the 60's, Point Judith was known as the "Tuna Capital of the World." In 1954, my father was going to participate in The Tuna Tournament the day Hurricane "Carol" wrecked part of the tuna fleet. The Bluefin tuna were as close as Nebraska shoal only 20 minutes from the harbor. Feeding on whiting was the key. The Rhode Island Tuna Club building was located just north of the State Pier where the Block Island ferries now dock.

The picture has a sign "Welcome to Rhode Island" then "United States Atlantic Tuna Tournament, Sept 8th-9th-10th-1965." The largest Bluefin shows a weight of 650 lbs. The fish were hung by the tail for display after being hoisted from the boat. At the end of each day, the fish were delivered to the Co-op for processing then shipped to markets in New York. Because of their condition sitting in the sun all day, they were lucky to be paid 10 cents/lb.

Over the years, 1990-1995 shipping Bluefin to Tokyo, the boat would get up to $20-28/lb. I recently read the caption under a picture of a 440 pound tuna being processed at Tsukiji Market that sold for $118,000. Think of the money that could have been made even selling locally if the fish had been cared for, especially that close to the dock. All the years I was at the Co-op, we always sold fresh whiting to the tuna boats. These days, the bluefin congregate in Cape Cod Bay up to New Hampshire, "the new whiting country."

Back when I was fishing with Sam Cottle on the *Dorothy & Betty* in the 1950's, there were very few fluke compared to the availability in the 1980's through 2015. I have heard that fluke is now being caught off the Maine Coast. Apparently "global warming" is not a new event although these days it may be a slightly accelerated process.

Again, back in the 1950's, we hardly ever saw a black sea bass. They started showing up in greater quantity in the 1990's and became a significant part of my rod and reel catch during the years when it was an "open" fishery. In 2015, there were so many they became a nuisance, and we could not keep them.

It was during the 1990's that I first noticed that the black sea bass would regurgitate partially digested lobster pieces into my live wells. After unloading a trip, it was always necessary to clean out the well with a fine mesh scoop net. As I became more observant, I found that the small bass, under 8", would have lobster pieces the size of shrimp protruding deep in the throat of the live fish. Most fish, especially fluke, regurgitate whatever they are feeding on when you bring them to the net. The stress to the fish when "fighting" them when rod and reel fishing causes this reaction. At the time, I asked Bob Smith, who owns the dock where I tie up, if he had noticed the occurrence. He owns a lobster boat that has a deck box where he keeps his live fish, and he confirmed that he had seen the same thing. I should mention that Bob fishes with specific pots to catch each specie including scup, sea bass, and lobster as well as rod and reel for fluke. He also goes fishing just about every consecutive day from mid-April through November. He started fishing the beach back in the 1950's, and as a result, he knows everything that goes on in the inshore waters.

When I started to write this book, I had intended to write my observations about issues in the fishing industry in this final chapter. That changed when I read a comprehensive commentary "From the Executive Directors Desk" in the October/November 2015 issue of the Atlantic Marine Fisheries Commission, ASMFC, Fisheries Focus. Bob Beal, the Director, had summarized the changes that were taking place as the Gulf of Maine is getting warmer. The statement that black sea bass were being caught in numbers never seen before north of Cape Cod caused me the most concern. A few pages later in Focus, the staff of ASMFC had stated that the Southern New England stock abundance of American Lobster had increased in the early 1980's, peaked in the 1990's to approximately 20 million lbs., then declined steeply to 3.3 million lbs. in 2013. In the summer of 2016 the local R.I. lobster fishery was practically non-existent.

On March 1, 2016, I emailed a two page letter to the Director, and I quote, "What nobody that I know of to date had done is to tie in the decline of lobster with the increase in black sea bass in the same area and same time frame. It is no coincidence that there is an all-time high in the stock abundance of lobster in the Gulf of Maine at the same time the cod stock is at an all-time low."

What I pointed out in my letter was that there was and continues to be a high probability that the black sea bass are eating the immature lobsters. Egg bearing lobsters, eggers, carry their eggs for eight or nine months until the water starts to warm in May and June. When the female sheds the eggs, the larvae are very small, almost like plankton. Talking to hatchery specialists, they agitate the water much like a washing machine effect because the larvae are very aggressive and eat each other. In the wild, they have more room and with tides, they stay disbursed. The juveniles sink to the bottom in the same configuration as a full-sized lobster. In order to grow, all lobsters shed their hard shell and for a time, they are very soft, like soft shell blue crabs that are a delicacy. On average, we always said it took 7 years before a lobster reached the gauge size and can be sold. I am convinced that the black sea bass are eating the young lobsters that are 1 to 3 years old. As I have said, I caught many sea bass back in the nineties that would regurgitate often soft lobsters when caught. The small bass that have the appearance of a mouth with a tail are dangerous predators for a small, especially a molting, lobster. Often these immature lobsters are located in the lobster traps. On many occasions, I have stuffed rags in the escape vents just to see what was going on.

My belief is that the black sea bass have been eating the immature lobsters since they appeared in quantity in the mid 1990's. There did not appear to be a problem for years because the survivors over 3 years old take another 4 years to reach gauge size, then years possibly before they are caught. The egg lobsters are released so the process continues.

The rocky area all around the Point Judith Lighthouse in Rhode Island was always a good place to set pots. My good friend Howard Holt had lobstering on his bucket list, and around 1995, we bought 10 inshore pots and set them in a line in 34-36 feet starting just north of the lighthouse. We would take turns hauling them by hand. We always caught 3 or 4 lobsters in each pot up to 3 lbs. After about a month, Howie was too busy, and I was now hauling all 10. I ended up giving the pots away. It was seriously interfering with my fluke fishing. In 2015, there were no pot buoys visible anywhere around that area. Some people speculated that the lobsters may have moved. If that was the case, the lobstermen would have found them. Bob Smith is still catching some lobsters, which is not a surprise, but he did tell me that he had never seen such a high proportion of egg-bearing lobsters. That confirms my premise that the egg bearers will be the only survivors. It is a hard story to tell, but the lobsters didn't move in Southern New England; they were consumed by the latest predator. In my opinion, there is no possibility that this lobster fishery will ever revive. To make matters worse, both the recreational and commercial fishermen could only keep one black sea bass per person all summer here in Rhode Island. This was because we have a minimal "historic" catch record. In 2016, the recreational fishermen can keep three fish per person.

When I was writing this segment of the book, I realized that when I was catching black sea bass, scup, squid, and fluke in Nantucket Sound back in the 1980's, I never caught any lobsters, although five miles south of the Island, there were plenty of lobsters.

I don't know if there ever were any lobsters in the past in the sound before the black sea bass showed up. There is no location along the East Coast that has a lobster fishery and a long-term history of a black seabass population.

The two page letter I sent to the director of ASMFC on March 1, 2016 was to give the chiefs of the marine fisheries in Massachusetts, New Hampshire, and Maine a heads up on what could happen to their lobster fisheries now that the black sea bass have started to penetrate their waters. Of course, the State of New Hampshire and Maine will probably have no allocation to land black sea bass because they have no historic catch record. I have talked to the heads of the marine fisheries in all three of the northern states because around May 1st of 2016, they will start to see the fish especially after such a mild winter. Their lobstermen will know what to do.

I believe this is a twenty-year event from the time the black sea bass start to show up in quantity until they reduce the lobster fishery to historic low population levels as in southern New England. I am concerned that the lobster population in Massachusetts south of Boston could already be in year 5 of the cycle.

As far as who is or was responsible for the loss of the millions of pounds of lost lobsters times their value per pound, I think it will be written off as one of the unknown consequences of global warming.

Another specie of fish that has all but disappeared from the commercial catch in the Point Judith area is the blackback or winter flounder. Back in the 1950's and 1960's, the Co-op had a fillet operation that I described when Joe Lewis was the manager. Blackbacks were relied on for most of the winter supply of fish and were caught primarily by the day-boats. The logo "freshest of fresh fish" certainly fit the description of the fillets from the Co-op. A high percentage of the fillets were sold fresh to local markets and restaurants. Yellowtail flounder caught by the larger boats south of Block Island, like I did in the early years with the *Jerry & Jimmy* in the 1960's, was always available and were usually sold to fillet houses in New Bedford.

Back then, it was normal that Narragansett Bay and Nantucket Sound would freeze over in the winter. We did not know the significance the freezing event had on blackbacks. Even in the early 1970's, we would experience freezing even in the ocean out as far as three miles south of Nantucket as I did with the *Alliance* in 1972.

Blackback flounder studies go back for years. Beginning in 1959, there were trawl surveys done twice/week in the West Passage of Narragansett Bay to study the fish species that are found in the Bay including the blackbacks. Extensive surveys have been carried out in the ponds and in the area along the southern beaches for all the years since.

Around 1980, I invited Dr. Perry Jeffries from the Graduate School of Oceanography, that I knew from my college days, to speak to the Co-op members about the condition of the blackback fishery. He explained that the key to recruitment for the blackback fishery was cold winters. He said there was a predator called a sand shrimp that would prey on juvenile blackbacks and that activity would increase with warmer winter waters. Although there has only been an average increase of 2 degrees since 1960, there have been very few cold spells where freezing has occurred. Prior to that, it was common to have the harbor of Point Judith freeze over with the exception of the fast moving current in the breachway.

With the generally accepted more rapid increase in water temperature due to global warming, it does not look good for any increase in the blackback flounder population; if anything, the situation continues to deteriorate. In my years of fishing, we caught a good run of blackbacks in the 1960's and 70's south of NoMans Land with most of the fish in the 2 lb. range. I also had George's Bank trips of extra-large and lemon sole in the 3 to 6 lb. range.

I would hope our local experience with the loss of the blackback fishery does not extend to the Greater New England Fishery. Warming waters seem to be a significant danger to fish eggs and juvenile fish that in time causes a permanent collapse of certain fisheries.

The predator-prey situation appears to be occurring at all levels when one or both species are protected. I may sound like a complainer when I tell my cormorant story. A cormorant is a diving bird that feeds on small fish. They were once used as a method of fishing in the Orient.

There are a half dozen cormorants that are stationed on

rocks fifty feet south of the dock that I use. Every day, all day, they are diving down all around the immediate area. The dock is one of the last ones on the west of the breachway.

Over the years, I have seen the birds surface close enough that I can see they are catching small flatfish about 3 inches long. This is a never-ending occurrence. Of greater concern is the estimated two-hundred cormorants that occupy the center wall of the breakwater that protects the harbor.

There was a study done on the consumption of blackback juveniles in Narragansett Bay that determined that 10% of juvenile blackback flounder were consumed by cormorants. Whether that percentage goes up considerably as the juvenile population diminishes seems likely if the cormorants continue to eat approximately the same amount each day year after year. It would certainly seem to make sense to permit the systematic reduction of the current number of cormorants in view of the near disappearance of the blackback flounder fishery. Everything helps.

Another specie that may not be considered a predator is the dogfish. They eat whatever is in the area. Not only that, but they are the ultimate nuisance. Once a huge shoal of dogfish moves into an area, they sometimes stay a week or more. This happens around Block Island every year, and on a calm day, they are often finning on the surface.

It was very encouraging when a market developed in Europe. Dr. Andreas Holmsen, a U.R.I. Professor, demonstrated how to clean a dogfish and what sections were sold in the European market during a learning session at the Co-op back around 1990. At one time, there was an effort made to change the name to "Cape Shark" because it sounded better for marketing purposes.

I applaud the efforts of the Chatham Massachusetts fishermen in developing the dogfish fishery. Why they have a 5,000 lb. daily limit is beyond me. The ocean is full of dogfish as everyone knows. I never thought I would see the day when dogfish became a controlled fishery. The fact that they are born alive as opposed to eggs just means that the survival rate is near 100%. No other fish that I know of feed on dogfish. At the current dockside price of 20 cents/lb. with a 5,000 lb. limit is tough going these days.

I was going to pass on commenting on the great white shark

issue on Cape Cod since it is not a commercial fishing issue. But, it is the master of all predator/prey situations. Since both the seal and the great white shark are considered as protected, the situation appears to be unsolvable. In a recent 2016 article in the newspaper, I read that Gregory Skomal, The Massachusetts Division of Marine Fisheries Shark Researcher, said that the white shark population in the Cape Cod area could be as many as 300 and in time could double that number.

Looking at aerial photographs of the number of seals on the various Cape Beaches it is not surprising that the area has been targeted by the sharks. There is a continuing effort to warn the public about the extreme danger of entering the water and new purple flags with a great white silhouette would fly at the lifeguard stands warning visitors of sharks.

Over the past six years, Skomal and his team have tagged 65 great white sharks with acoustic tags. Detection receivers have been moored that broadcast shark detections and which shark it was. Off Chatham during 2015, for example, there were 14,124 contacts by 28 sharks. Based on the possibility that there could be up to 300 great whites in the area, there are many more that go undetected.

I have been concerned for years that our Rhode Island beaches may be subjected to great white shark "visits" since we have no system in place that I know of to detect the sharks except visually by lifeguards which is probably not their priority. I know of only one great white that was caught in a fish trap off Black Point about a mile north of Scarborough Beach in Narragansett in about 2010. The shark was released with difficulty by the trap boat crew. There was one other South of Point Judith that was sighted feeding on a floating dead whale about the same year.

I have no solution to this dangerous situation. The Canadian government has had a long history of "population control" of seals, and they should be consulted. The other long-term solution would be to install shark nets enclosing the main beaches. The most successful of this type of net has been used at 32 beaches in Hong Kong that has prevented all shark attacks since being installed. No doubt there would have to be significant government funding and involvement to meet this threat.

To get a complete view of the great whites, visit oceanaerials.com by Wayne Davis, Gregory Skomal's pilot and photographer. While you are at it, view all the categories listed. By the way, Wayne was in one of my wife's first grade classes when she was a teacher in Narragansett, R.I.

The most important concern I have for the future of the northeast commercial fishing industry is the age and condition of the finfish fishing fleet. There are no new boats coming into the Point Judith fleet, in fact, the last one that I recall was built by Harold Loftes, Jr. back around 2000.

This fleet has been well-maintained over the years because the owners have put money back into the boats as needed or as required to keep the vessels insurable. In the "old days," it was the common practice to sell your older, usually wooden, boat and use the money to build a new steel boat. I did this when I sold the *Jerry & Jimmy* soon after I had the *Alliance* built.

Most of our boats in Point Judith were built during the "good times" of the mid 1980's when the government agencies were encouraging investments in new boats. The URI Fisheries School was providing young, new, trained fishermen to fill out the crews, and the future looked bright.

Since that time, between 1991 and 1997, when I was on the New England Fisheries Management Council, the federal fishing license became a requirement. There was a decision made to have the license in the name of the boat as opposed to the name of the owner as it is in our Rhode Island seller's license.

The federal log books came next, which over the years has established the catch record of the boat. In order to stop the increase in effort, no new federal licenses were issued, in fact, there was a buy-back program, as I recall, to reduce the number of boats participating in the groundfish, principally cod fishery.

The importance of the catch record was demonstrated by what happened to the *Alliance* after I sold the boat in 1990. After 2 or 3 years Ed Todd, the owner, replaced the main engine and had to plate over the area toward the bow where the portholes were. The boat was painted a dark green without the distinctive "A" on the bow.

I didn't keep track of the boat's activity over the years, then about 2002, the boat went bankrupt. Ed Todd was able to buy it back at the auction. I heard that Ed was in poor health and for a year or more, the *Alliance* was tied up at a dock on the west end of the Company. I heard that the boat was for sale, but there was no interest primarily because there was no significant catch record and its age.

I came home from Florida in the spring of 2009, and the *Alliance* was in the process of being cut up for scrap. I heard from a reliable source, that in 2008, the boat was given to Paul "Joe" Champlin, owner of Champlin Welding, to dispose of the *Alliance*. While I was standing close to the bulkhead looking at the boat, one of the other boat owners came over to talk about the dismantling of the *Alliance*. One of his comments was that "the steel looks good, probably better than some of the other boats." The last I saw of the *Alliance*, it looked like an 80-foot canoe.

In order to replace a boat today, it would be necessary to dispose of the fishermen's current boat, to be able to transfer the license and the catch record. It is unlikely that a newer used boat could be found since there are few boats in that category available. It is important to realize that most of the existing fleet in the Northeast, built in the mid-eighties, is now 30 years old. The *Alliance* was 37 years old when it was disposed of. The expected service life of U.S. Navy vessels is 35 years as an example.

At some point in the next 15 to 20 years, it will be necessary to build new boats or there will be no fishing fleet. Even now to replace a boat the size of the *Alliance* would probably cost over two million dollars based on the marine surveyor's estimate of a replacement value for the *Alliance* of $950,000 in March 1989.

When I built the *Alliance* in 1971, it cost $240,000. At the time, I had witnessed first-hand how I could catch a large amount of lobsters based on trials using pots on the *Jerry & Jimmy*. The *Alliance* was a sure venture, and we did catch the lobsters as expected and made "big money" right away. As one of the early true stern trawlers, we also caught fish better than expected. The boat was also big enough to fish anywhere you had a mind to go, and we did. Back in those days, there were no restrictions. The marketplace determined where and what you fished for.

The question all fin fishermen will be faced with is are they going to go in debt for two million dollars of new money, recognizing the old boat will be worthless, to continue in this business. Those fishermen who do decide to build new may decide to downsize assuming the boat would cost less. Making that choice would limit the boat from fishing the more lucrative areas farther offshore. Even with the decent weather reports we now have, I personally would never have gone fishing where I made the most money unless I was fishing with a boat in the size range of the *Alliance*. Also, who is going to finance a new boat unless government agencies participate? In the last four or five years, a number of captain/owners have sold their draggers and offshore lobster boats along with their licenses, etc. to fish or lobster dealers. I assume the buyers are accumulating these boats to be assured of continued landings in the future. The replacement of the vessels, because of age, is still a factor. Most of those that have decided to sell have had enough of the hassle of trying to make a living with all the restrictions. Also, most that have sold have no family members who are interested in the business after witnessing first-hand the number of days their father had to be away from the family. The fishermen's children that I know of have college degrees in most cases and are doing very well in the outside world.

This is an indication, in my opinion, that when it comes time in the next 10 to 15 years to invest in a new boat, the original owners will be too old to consider new debt. Florida is a likely choice.

By buying up the licenses, eventually, it will be like buying the right to fish and could end up in the hands of a very few people compared to the current, although diminishing, number of owner/operators.

When I was on the Board of Directors of Sunderland Marine Mutual, we visited Nelson, New Zealand, the home of one of our directors. He was one of the major fish company operators in the country and over time had bought a significant allocation of fish. Along with his own large boats, he chose other owner/operator boats to fish using his quota. They in turn sold the fish they caught exclusively to him. It was the recognized system. Is this our future?

There has to be a real incentive very soon that will encourage future investment to replace the current fishing fleet. I would hate to think that the license/log book requirement was actually devised with the intent of eliminating fishing effort when the age of the fleet will require the vessels to retire from service.

On April 14, 2016, I attended a two-hour meeting at Rhode Island College in Providence, RI. The subject was "Is Commercial Fishing Sustainable?" There were six speakers with a broad range of interest in the fishing industry. One of the issues was the need for observers on fishing vessels engaged primarily in the Groundfish Fishery. In the past years, the NMFS has paid for the observers. To date, the observers have been required to insure the boat captain is observing all the regulations, especially discards. More important, the observer is charged with collecting data in the same way as a vessel hired to do stock surveys. The scientists at Woods Hole need this information if they are going to get a handle on the status of the various stocks because in my opinion, the information gathered by their own survey vessels is seriously inadequate. The problem this season is that each vessel is required to pay $700/day for the observer. The fishermen on the panel indicate that this cost was beyond their ability to absorb the expense. I see this response by the fishermen as an indication of just how bad things are from an economic point of view. The congressional delegations of the New England states should be able to find funding for the observer program. I have heard since that time, that funding has become available.

The more important observation was how involved everyone on the panel was in what I call the "process." To me, this was all the different ways the Fishery Councils had to come up with to allocate the ever decreasing numbers from the stock assessments coming out of Woods Hole, especially if it includes cod. If the vessel catches its allowance of cod, it cannot continue to fish for haddock that is abundant and very marketable. The obsession with cod tends to drive the whole system.

The situation today revolves around the fish allocation a vessel "owns" based on catch records. The states own their allocations based on their historical catch which in these days of accelerated global warming is not a valid concept. None of these owners are going to give up a single pound in the future although they never paid dime one to the government for the fish as I described in the New Zealand Fishery.

The Fishery Councils should start to focus on an orderly reduction in the current restrictions with the eventual target of an open fishery as it was in the 1980's, instead of looking at new avenues that lead to even more restrictions. Black sea bass, for example, could easily take the place of codfish in the marketplace, and they taste better than cod and bring a better price.

From everything I have heard from active fishermen, there are plenty of fish to be caught. The fish stocks are certainly sustainable. I doubt if the fishermen and their vessels are "sustainable" under the existing conditions facing the industry.

"In My Wake" has turned out to be an endless story, but at my age, "I have seen and have done more than my share." I turned 85 in September 2016.

James A. McCauley, author

Appendix 1

JAMES A. McCAULEY

WORK EXPERIENCE:

1996-Present	Rod & Reel Commercial Fishing
1995-1998	Slavin Point Judith Company, Administrative Liaison
1985-1995	President & Chairman of the Board of the Point Judith Fishermen's Cooperative Association, Inc., RI
1985-1990	Owner of F/V *Alliance*, Point Judith, RI
1971-1984	Captain & Owner of F/V *Alliance*, Point Judith, RI
1970-1974	Assistant Professor, Fisheries School, URI College of Resource Development Subjects: Diesel & Hydraulic Engineering, Fishing Gear Design, Fishing Methods & Vessel Operations
1961-1970	Captain & Owner of F/V *Jerry & Jimmy*, Point Judith, RI
1957-1961	Crewman on Point Judith commercial fishing vessels
1956-1957	Administrative Assistant in Inventory Control, Electric Boat Division, General Dynamics, Groton, CT
1954-1956	1st Lt. U.S. Army Infantry, Ft. Dix, NJ

EDUCATION:

1954	B.S. Degree, General Business, URI 2nd Lt. Infantry Commission U.S. Army Infantry School, Ft. Benning, GA
1956	Submarine Familiarization Course, Electric Boat Division, General Dynamics Corp., Groton, CT

ACTIVITIES:

1991-1997	Member: New England Fishery Management Council. Committee Chairman: Gear Conflict. Committees: Groundfish, Sea Herring, Ocean Quahaug. Liaison: Mid-Atlantic Fishery Management Council. Committees: Squid, Mackerel and Butterfish, Dimersal Finfish.
1989-1990	Appointed to the Rhode Island Aqua Fund Advisory Council
1988-1997	Board of Directors, Sunderland Marine Mutual Insurance Company Limited, Sunderland, England
1986-1997	President: Point Club, Fishing Vessel Self Insurance Mutual, renamed in 1991 to Nor' East Point Group
1985-1996	URI Graduate School of Oceanography Advisory Council
1992-1993, 1996-1997	Executive Committee of the New England Council
1987-1991	Appointed to National Fish and Seafood Promotional Council, U.S. Department of Commerce
1987-1991	Regional Director: National Fisheries Institute
1985-1990	Director: New England Fisheries Development Association
1984-1988	URI College of Resource Development Advisory Council
1982-1983	Vice President and Board of Directors, Atlantic Offshore Fishermen's Association

1984	Governor's Panel for the Administration of State Technical Services Act Funds

AWARDS

1992	National Fisherman Magazine Highliner Award

Appendix 2

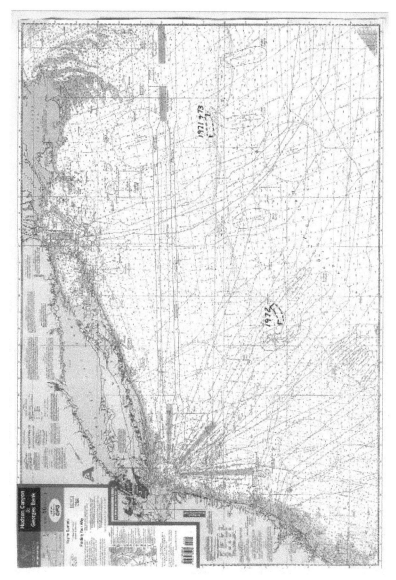

The *Alliance* fishing grounds

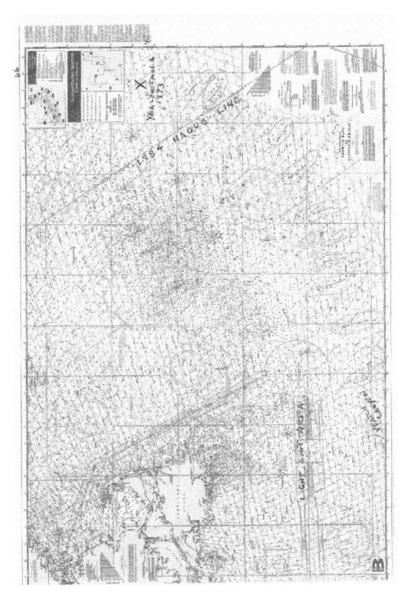

The *Alliance* fishing grounds